Personalising Learning in Teacher Education

Mellita Jones • Karen McLean

Personalising Learning in Teacher Education

Mellita Jones
Australian Catholic University
Ballarat, VIC, Australia

Karen McLean
Australian Catholic University
Ballarat, VIC, Australia

ISBN 978-981-10-7928-3   ISBN 978-981-10-7930-6   (eBook)
https://doi.org/10.1007/978-981-10-7930-6

Library of Congress Control Number: 2017964510

Printed on acid-free paper

This Springer imprint is published by the registered company Springer Nature Singapore Pte Ltd. part of Springer Nature.
The registered company address is: 152 Beach Road, #21-01/04 Gateway East, Singapore 189721, Singapore

Foreword

An inquiry into education does not begin merely in an experience of curiosity, but rather with a tangible sense of its problematic nature. Many educational researchers have developed their standpoints on learning and teaching practices from the idea of emancipatory and democratic education that empowers people's agency and participation in all the spheres of social-political life, including their capabilities to live and learn with others. The project of building an educated and democratic society through schooling has been inherently difficult to achieve in so far as, according to Illich (1973, p. 9), policymakers, teachers and students continue to confuse "teaching with learning, grade advancement with education, a diploma with competence, and fluency with the ability to say something new". This view of education as schooling has intensified over the last three decades, in particular with the rise of neo-liberal policies of educational accountability and standards-based reforms.

Today, the standardisation of schooling and teacher education and the accountability of teachers and teacher educators for delivering standardised learning experiences have become a core concept of neo-liberal policymaking, both fashioning and normalising what counts as effectiveness and quality in the "audit society". The steady drift towards the delivery of standards-based education has produced a number of effects and one of them is reification. In schools, standards-based reforms mediate the delivery of identical curricular to all students, mapping students' stage-like progression and common everyday learning experiences in classrooms. Equally, teacher educators are forced to prepare teachers that are ready to work in a standard classroom. To ensure the implementation of standards-based reforms, schools and teacher education programmes are made accountable for high-stakes test results. As a result, learning is increasingly understood and treated as a set of measurable outputs and as an object of scrutiny for which educators can be rewarded or punished. This reifies both teachers and students into objects to be acted upon rather than seeing them as human beings who come into the world as unique individuals and who, in and through education, learn to assume responsibility for others and the world.

Personalising Learning in Teacher Education, written by Mellita Jones and Karen McLean, challenges precisely the idea and practice of schooling and teacher education in which people have to fit into the standardised curriculum and learning experience. Placing learners and learning in the centre of education is by no means a new idea, but the book invites us to re-engage with the impact of current policy environment in Australia, and elsewhere, on education that decentres learners and learning in practice. Jones and McLean's starting point, in this regard, is not only to identify "personalising learning" as a powerful alternative to neo-liberal discourses of standardisation that marginalise and reify many learners. They also, and importantly, differentiate this concept from "individualised learning" that is constitutive of the larger neo-liberal discourse of education where knowledge is represented as goods designed for individual consumption. Recognising the centrality and prominence of "learning" in contemporary educational research, Jones and McLean argue that the shift from teaching to learners and their needs is not representative of a single or common agenda in education. "Individualised learning", as the term suggests, starts with the individual, while "personalised learning" starts with and within the social. The book, therefore, situates itself in an alternative political and theoretical camp in developing the concept of "personalising learning" and applying it to teacher education.

Jones and McLean have identified four trends that, in one way or another, have contributed to personalising learning as an approach to teaching, learning and assessment. First, the book emphasises sociocultural and constructivist theories of learning as a foundation for the social and collaborative forms of education that shift attention away from teaching to learning. As a result, not only learning becomes more central in the process of education but also the discourses, relations and processes through which participation in learning communities can be understood and new opportunities can be created. To reframe this theoretical foundation in terms of personalising learning is then to recognise learners as active participants in the context-oriented appropriation of knowledge and meanings, within the framework of guided or scaffolded participation. Personalising learning, as this book demonstrates, enables one to reconceptualise the metaphor of scaffolding students' learning. Scaffolding implies not so much "assistance" in acquiring fixed knowledge but the exhibition of a critical-reflexive practice in which both educators and students as sociohistorical individuals create possibilities of articulating new knowledge and associated set of new meanings, identities and representations.

Second, personalising learning allows researchers and educators to trace the influence of technological tools, such as ICT, on intersubjective activities of learning and, ultimately, on the possibilities of intrapersonal transformations. The first step towards the substantiation of this principle in *personalising learning* is a proposal that individual learning is built through relations with others that are increasingly ICT mediated. Individual learning must therefore be viewed as a product of social activity, in which material-semiotic tools and means of interpersonal communication are mediators of psychological processes, both interpersonal and intrapersonal. From this perspective, virtually all learning activities today are embedded in a social matrix composed of people and artefacts. In learning environments, artefacts are themselves "participants" that can resist some and afford other practices, shaping understandings and actions of those who use them. Because of this dialectical relationship, neither an individual nor ICT functions in isolation; a disjunctive approach to the individual-artefact interaction cannot provide the necessary grounds for an account of the ongoing learning activity. As Jones and McLean argue, this creates a number of affordances as well as challenges, many of which are social-emotional and ethical in their nature.

Third, the book is influenced by and develops personalising learning approach further through a student-centred perspective on education. Jones and McLean, in this regard, emphasise that making sense in learning environments embodies contextual experiences of individuals, through which an internal relationship with reality is established. The relationship here is not a passive relationship of perceiving or processing incoming information, but a relationship defined by the learner's needs and goals – a relationship defined by the forms of social practice that relate learners to an objective environment and define what the environment means for them. This learner-centredness – contextually defined needs and goals – functions in this book to show an active understanding of learning that, so to speak, goes beyond a mere duplication of someone else's ideas. Consequently, the concept of learner-centredness is central in Jones and McLean's book for an understanding of how meanings and personality interrelate in the context of situated activity be it in a school or a teacher education context. It is through this concept that Jones and McLean come to focus on concrete particularities in terms of which the general learning trajectory of an individual in society can be conceived.

And, finally, the book mobilises the concept of lifelong learning as a recognition that people today spend increasingly more time and effort on different forms of learning, both inside and outside of classrooms. Indeed, some researchers have recognised this as the "silent explosion of learning", occurring in formal and informal settings, as well as through the Internet and other forms of digital mediation. Personalising learning becomes central in capturing the multiplicity of learning experiences across the time-space(s) of learning. Thus, while the general sociocultural and constructivist principles of learning work across social contexts, lifelong learning adds an important dimension in thinking about personalisation as it is tied to particular forms of learning and to particular goals in the stream of one's life. In this connection, the book suggests that the personalising of learning is characterised by unevenness and qualitative transformations in the process of one's knowing. This is due to the interaction between external and internal, meaning and sense and internalisation and externalisation in contextually specific practices and across time.

These four broader trends are illustrated in the second part of the book in relation to teacher education more specifically. If this suffices as an indication of why the book of Jones and McLean is important today to counteract some trends in standardising students' experiences of schooling, the question is whether they have provided the new language for practising teacher education in times of major education reforms. The beauty of this book is that it is at once intensely theoretical and incredibly pragmatic. Hence, it definitely provides an alternative language and an understanding of what may count as "profession-ready" teachers. The book creates multiple entry points for educators to understand the complexity of learning and, more specifically, professional learning today. It invites the readers to look at professional education of teachers from various focal points and to reflect on their own practices and research agendas in light of ideas and projects discussed in this book. Jones and McLean are optimistic in conceptualising their alternative view of teacher education. If standards-based reforms attempt to interrupt the project of democratic and responsive teacher education, *personalising learning* holds out the prospect of professional agency that can continue this project.

Faculty of Education   Alex Kostogriz
Monash University
Melbourne, Australia

Acknowledgements

No writing project is accomplished easily, and a full manuscript is, we have discovered, no exception. We are indebted to a number of people for their support, advice, encouragement and assistance in (finally) reaching the completion of this particular project.

Firstly, to Sue McNamara, who stepped in to assist with some of the writing, very late in the project, when neither of us were managing anything well, particularly our stress levels. With her usual grace and positivity, Sue wrote the first drafts of Chaps. 4 (ICT for Learning) and 6 (Lifelong Learning) and assisted with proofreading to enhance the final product.

To Dan Schweinzer, budding graphic artist, who provided the drawing of the tree that represents our culminating visualisation of personalising learning in teacher education, found in Chap. 12. This was a first draft hit – something quite notable given the vague directions provided – "roots something like this, not too many; a short trunk, limbs and branches with lots of leaves, all drawn slightly differently". I'm not quite sure how he managed to translate such a description into something that was even better than what was in our heads. Thanks Dan!

Ben Clark at Hightech Printing who took Dan's tree diagram, digitalised the image and incorporated the theories, strategies and approaches we wanted to represent. "When do you need it by?" Ben asks innocently, as we discuss the details of the work. "Yesterday", which is becoming the usual response to everything. So, thank you Ben, not only for your excellent work but for your good-natured attitude in the face of our many and ongoing last minute requests and your record speed turnaround.

We each have important people in our personal lives who are forever supporting us.

I (Mellita) would like to extend my love and gratitude to my husband, David, who loves and supports me unconditionally and always knows exactly what I need and when I need it. Thank you also for your suggested alternative title for this book – The Neverending Story. Sorry it didn't quite pass the final edit. Also to my wonderful children, Jesse and Marne, who make me proud every single day. To my parents, Mike and Mary, and my parents-in-law, Des and Pauline: you all put up with the worst from me and seem to love me anyway. I love you all too. I also want to say a big thank you to my friend, colleague and co-author, Karen McLean. Academia is lucky to have you as a teacher and researcher, and I am blessed to count you among my closest of friends.

I (Karen) would like to acknowledge the support of my amazing family. My husband, Stephen, has been my "rock" throughout this writing project. Thank you, Steve, for your patience with my mood swings following those late nights of writing and for being the most generous, kind-hearted person I know! To my children, Luke and Hayley, who although each busy with their own lives still generously take an interest in my work. To my parents, Russell and Carolyn, who have become accustomed to visits that entail me disappearing into the office to write that extra line. To my parents-in-law, Malcolm and Leselie, and extended family members who are genuinely mystified by the many hours that I spend in front of a computer screen – and accept this as just another of my quirks! This book would not have happened without the love and support from each of you. I love you dearly and thank you from the bottom of my heart! I also extend my sincere thanks to my co-author Mellita Jones. My dear friend and colleague Mellita, this book has taken us on quite a journey and I cannot think of anyone that I'd rather share that journey with than you! Your friendship is an absolute blessing in *my* life and I thank you for the privilege it has been to write this book with you.

Contents

About the Authors

Mellita Jones is the deputy head of Education Victoria at the Ballarat Campus of Australian Catholic University where she also teaches in science teacher education. Her research is concerned with effective teacher education where her focus has been on school-university partnerships, reflective practice and authentic uses of technology for personalising learning. Her recent work has involved practicum partnerships for rural and regional teacher education courses and reflective theory and practice in teacher education. She also has an interest in working with teachers in the Pacific region and has had significant involvement in the Solomon Islands. Mellita has won a number of teaching excellence awards including an Australian Learning and Teaching Council Citation for Outstanding Contribution to Student Learning and has reviewed and written teacher education units for UNESCO's teacher education programme for the Pacific region.

Karen McLean is a senior lecturer in the Faculty of Education and Arts and researcher in the Early Childhood Futures research programme in the Learning Sciences Institute of Australia (LSIA), Australian Catholic University. Dr. McLean commenced her career in primary and early years' education in regional Victoria. She has been working in early childhood and primary teacher education for over 10 years. She has been the recipient of an Australian Learning and Teaching Council Citation for Outstanding Contribution to Student Learning. Karen's research uses sociocultural perspectives to understand *learning for contemporary times*. Karen's research interests encompass children and adult learning with a focus on literacy, technologies and play-based learning.

Chapter 1
Introduction

This volume, *Personalising Learning in Teacher Education*, portrays something of a learning journey that we, the authors, have been travelling since our commencement as educators in the tertiary learning scene. We have both come from a school teaching background: Karen from the primary school sector, where she worked predominantly in the early years of primary schooling with a strong focus on literacy and technologies education, and Mellita from the secondary school sector where she taught science and mathematics across years 7–11 and specialised in teaching Physics at the senior secondary level (years 11 and 12). Given these diverse backgrounds, it is both interesting and refreshing (and, quite often, life-saving!) that we have grown together in our roles as teacher educators and been inspired by similar pedagogies and theories of learning.

We commenced as teacher educators approximately 6 months apart and were fortunate enough to be located in offices near one another, but distant from (in another building) other staff in our Faculty. This led to a heavy reliance on one another as we forged our identities as teacher educators. Many office and corridor conversations revealed that despite our contrasting backgrounds, we shared very similar philosophies of education.

We are both inspired by the creativity that we believe needs to be embedded in education, regardless of the level – primary, secondary or tertiary – and through our shared learning, we have aspired to bring this creativity into our own teaching practices. We are both also driven by holistic approaches to teaching, learning and assessment. We believe in nurturing the whole person – not just their cognitive function, but their mental, emotional and spiritual learning as well. Such a philosophy of teaching has permeated through our approaches to teacher education.

Being influenced by such holistic bases in how to accomplish our roles as teacher educators, it is not surprising that we both found ourselves aligned with sociocultural and systems theories of learning and development. The incorporation of creativity in sociocultural approaches to teaching, learning and assessment saw each of us striving to constantly enhance our own practice and, through this, enrich our pre-service teachers' learning experience at university. On the most part, we applied

© Springer Nature Singapore Pte Ltd. 2018
M. Jones, K. McLean, *Personalising Learning in Teacher Education*,
https://doi.org/10.1007/978-981-10-7930-6_1

such theories and approaches to our areas of specialisation in literacy and science education.

One semester, a couple of years after we commenced at the university, we were given the opportunity to teach a foundation education unit that was a part of the core course work in the first semester of the first year of a Bachelor of Education (Primary) course. This provided an opportunity to work together and apply some of the many creative and inspired (we thought) approaches to teaching, learning and assessment that we often discussed. The unit, which is reported in Chap. 11 of this volume, and elsewhere (Jones and McLean 2012), provided the foundations for our ongoing work in personalising learning in teacher education. The book is the culmination of this personalising learning work and portrays the underpinning theories, cautions and applications of personalising learning in teacher education. Here, it is important to consider what we mean by teacher education and hence how this book sets out to explore personalising learning *in* teacher education.

It is often difficult to clearly articulate what is meant by teacher education. Is it the education of the pre-service teacher or the in-service teacher? Or both? Or does it refer to the education of the teacher educator? A myriad of terms have been adopted to help distinguish between these different forms of teacher education. For example, pre-service teacher education is often referred to as *initial* teacher education, whilst education of in-service teachers is commonly called teacher professional development or teacher professional learning. There has been little in the way of describing the explicit education of the teacher educator, although recently, notions of *self-study* and the *pedagogy of teacher education* through reflection, congruent teaching and core practices have emerged in the literature (e.g. Grossman et al. 2009; Loughran and Hamilton 2016; Swennen et al. 2008).

It is well established (at least among scholars and no doubt for teaching practitioners themselves) that teaching is a complex, challenging and sophisticated endeavour. This is in contrast to the conception of teaching held by the majority of those who have attended school that it is relatively easy – a conception arising from what Larabee (2010) describes of teaching as "an extraordinarily difficult job that looks easy" (p. 298) and what Lortie (1975) attributes to the 10–12 years of "apprenticeship of observation" that anyone who has been through school has experienced. Teaching is easy in the same way that petrol is all you need to make a car go. The intricacies of the different components of the engine and how they work together to transform the chemical potential energy of petrol into the movement of the car are largely unseen and uncomprehended. For teaching it is both the "behind the scenes" work of a teacher as well as the explicit and tacit knowledge that a teacher brings to their decisions about the teaching process that are largely unseen and uncomprehended. Extrapolating this to the notion of teacher education adds to the complexity of what must be done; and extrapolating further again to the work of the teacher educator makes their role intricate, convoluted, esoteric and somewhat elusive.

The role of the teacher educator is to take the intricacy, convolution, esotericism and elusiveness of understanding teaching and learning and make it intelligible, coherent and accessible. To achieve such a task, the teacher educator must have a multidimensional understanding of learning. They need to know how children learn, how they are motivated, and how these elements change through childhood development into adolescence and pre-adulthood. They must then know how to articulate this knowledge and the skills associated with its practice to students of teaching. To succeed in this, teacher educators must know of teacher education students, what teachers must know of children, what is it that motivates them, how they learn and, indeed, how their preconceptions of learning, teaching and schooling are *unlearned* to combat the prevailing belief that teaching is easy. In the same way, it is universally accepted that teachers need a formal and professional education that provides both theory and practice about how to best teach children; then surely teacher educators need a similar formal and professional education on how to best teach students of teaching. Yet the prevailing culture of teacher education preparation consists of either an apprenticeship itself, that of being a teacher and then moving into teacher education, or an academic pathway from schooling into university as a student and ultimately as a teacher. Neither pathway supports the emerging understanding that there is a pedagogy of teaching that is specific to teacher education. In fact, it is quite possible that the almost entirely practice-based or theoretical-based pathways into teacher education exacerbate at best, and precipitate at worst, the whole theory-practice divide that (albeit contentiously) bedevils teacher education.

So how are these forms of education addressed in this book? Well, in many ways it attempts to encompass all the forms of teaching and learning noted above. Personalising learning, as we explain further in Chap. 2, is an assemblage of a number of theories and approaches to education. As such, it has application for how children learn and hence informs how they could/should be taught. It also has relevance for the adult learning associated with teacher professional learning and initial teacher education. Moreover, it has implications for how teacher educators themselves might learn about teacher educator practice. We hope that elements of these different forms of teacher learning are at least implicit in what we have presented. However, the key ways in which we are explicit about teacher learning in this manuscript are twofold, and thus, the book is presented in two parts.

In the first part of the book, we discuss elements of what we see personalising learning offering teaching, learning and education in general. We explore the theoretical foundations that we believe are fundamental to informing personalising learning as an approach to teaching, learning and assessment across the *different* sectors of education. We draw heavily on the work of Keamy et al. (2007) who were the first Australian authors to present personalising learning as a recommended approach for contemporary education practice. In this work, Keamy et al. propose four tenets for personalising learning for the compulsory years of education (which in Australia range from approximately age 5–15). These four tenets are Learner as Central, Communities of Collaboration, ICT and Lifelong Learning. We present these tenets, in a summary of personalising learning in Chap. 2, and then discuss each in more detail in Chaps. 3, 4, 5 and 6 where we consider in particular, each tenet in relation to its underpinning theoretical foundations. The first part of the book concludes with Chap. 7 in which we present personalising learning in the context of teacher education and make links between its use in teacher education and other established ideas around teacher education pedagogy.

The second part of the book provides a number of examples of our own practice in which personalising learning, or elements of it, is applied to our various experiences as teacher educators. Through this, we make explicit the applications of personalising learning in our own practice as teacher educators. Whilst this does not explore in depth the more specific ideas regarding a pedagogy of teacher education, it does present links to some of the ideas and the terminology that stems from this relatively recent field of scholarship. The second part is primarily concerned with depicting the enactment of personalising learning rather than exploring the scholarly discussion on education for the teacher educator. Through this depiction, we aim to provide a springboard for discussion and practice among other teacher educators. As such, we present the four tenets of personalising learning explicated in Part I of the book as they have been applied in various aspects of our teaching in initial teacher education contexts.

The tenets of Learner as Central and Communities of Collaboration are represented in Chap. 8 and 9 as they apply to two community-based, after-school, literacy-focused learning clubs *Tell Tales* and *Digi-tell*. In Chap. 9, the tenet of ICT as a key enabler of learning is also represented in the *Digi-tell* example of personalising learning. Chap. 10 also explores the tenet of Learner as Central and Communities of Collaboration as they apply to a Science Teaching in Schools Experience (*STISE*) that is a situated, concurrent school- and university-based programme. As noted above, Chap. 11 depicts the unit of study that served as the impetus for our journey in personalising learning in teacher education. It describes a *Transition to University* context used in a first-year, first-semester core unit of study in a Bachelor of Education course that explored the content of Human Development and Contexts for Learning. All four tenets of personalising learning were embedded into the approach taken to teaching, learning and assessment in this Chapter.

Chapter 12 provides a synthesis of applications of personalising learning in teacher education that have been presented in Part II of this book. The four key tenets of personalising learning as identified by Keamy et al. (2007) are revisited and described with a particular emphasis on the adult learning associated with tertiary education. The final chapter of the book, Chap. 13, concludes with an analogy of personalising learning in teacher education to the growth of a tree: rooted in existing, proven theories of learning; given structure through the "trunk" of personalising learning; and supported in various ways through the branches of individual support to the individual learners for whom the learning is all about, our pre-service teachers and the children they in turn will teach.

Whilst limited to application in our own practice, we hope that our focused depiction of personalising learning in our practice acts to affirm, challenge and inspire others' views of effective, theory-informed, and holistic approaches to teacher education and that it may act as a stimulus for personalising the approaches of other teacher educators in their own teacher education contexts. We hope you enjoy it!

References

Grossman, P., Hammerness, K., & McDonald, M. (2009). Redefining teaching, re-imagining teacher education. *Teachers and Teaching, 15*(2), 273–289.

Jones, M., & McLean, K. J. (2012). Personalising learning in teacher education through the use of technology. *Australian Journal of Teacher Education, 37*(1), 75–92. https://doi.org/10.14221/ajte.2012v37n1.1.

Keamy, K., Nicholas, H., Mahar, S., & Herrrick, C. (2007). *Personalising education: From research to policy and practice*. Melbourne: Department of Education and Early Childhood Development. 0.1080/00461520.1996.9653266.

Larabee, D. (2010). An uneasy relationship: The history of teacher education in the university. In M. Cochran-Smith, S. Feiman-Nemser, D. McIntyre, & K. Demers (Eds.), *Handbook of research on teacher education: Enduring questions in changing contexts* (3rd ed., pp. 290–306). New York: Routledge.

Lortie, D. C. (1975). *Schoolteacher*. Chicago: Chicago University Press.

Loughran, J., & Hamilton, M. (2016). Developing an understanding of teacher education. In J. Loughran & M. Hamilton (Eds.), *International handbook on teacher education* (Vol. 1, pp. 3–22). Singapore: Springer.

Swennen, A., Lunenberg, M., & Korthagen, F. (2008). Preach what you teach! Teacher educators and congruent teaching. *Teachers and Teaching: Theory and Practice, 14*(5-6), 531–542.

Part I
Personalising Learning: Theoretical Underpinnings

Chapter 2
Personalising Learning: An Overview

Personalising learning is an approach to teaching and learning that is only just emerging in educational research. This recent emergence in research follows a fairly rapid increase of personalising learning in the education policy discourses of a number of countries around the world. As an initial concept, personalising learning originated in the United States, but it has gained its popularity through its emphasis in education policy of the United Kingdom. More recently its prevalence has grown in other education systems, particularly Organisation for Economic Co-operation and Development (OECD) countries including Canada, the United States, Australia and New Zealand. This international focus on personalising learning as an educational concept in the compulsory years of schooling provides an opening in the field of education research to examine arguments for and against its inclusion in a twenty-first-century approach to education, and subsequently, what place, if any, it should have in teacher education.

This book considers such arguments by outlining how personalising learning is defined and enacted and how its subsidiary parts align with what is already established and accepted in effective education practice. In beginning this discussion, this chapter examines in particular what is meant by personalising learning and how it is defined by different educational organisations. This chapter also distinguishes between notions of personalis*ing*, personalis*ed* and individualised learning and considers the ways in which it is characterised in different countries. These ideas, along with the educational theories underpinning the approach, are presented to consider an argument for personalising learning in teacher education.

2.1   What Is Personalising Learning?

Personalising learning has been described and defined in a range of ways such that it can mean quite different things to different stakeholders (de Freitas et al. 2005). This lack of consistency in what is meant by "personalising learning" complicates attempts

© Springer Nature Singapore Pte Ltd. 2018
M. Jones, K. McLean, *Personalising Learning in Teacher Education*,
https://doi.org/10.1007/978-981-10-7930-6_2

made to provide a common definition and a shared understanding within and across sectors, let alone across the world. The OECD (2006a) describes personalising learning as a "holistic, person-centred approach to learner development" (p. 4) that stems from the realisation that "'one-size-fits-all' approaches to school knowledge and organisation" (p. 4) are incapable of meeting the needs of both the individual learner and society at large. Australian authors, Keamy, Nicholas, Mahar and Herrick (2007), describe it as learning that responds "directly to the diverse needs of students" (p. 2); and the UK Department for Education and Skills [DfES] (2004a) portrays it as an approach that "tailor[s] education to individual need, interest and aptitude so as to fulfill every young person's potential" (p. 4). Here there is some commonality, if not in definition then at least in intention, where personalising learning essentially means being responsive to the social, emotional and cognitive needs of the child and to their aspirations for both their educational and their lifelong goals. As such, personalising learning is focused on the learner as opposed to the teacher and requires a student-centred approach to teaching, learning and assessment.

2.2 Individualised, Personalis*ed* or Personalis*ing* Learning?

A further challenge that complicates the shared understanding of personalis*ing* learning is its common confusion with the constructs of personalis*ed* and individualised learning. Individualised learning is technically viewed as a teacher-centred activity, because the teacher controls the level and nature of differentiation, the content, and determines when and what sorts of accommodations will be made for individual students (Bray and McClaskey 2013). Personalised learning, they see, is student-centred, because the learner drives the learning by setting goals, building networks and connecting with interests and aspirations, and is responsible for the voice and choice made in the learning process. This aligns with Miliband's (2006) assertion that the focus in personalising learning is on the process of learning rather than the learning product.

In providing their own definition, the United States Department of Education [USDOE] (2010) purports that personalis*ed* learning is:

> instruction that is paced to learning needs, tailored to learning preferences, and tailored to the specific interests of different learners. In an environment that is fully personalized, the learning objectives and content as well as the method and pace may all vary. (p. 12)

This definition relies heavily on the notion of individualisation and differentiation, highlighting the distinctive features of these approaches as unique in content, style, outcomes and pace for individual learners. This individualisation and differentiation often risk leaving the learner to work alone on an individual pathway, time-table and programme (Sebba et al. 2007), something that may isolate students. This is in contrast to the notion of personalis*ing* learning, which is far more focused on the social aspects of learning through collaboration with peers and the wider community (Jones and McLean 2012). In fact, community is identified as a key tenet of personalising learning in Australia (Keamy et al. 2007) and in New Zealand (Ministry of

Education NZ 2006). The social and community focus personalising learning takes addresses the "personal" through the motivation that students gain through their sense of belonging (Sebba et al. 2007). In this way, personalising learning differs from personalised learning, and the two each differ from individualised learning.

The general notion of catering for personal needs, interests and aptitudes does not automatically imply agreement with the social element that is emphasised in personalising learning. In privileging collaborative group work in personalising learning, the needs of the collective often take precedence over the needs of individual group members, which indeed sounds contradictory to personalisation. However, this is not necessarily the case. Personalising learning is concerned with social and community-based groups within which the individual is encouraged to have a voice. Furthermore, the strategies used to personalise the learning are those that elicit and build on group members' prior knowledge and experiences and provide a balance between individual, small group and large group cooperation (Sebba et al. 2007). As de Freitas et al. (2005) explain:

> personalisation in this context means more than choice and selection of what and where to learn; it means formalizing a commitment to bring different communities together to enrich and broaden the learner's experience, through empowering the learner to take more control over what and how they learn. (p. 109)

This broader view of personalising learning thus takes into account the importance of teaching "learnacy" (Johnson 2004, p. 6) "where students learn to learn in a variety of ways" (Jones and McLean 2012, p. 76) and from a variety of others. In achieving this within an approach that still aligns with personalising learning, Johnson (2004) suggests that students' needs and interests can be categorised in groups rather than being viewed as strictly individual. It is this viewing of needs and interests within student-driven categories that the social nature of learning that is fundamental to personalising learning can be achieved.

There is significant overlap between the notions of personalised and personalising learning, which has also led to a level of interchangeability between the two terms in much of the literature. For example, although Miliband (2006) discusses personalised learning in the United Kingdom, the descriptions used to illustrate its achievement align with the notion of personalising learning. That is, it encourages a focus on collaborative and social learning in conjunction with catering for students' individual needs and interests. In this book, we also adopt a view of personalisation that includes this collaborative and social element of learning, and henceforth, all references to personalised learning and personalisation are intended within the framework of personalising learning that is described in this section.

2.3 The Emergence of Personalising Learning

Personalising learning gained its notoriety in the United Kingdom where the phrase "personalised learning" was coined by the then minister for state for School Standards, the Honourable David Milliband, during a 2003 speech at the North

England Education Conference. Following Milliband's speech, the concept of personalised learning attracted further government interest found its way on to political agendas and was reflected in policy aimed at informing classroom practices for improved educational outcomes (Sebba et al. 2007). The expansion of the discussion around personalised learning in the United Kingdom was particularly evident in *The Five Year Strategy for Children and Learners* (DfES 2004b) and *Higher Standards, Better Schools for All: More Choice for Parents and Pupils* (Her Majesty's Stationary Office 2005). However, personalised learning agendas in the United Kingdom were also driven by the imperative to improve public perception of government institutions (McRae 2010), and this led to a personalisation agenda of "reforming public services more broadly" (OECD 2006b, p. 3). In the United Kingdom, this approach to personalising learning led to a whole-of-government approach and extended beyond the school into the wider community (Keamy et al. 2007).

A growing awareness of a need to change service delivery models to meet the needs of individuals and society as a whole became the impetus for OECD interest in personalising education. *Schools for Tomorrow: Personalising Education* was the publication from the 2006 OECD London conference (OECD 2006b) that aimed to provide clarification of issues around personalising learning and its concomitant focus on moving thinking beyond the one-size-fits-all mentality that has permeated education since its formalisation in the eighteenth and nineteenth centuries. In this document, Milliband discusses five components that characterise the approach to personalised learning in the United Kingdom that aim to differentiate it from other learning theories. These components are:

1. Assessment for Learning (emphasising formative rather than summative assessment practices)
2. Effective Teaching and Learning (utilising student-centred approaches);
3. Curriculum Entitlement and Choice (providing a range of pathways for student learning)
4. Organising the School (using a whole-school approach to student learning and wellbeing)
5. Beyond the Classroom (establishing strong links and relationships with the wider community) (DfES 2004a)

Milliband suggests that these five components must be developed in the interests of the learner rather than in the interests of the school or institution (OECD 2006b). Various interpretations of these components of personalising learning can be found in educational strategies internationally and particularly in the educational policies of OECD countries.

In the United States, personalised learning is more closely aligned with differentiated instruction (Fullan 2009), where there is a focus on improving the performance of underachieving children (Keamy et al. 2007). Fullan (2009) purports that this is difficult to achieve because it suggests that schools, as a part of a complex system with limited resources, must meet the individual learning needs of all learners. He suggests that one possible way forwards may be to ensure that learners are engaged in meaningful learning experiences that connect learning in and out of school through a focus on personal relationships and providing learners with a voice in the decisions that affect their learning. For this to occur, it would seem to be important for teacher education programmes to engage more fully in preparing graduates whose university experiences contribute to a preparedness to enact approaches that can better personalise learning when they enter the profession as teachers.

Personalising learning has been embraced in New Zealand in similar ways to that of the United Kingdom. New Zealand's six components for personalising learning, outlined in *Let's Talk about Personalising Learning* (Ministry of Education NZ 2006), are similar to those described by Milliband in *Schools for Tomorrow: Personalising Education* (OECD 2006b). The six New Zealand components are:

1. Effective Teaching
2. Assessment for Learning
3. Curriculum
4. Professional Leadership (which aligns with the UK's Organising the School)
5. A Highly Supportive System (an additional component compared to the United Kingdom)
6. Strong and Engaged Communities (Ministry of Education NZ 2006)

The similarities between the ways in which the United Kingdom and New Zealand characterise personalising learning are clear. Both make explicit the requirement of assessment *for* learning or, in other words, formative assessment. They both emphasise the need for *effective* teaching and for a curriculum that provides pathways and choice for students. Engagement with communities beyond that of the classroom and school is also a feature of these models of personalising learning, as it is the notion of professional support, learning and wellbeing through the way in which schools are organised.

Whilst these features of personalising learning are noted and explained in these countries' education documents, the extent to which they are enacted by teachers and schools is less clear. A study reported by Bevan-Brown, McGee, Ward and MacIntyre (2011) aimed to investigate "whether components of personalised learning were being put into practice in New Zealand schools" (p. 76). This study was carried out using survey methodology and provided a return rate of 16% from 2473 questionnaires. Although personalising learning continues to be advocated in ministerial initiatives in New Zealand (e.g. see Statement of Intent 2007–2012), the findings of this study indicate that interpretations of personalising learning among the educational establishments are varied and do not always include all components. Similar findings were noted by Sabba et al. (2007) in the United Kingdom in relation to interpretations of personalised learning. In particular, Sabba et al.'s large-scale study highlighted confusion among teachers as to what difference there was between definitions of individualised and personalised learning. A stronger focus on personalising learning in teacher education programmes may assist in addressing this issue by providing teacher education students with learning experiences that are more akin to what they would be expected to provide in the field.

In the Australian context, and the state of Victoria in particular, personalising learning approaches have been largely influenced by Keamy et al. (2007). Their paper *Personalising education: From research to policy and practice* points to evidence from around the world that shows the success of learning approaches that personalise learning. This paper aimed to generate intellectual discussion around personalisation in education and to provide the basis for the exploration of learning approaches in Victorian schools through four tenets of personalising learning to drive educational reform. These tenets, drawn from national and international research, are:

1. Learners as Central
2. Information and Communications Technology (ICT)
3. Lifelong Learning
4. Communities of Collaboration

These tenets embed similar principles as the UK and US models of personalising learning described above. We have drawn on these four tenets throughout this book to explore personalising learning within the Australian context. The remainder of this chapter briefly outlines each of the tenets and introduces the theoretical underpinnings of personalising learning.

2.4   The Tenets of Personalising Learning

With its origins in Australia, this book explores personalising learning by drawing on Keamy et al.'s (2007) four key tenets of Learners as Central, ICT, Lifelong Learning and Communities of Collaboration. Keamy et al. (2007) claim that each of these tenets emerges from themes that are common to international personalising/personalised learning frameworks. The links to these international frameworks are explicated in the outline of the each of tenets below.

2.4.1   Learners as Central

The notion of learners being central in an approach that personalises learning stems from the idea that students' needs, interests and learning styles must be catered for in the learning process. In other words, it is an approach that is primarily concerned with teaching and learning that is student-centred. Student-centred learning is achieved when there are a variety of teaching strategies, where students find relevance in their learning through choice and when the contexts of learning are linked in meaningful ways to the world around them (Keamy et al. 2007). Student-centred learning also requires a focus on assessment *for* learning, whereby students' knowledge and abilities are assessed before and during the learning process in order to inform ongoing teaching practice. These ideas associated with Learners as Central are also evident in New Zealand's *Effective Teaching* and *Assessment for Learning* elements of personalising learning (Ministry of Education NZ 2006). The

United Kingdom's *Assessment for Learning, Teaching and Learning Strategies, Curriculum Entitlement and Choice* and a *Student-Centred Approach* (DfES 2004a) also capture these same elements of variety, choice, relevance and assessment to inform teaching practice.

2.4.2   Information and Communications Technology (ICT)

Keamy et al. (2007) identify ICT as a "key enabler" (p. 2) of learning due to its capacity to cater for diversity, enhance interactivity, connect with the globalised world and, for its mobility, allow learning to extend beyond the physical classroom. ICT is discussed in a similar way in the personalising/personalised learning frameworks of all other countries. For other countries, however, it is embedded in components of personalising learning rather than being an element in its own right. For example, in the United Kingdom, the component *Organising the School* is explicit about teachers learning how to use ICT effectively, and in *Effective Teaching and Learning*, ICT is highlighted as a focus area for accommodating differences in the pace at which students learn (DfES 2004a). The OECD (2006b) also refers to technology as "a personal cognitive and social tool" (p. 11). Hence the place of ICT in a personalising learning approach is ubiquitous, despite it being a tenet in its own right only within the Australian framework.

2.4.3   Lifelong Learning

Personalising learning is concerned with fostering habits and motivation for learning that stay with a person beyond the compulsory years of schooling. This lifelong interest and engagement in learning is identified by Keamy et al. (2007) as another tenet for personalising learning. Fostering the habits and mindsets associated with Lifelong Learning requires provision of flexible learning environments and a range of pathways that cater for all students (Keamy et al. 2007). These ideas are also evident in the "flexible curriculum" described in the United Kingdom's personalising learning elements of Curriculum *Entitlement and Choice* and *Beyond the Classroom*. Within these elements of the UK framework, there are multiple pathways within the school curriculum as well as opportunities for extracurricular and further education (DfES 2004a). For New Zealand, this same flexibility is referred to through opportunities for learning across and beyond the compulsory years of schooling in their component addressing *Strong and Engaged Communities* (Ministry of Education NZ 2006). These characteristics of achieving Lifelong Learning are embedded in the general teaching and learning approaches and are thought to create an attitude towards learning rather than being an teaching and learning strategy per se.

2.4.4   Communities of Collaboration

Communities of Collaboration refer to the need for students to be connected to one another, to their teachers and to other adults, in strong, supportive learning relationships. This notion of relationships within communities promotes the idea of learning networks rather than the more traditional view of learning as being a process that occurs in isolation from others (Keamy et al. 2007). This tenet also promotes approaches to learning in which there are strong and meaningful links to the wider community including the home, local institutions, community and businesses (Keamy et al. 2007). The notion of Communities of Collaboration is representative of New Zealand's *Strong and Engaged Communities* component of personalised learning which also encourages partnerships between schools, home and early childhood services (Ministry of Education NZ 2006). It is also apparent in the United Kingdom's *Beyond the Classroom* where support for student wellbeing is promoted through partnerships with the school and wider community (USDOE 2010).

These tenets of personalising learning and how they are supported by research and scholarship are explored in detail in Chaps. 3, 4, 5 and 6. In Chap. 7, we also provide connections between these tenets and research about effective teacher education. Before exploring the tenets themselves further, however, the core theoretical ideas informing personalising learning are introduced.

2.5   Theoretical Perspectives Informing Personalising Learning

One of the criticisms of personalising learning is that it does not offer anything new but, rather, is fairly typical about what is already known about "good" teaching (Johnson 2004; Sebba et al. 2007). In fact Beetham (2005) proposes that all learning is personal and that this is represented in the work of many learning theorists including Piaget, Bruner and Vygotsky, where Beetham argues that the process of constructing or internalising knowledge is in fact the same thing as personalising learning. We argue that whilst this may indeed be the case, what personalising learning does do is bring together a range of ideas and practices known about effective teaching into a useful framework that supports holistic learning for the twenty-first century. It "cherry-picks" the fundamental aspects of a range of learning theories. "Cherry-picking and cross-pollination" from different theories is how Murphy (2013, p. 7) proposes that new ideas and knowledge are formed. As such, there is no issue that aspects of the personalising learning philosophy are representative not only of Piaget's assimilation and Vygotsky's mediation and sociocultural theory but can also be likened to Dewey's (1897) progressive education, linked to Habermas' theories of knowing and connected to Freire's pedagogy of the oppressed.

Generally, most of the theoretical bases for personalising learning can be traced back to Marxist influences and the focus of these influences on reifying the status quo. Educationally, this would refer to the position that educational institutions play in reifying the power dynamics within societies, an upshot of schooling's early function to induct those of privilege and power into society, and as such, providing education for the elite. In line with the varying theories and theorists underpinning it, personalising learning belongs to the progressive education movement in which "ideas and practices aim to make schools more effective agencies of a democratic society" (College of Education and Social Services 2002). It endeavours to achieve this through the provision of "voice and choice" that is availed to students in shaping the teaching and learning process, through the fostering of habits of mind and attitudes for lifelong learning, and by cultivating communities of practice that value individuals as active participants and contributors to the community.

2.5.1 Learning as Active and Process Driven

The various definitions and elements of personalising learning culminate in the notion of student-centred, holistic learning focused on learning processes. Dewey (1897) recognised the importance of education as a "process of living and not a preparation for future living" (p. 76), a sentiment redolent of Millibrand's (2006) assertion that personalising learning emphasises process rather than product. This requires a distinct movement away from the more traditional forms of didactic teaching, which unfortunately still tend to dominate many teaching practices, and reinforces what Freire (1998) views as an example of oppression in education. This is particularly the case as formal learning progresses: more prevalent in secondary schools than primary and more prevalent in the lecture-style environment of tertiary institutions than in schools. Freire argued that education needed to be situated in the lived experiences of learners (Smith 2002), and a focus on student-centred nature of personalising learning and its concomitant elements help to achieve this.

In a similar vein to Freire, de Freitas and Yapp (2005) depict personalising learning as an active process where "the learner is an active agent rather than a passive recipient of learning" (p. xi). Passive learning aligns with Freire's criticism of conventional education as being analogous with "banking", where teachers make "deposits" of knowledge in the children they teach in a passive and oppressive manner (Freire 1998). This is counter to the more active approach to learning, where learners have far greater involvement and control over what is learnt and how it is learned, and teachers take on a role that is less sermonic and more one of facilitation and guidance. In this way, teachers are responsive to learners rather than requiring learners to be responsive to teachers and teaching. Dewey relayed a similar criticism of passive compared to active approaches to learning over a century ago:

> the active side precedes the passive in the development of the child nature...the neglect of this principle is the cause of a large part of the waste of time and strength in school work. (Dewey 1897, p. 79)

Informed by Dewey, Habermas also queries the role of the teacher and the types of pedagogies that are most effective for learning (Lovat 2013). Lovat describes Habermas' concern with authentic learning that is "infused with the subjectivity of the person doing the knowing" (p. 71). This is consistent with the ideas of personalising learning where the student is an active participant, central to the learning process. This centrality is important if the diversity of language, culture, interests and needs is to be taken into account in the learning process, and it is attention to these elements that indeed make the learner central. Of course, this is where some criticism comes for personalising learning where "the danger of creating an image of the learner as an isolated individual" (de Freitas and Yapp 2005, p. xi) has been expressed as a concern. Keamy et al.'s (2007) focus on "Communities of Collaboration" helps to ensure that this individualisation and isolation do not occur in personalising learning.

2.5.2   *Learning as Collaboration*

Personalisation "is not simply about supporting the single learner, but rather about supporting collaborative learning" (de Freitas et al. 2005, p. 109). Keamy et al. (2007) purport a similar view that manifests in their identification of collaboration as a key tenet of personalising learning. New Zealand's personalised learning also highlights learning through collaboration in their *Strong and Engaged Communities* in which the collaborative nature of a personalised approach is stipulated (Ministry of Education NZ 2006).

The emphasis on collaboration in personalising learning links strongly to the concept of sociocultural theory (Vygotsky 1978). Sociocultural theory recognises that teaching and learning, at its basis, is an interpersonal activity. As such, recognition of social and cultural influences is a fundamental component of any teaching and learning situation. Within sociocultural theory, John-Steiner and Mahn (1996) highlight Vygosky's well-known zone of proximal development (ZPD), where initially learners depend on more informed others to maximise their learning experience. Over time, the learner becomes more autonomous, and upon achieving independent knowledge, the scaffolds associated with the "guided participation" of ZPD are removed (Rogoff, as cited in John-Steiner and Mahn 1996). This is not dissimilar to Habermas' theory of knowing which also contains an element of the social through "communicative knowledge" – that which comes from interaction and dialogue with others – and ultimately "emancipation" when the learner is truly a free agent of knowing (Lovat 2013). Freire (1998) also emphasises dialogue in education, arguing that it needs to involve respect and people working with one another to enhance community and social capital (Freire 1998). As such, the notion of social, collaborative and community is ubiquitous in the thinking throughout the history of many educational scholars, positioning it as an established and valued practice of effective teaching and learning.

2.5.3 Learning as Construction of Knowledge

Another key similarity between the works of Vygotsky and Habermas that aligns with personalising learning is the interplay between individual and social processes that lead to construction of knowledge. Construction of knowledge as an effective means of learning is emphasised in sociocultural theory (John-Steiner and Mahn 1996) and underpins Habermas' notion of the emancipation of an informed person (Lovat 2013). The individual and social interplay is evident in most interpretations of Vygotsky's work, which acknowledges the interdependence on internal and external conditions. This interdependence claims that an individual's social experiences, from caregivers in infancy and childhood, to peers and mentors in life's later stages, all influence the participation and interpretation that the individual places on different experiences. This interpretation is otherwise known as the individual's construction of knowledge. Combining the social aspect of learning with the internalisation process, where individuals process and synthesise their experiences, allows these individuals to construct new ideas, perspectives and knowledge that ultimately become his/her own. Thus, it is claimed, "Vygotsky conceptualised development as the transformation of socially shared activities into internalised processes" (John-Steiner and Mahn 1996, p. 192).

Lovat (2013) also discusses internal and external influences on learning and purports that the connection between these is fundamental to Habermas' thesis. Lovat (2013) states of Habermas' theory:

> [e]xternally, one confronts one's enculturated past, one's corporate beliefs and community values, one's family, school, political and religious heritage. Internally, one confronts one's self: there is no knowing without knowing the knower. (p. 72)

Both Vygotsky, through sociocultural theory, and Habermas note the important features that characterise the diversity of learners that we encounter in education. This diversity needs to be taken into account in order to achieve authentic and meaningful learning for everyone. This is acknowledged in personalising learning where it is through this interplay between internal and external and individual and social that a Community of Collaboration can be achieved and where the diversity of individual learner needs is catered for. These connections firstly, demonstrate how personalising learning is situated within well-founded and well-argued elements of learning theory, and secondly, help to frame the place for each of the components important in personalising learning: those of effective teaching, learning and assessment, learner centredness, opportunities for collaboration, and the propensity for lifelong learning that stems from these types of learning experiences.

2.5.4   Learning with ICT

What is not addressed well by the theoretical perspectives outlined above is Keamy et al.'s (2007) identification of ICT as a key tenet of personalising learning. Technology is viewed as a generic skill in modern society, one required for active participation and citizenship (US Department of Education 2010). This pervasiveness in society makes ICT an important focus for twenty-first-century education. Such prevalence is also recognised in Hargreave's (2006) discussion of the place of technology in education where it is described as one of nine gateways to personalising learning. According to Hargreaves (2006), new technologies are associated with flexible and customised learning environments. In this way, technologies are essential for supporting a student-centred approach to learning as well as having their broader importance in regard to functioning adequately in an increasingly technologised society.

There is some criticism of the view of new technologies in not meeting the transformation of learning that they should, and that rather, current use of ICT does little more than manage approaches to learning (Hargreaves and Shirley 2009). Despite this criticism the view that technologies are key enablers in personalising learning persists. It is in recognition of this potential that Keamy et al. (2007) describe ICT as a key enabler through personalisation. Similar references are noted in the New Zealand document *Let's Talk about Personalising Learning* (Ministry of Education 2006) where ICT is described as "enabling students to be more in control of their own learning and work at a level that challenges them" (p. 5). A discussion paper entitled *Inspiring Action on Education* published by the Alberta government in Canada (2010) provides a link between "technology- and community-based activities" (p. 14) within personalised learning approaches that offer "flexible timing and pacing through a range of learning environments" (p. 14) and hence supports similar notions that technology is paramount in achieving a personalised approach. In this way ICT can be linked to Vygotsky's semiotic mediation: tools that "mediate social and individual functioning and connect the external and internal, the social and the individual" (John-Steiner and Mahn 1996, p. 192).

Despite the recognition of the importance of technology for twenty-first-century learning, findings of some studies (e.g. Robinson and Sebba 2010) examining the use of technology continue to find gaps in the ways in which it is used to personalise learning. Robinson and Sebba (2010) found that "genuine learner-led personalised learning using digital technologies was relatively rare in the ten case study institutions" (p. 774) of their study and indicated that curriculum and assessment requirements hindered effective use of technology for personalising learning. Their findings also suggested that personalising learning through the use of ICT required both students and teachers to possess "good technology skills" (p. 774), have an interest in technology and to be actively and collaboratively involved in decisions about learning. These findings would seem to support arguments for personalising learning in teacher education in order to provide graduates who are competent and confident to embrace personalising learning through the use of technology in their practice. Studies like that of Robinson and Sebba (2010) demonstrate the challenge that exists for educators to learn how to use ICT in ways that better meet its potential to transform learning.

2.6 Looking to the Future

In the current educational climate, personalising learning agendas remain key drivers of educational reform. However, there remains some confusion about the use of the term and what it means in different contexts. It is suggested that what is needed is a shared vision (McRae 2010) that will enable policy into practice. Other barriers to personalised learning as identified by Fullan (2009) are associated with the enduring nature of traditional views and approaches to schooling. Fullan (2009) states that "the traditions of schooling" (p. 2) stemming from the "factory" model or "one-size-fits-all" approaches impede personalisation of learning. Four other barriers he identifies are (1) international trends in relation to prescribed curriculum and standards-based reforms; (2) the overwhelming nature of the task of designing a programme that meets the individual needs and interests of all learners, particularly on a large scale; (3) a need to carry out assessment before, during and after learning in order to provide differentiated instruction; and (4) "gaps in teacher education and professional learning" (p. 2).

Looking to the future, it is perhaps through teacher education that these barriers can be addressed. Teacher education that engages students in active inquiry needs to challenge these barriers. This could occur through the provision of learning experiences that enable teacher graduates to be competent and confident in new ways of teaching and learning. Such strategies are already evident in some pedagogies specific to teacher education, such as critical reflective practice (Loughran and Hamilton 2016; Korthagen 2001) and study of core practices (Grossman et al. 2009). Tying these and other established approaches such as congruent teaching (Swennen et al. 2008), which privileges ideas around "meta-commentary" and explicit modelling (Loughran 2006), with the tenets of personalising learning and bringing these to the fore in teacher education programmes, offers another way forward. Hargreaves and Shirley (2009) point to "creativity, innovation, intellectual agility, teamwork, problem solving, flexibility and adaptability" (p. 85) as essential skills for the twenty-first century. In preparing teachers for the field, these skills need to be fostered in communities of inquiry. Perhaps through embedding the tenets of personalising learning (Keamy et al. 2007) in communities of inquiry within teacher education contexts, these tenets may act as seeds of change necessary for nurturing these skills in our future educational leaders.

References

Beetham, H. (2005). Personalisation in the curriculum: A view from learning theory. In S. de Freitas & C. Yapp (Eds.), *Personalizing learning in the 21st century* (pp. 17–24). London: Continuum International Publishing Group.

Bevan-Brown, J., McGee, A., Ward, A., & MacIntyre, L. (2011). Personalising learning: A fad or a cornerstone of education? *New Zealand Journal of Educational Studies, 46*(2), 75–88.

Bray, B., & McClaskey, K. (2013). A step-by-step guide to personalize learning. *Learning & Leading with Technology, 40*(7), 12–19.

College of Education and Social Services. (2002). *The John Dewey project on progressive education*, University of Vermont. Retrieved from http://www.uvm.edu/~dewey/articles/proged.html

Department for Education and Skills (DfES). (2004a). *A national conversation about personalised learning*. Nottingham: DfES Publications. Retrieved from www.standards.dfes.gov.uk/personalisedlearning

Department for Education and Skills (DfES). (2004b). *Five year strategy for children and learners*. Nottingham: DfES.

Dewey, J. (1897, 1929). My pedagogic creed. *School Journal, 54*, 75–81.

de Freitas, S., & Yapp, C. (Eds.). (2005). *Personalizing learning in the 21st century*. London: Continuum International Publishing Group.

de Freitas, S., Dickinson, C., & Yapp, C. (2005). Personalizing learning: Is there a shared vision? In S. de Freitas & C. Yapp (Eds.), *Personalizing learning in the 21st century* (pp. 109–112). London: Continuum International Publishing Group.

Freire, P. (1998). *Pedagogy of the oppressed* (New revised 20th anniversary ed.). New York: Continuum.

Fullan, M. (2009). Michael Fullan's answer to "what is personalized learning?" *Microsoft Education Partner Network*. Retrieved from http://www.michaelfullan.ca/media/13435863160.html

Grossman, P., Hammerness, K., & McDonald, M. (2009). Redefining teaching, re-imagining teacher education. *Teachers and Teaching, 15*(2), 273–289.

Hargreaves, D. (2006). *Personalising learning 2: Student voice and assessment for learning*. London: Specialist Schools Trust.

Hargreaves, A., & Shirley, D. (2009). *The fourth way: The inspiring future for educational change*. Thousand Oaks: Corwin Press. https://doi.org/10.4135/9781452219523.n4.

Her Majesty's Standards Office. (2005). *Higher standards, better schools for all: More choice for parents and pupils*. White Paper. London: HMSO.

Johnson, M. (2004). *Personalised learning: An emperor's outfit*. London: Institute for Public Policy Research (IPPR).

John-Steiner, V., & Mahn, H. (1996). Sociocultural approaches to learning and development: A Vygotskian framework. *Educational Psychologist, 31*(3–4), 191–206.

Jones, M., & McLean, K. J. (2012). Personalising learning in teacher education through the use of technology. *Australian Journal of Teacher Education, 37*(1). https://doi.org/10.14221/ajte.2012v37n1.1.

Keamy, K., Nicholas, H., Mahar, S., & Herrrick, C. (2007). *Personalising education: From research to policy and practice*. Melbourne: Department of Education and Early Childhood Development. 10.1080/00461520.1996.9653266.

Korthagen, F. (2001). *Teacher education: A problematic enterprise in linking practice and theory: The pedagogy of realistic teacher education*. Mahwah: Lawrence Erlbaum Associates.

Loughran, J. (2006). *Developing a pedagogy of teacher education: Understanding teaching and learning about teaching*. Abingdon, Oxon: Routledge.

Loughran, J., & Hamilton, M. (2016). Developing an understanding of teacher education. In J. Loughran & M. Hamilton (Eds.), *International handbook on teacher education* (Vol. 1, pp. 3–22). Singapore: Springer.

Lovat, T. (2013). Jurgen Habermas: Education's reluctant hero. In M. Murphy (Ed.), *Social theory and education research: Understanding Foucault, Habermas, Bordieu and Derrida*. Abingdon: Routledge.

McRae, P. (2010). The politics of personalization in the 21st century. *Alberta Teachers' Association Magazine, 91*(1), Retrieved from http://www.teachers.ab.ca/Publications/ATA%20Magazine/Volume-91/Number-1/Pages/The-Politics-of-Personalization-in-the-21st-Century.aspx

Miliband, D. (2006). Choice and voice in personalized learning. In OECD (Ed.), *Schooling for tomorrow: Personalising education* (pp. 21–30). Paris: OECD Publishing.

Ministry of Education NZ. (2006). *Let's talk about: Personalising learning*. Wellington: Learning Media.

Murphy, M. (Ed.). (2013). *Social theory and education research: Understanding Foucault, Habermas, Bordieu and Derrida*. Abingdon: Routledge.

Organisation for Economic Co-operation and Development (OECD). (2006a). *21st century learning: Research, innovation and policy. Directions from recent OECD analysis*. Paris: OECD Publishing. Retrieved from http://www.oecd.org/site/educeri21st/40554299.pdf

Organisation for Economic Co-operation and Development (OECD). (2006b). *Schooling for tomorrow: Personalising education*. Paris: Centre for Educational Research and Innovation, OECD.

Robinson, C., & Sebba, J. (2010). Personalising learning through the use of technology. *Computers and Education, 54*, 767–775.

Sebba, J., Brown, N., Steward, M., Galton, M., & James, M. (2007). *An investigation of personalising learning approaches used by schools* (Research report No. 843, University of Sussex). England: DfEs.

Smith, M. K. (2002). Paulo Freire and informal education. *The encyclopaedia of informal education*. Retrieved from http://infed.org/mobi/paulo-freire-dialogue-praxis-and-education/

Swennen, A., Lunenberg, M., & Korthagen, F. (2008a). Preach what you teach! Teacher educators and congruent teaching. *Teachers and Teaching: Theory and Practice, 14*(5-6), 531–542.

United States Department of Education (USDOE). (2010). *Transforming America education: Learning powered by technology*. Alexandria: US Department of Education. Retrieved from http://www.ed.gov/technology/netp-2010.

Vygotsky, L. S. (1978). *Mind in society. The development of higher psychological processes*. Cambridge, MA: Harvard University Press.

Chapter 3
Personalising Learning Through Communities of Collaboration

In Chap. 2 the notion of Communities of Collaboration as being fundamental to personalising learning was introduced. This chapter expands on the idea of Communities of Collaboration, explicating what they are, how they can be established and how they might be utilised for effective and collaborative learning. This explanation will demonstrate the importance of Communities of Collaboration and thus explore this tenet in relation to personalising learning. The "Communities of Practice" work of Lave and Wenger (1991) is heavily drawn on in this exploration, as it has been significant in informing the Communities of Collaboration ideas that Keamy et al. (2007) have identified in personalising learning. By examining Communities of Practice closely in this chapter, we are able to demonstrate the nuanced shift from this powerful and pervasive approach to learning and how this nuanced shift is important for considering collaborative and community-focused approaches to learning in formal education settings.

3.1 An Introduction to Communities of Collaboration

The notion of "Communities of Collaboration" within which the social aspect of learning is emphasised is not a new approach to learning per se but, rather, provides a relatively new phrase with a subtle difference from its foregrounding theory "Communities of Practice". Communities of Practice, an expression introduced by Lave and Wenger (1991) through their seminal work in situated learning theory, is drawn on heavily in this chapter due to what we see as its dominating influence in Keamy et al.'s (2007) conception of Communities of Collaborations. In their Communities of Practice work, Lave and Wenger (1991) provided a shift in the positioning of social participation from what Hughes et al. (2007) describe as an "adjunct to learning" to "the vehicle for learning itself" (p. 3). Despite this shift in the positioning of social participation as a part of the learning process, Wenger (2011) acknowledges that their coinage of the phrase is merely a description for an

© Springer Nature Singapore Pte Ltd. 2018
M. Jones, K. McLean, *Personalising Learning in Teacher Education*,
https://doi.org/10.1007/978-981-10-7930-6_3

age-old phenomenon that recognises the importance and centrality of the social condition for learning.

Since the release of their seminal work (Lave and Wenger 1991), Wenger in particular has expanded and refined the ideas behind Communities of Practice (cf. Wenger 1998, 2009, 2011). One initial refinement included an extrapolation on what is actually meant by the expression "Communities of Practice". In explaining this, Wenger (1998) referred to the notions of "learning, meaning and identity". In basic terms, "meaning" is represented by the negotiation that occurs through participation in and reification of practice "as an experience of everyday life" (p. 52). Through this practice of meaning making, identity as a member of and learner in the community is formed.

More recently, Wenger (2011) describes a Community of Practice as one that involves a group of people "who engage in a process of collective learning in a shared domain of human endeavor" (p. 1). He differentiates this from the generic term "community" because Communities of Practice have, at their basis, a collective learning outcome around which practice is discussed and enacted. This focused learning purpose is not a characteristic of the more universal understanding of the notion of community. As such, Wenger (2011) identifies three necessary criteria to qualify a Community of Practice. These are:

1. A domain, defined by the common interest that brings people together
2. A community, defined by the relationship between its members where there is collaboration, interaction and learning
3. Practice, a shared repertoire of resources, experiences, stories and tools; i.e. ways of practice within the domain

Together the elements of domain, community and practice constitute a Community of Practice.

3.2 Vygotsky and Social Learning

Prior to the popularity of the Communities of Practice approach, notions of social learning were generally (and for many, still are) attributed to the early work of Dewey (1916) and the following works of Lev Vygotsky (1978) through his sociocultural theory of learning, which is frequently termed social constructivism. Social constructivism is a theory of knowledge that asserts that the construction of knowledge is dependent on the social and cultural context in which a learner is situated. In this theory, Vygotsky recognises that there is interplay between the personal and the social experience that relates to an individual's cognitive development. Wenger (2009) recognises this interplay in Communities of Practice through his description of learning as a "two-way relationship between people and the social learning systems in which they participate" (p. 227).

Vygotsky's view of a child's development was "structured through, embedded in, and mediated in and by relationships with peers and adults" (Haenen et al. 2003,

Victorian School Room – 19th Century
Goring, Jack, Autobiographical notes, MS, pp.332
(c. 27,000 words). Brunel University Library.

Traditional dance of Solomon Islanders
Soka Village, Buena Vista Island. M. Jones, 2011, with
kind permission from Cultural Survival.

Fig. 3.1 Images depicting the cultural influences on approaches to teaching and learning

p. 251). Haenen et al. relate Vygotsky's words that "it is through others that we develop into ourselves" (p. 161). Vygotsky developed this notion into what is now commonly known as the "zone of proximal development" (ZPD). Through the ZPD, Vygotsky describes the increased learning potential that a person gains through interaction with an adult or more-able peer. Thus, the ZPD underpins the notion of a teaching-learning relationship where the teacher's role is the one of "more-able" and where she can organise and guide learning in a way such that the learner can achieve beyond the level he would be capable of achieving on his own. In this relationship, Vygotsky recognised that societal and cultural factors also shape the content and nature of learning. For example, in Victorian times, British children learned from their teachers by listening, reading and writing in large groups, where in contrast, many indigenous cultures around the world passed (and still pass) on knowledge and wisdom through oral story and dance (Fig. 3.1). Both examples are embedded within a type of community that is facilitated by experts, but different cultural norms influence the manner in which the teaching and learning occurs. These Vygotskian ideas about the social and cultural construction of knowledge and its characteristic ZPD provide the foundation for the more contemporary ideas of learning in Communities of Practice.

3.3   Communities of Practice as Distinct from Sociocultural Learning Theory

Whilst there are many commonalities between sociocultural theories of learning and the notion of Communities of Practice, there are some subtle but important differences that distinguish these two learning philosophies. Key similarities include the way in which both Communities of Practice through its situated learning theory, and sociocultural theory, embed learning within the social interactions that occur between learners. Such similarities stem, no doubt, from the development of situated learning theory as a contemporary form of sociocultural theory. Vygotsky's broad notions of learning are founded on the belief that learning occurs first externally, on a social plane and through social interaction, and then internally, within the individual (Vygotsky 1978). Communities of Practice also highlight learning embedded in social interaction, or as they refer to it, through social participation. In this way, both Vygotsky (1978) and Lave and Wenger (1991) situate the potential for learning in broad social settings.

The zone of proximal development, or ZPD, is probably the best-known aspect of Vygotsky's work in learning theory (Verenikina 2003), even though it was only quite a small component of his overall life work. ZPD has had a resounding impact in the applications of Vygotsky's work in formal education settings. In having this impact, and despite the warning of some researchers that it can be too narrowly interpreted and applied (Verenikina 2003), the role of the more-able peer associated with ZPD theory tends to be heavily emphasised in approaches to teaching and learning that are attributed to Vygotskian influences. A subtle difference that occurs here for the Communities of Practice approach is the emphasis on learning from interactions with the entire community rather than just on more-able peers. In Communities of Practice, there is a community of practitioners whose various behaviours, expectations and norms are gradually adopted by participating individuals as they forge their identity as a member of the community. Lave and Wenger (1991) liken this induction process to the notion of apprenticeship. They discuss the newcomer (or apprentice) entering a community and interacting with "old-timers" (p. 29) and the subsequent process of learning and identity formation that this instils. Lave and Wenger (1991) describe this process of transition from newcomer to established community member (or "old-timer") as "legitimate peripheral participation" (Lave and Wenger 1991, p. 29).

Legitimate peripheral participation represents the process of learning that takes the apprentice or newcomer from an entry level of participation through to increasing levels of "intense, interconnected and "knowledgeably skilled" participation" (Lave 1991, p. 69). This sounds somewhat similar to sociocultural ideas around scaffolding and even ZPD, but in fact it differs at a very fundamental level. In defining ZPD, Vygotsky was concerned with cognitive development of the learner and, as such, teacher-guided learning of concepts. Wood et al. (1976) introduced the term scaffolding to extend on Vygotsky's notion of guidance and, thus, describe the "help" given by an expert to support an individual's learning and development. Scaffolding has also been described as the way in which ZPD can be operationalised, although it is important to note that the interpretation of scaffolding is often inconsistent throughout the literature, particularly in terms of how much it is teacher controlled (Verenikina 2003). In general, whether scaffolding within the ZPD is imposed by the teacher or negotiated through collaboration with the learner, the idea of scaffolding is to facilitate appropriate support mechanisms until a certain independent stability in the learning is achieved. As this independence emerges, as with the scaffolding on a building site, the learning scaffold is gradually removed until the learner (or the building) is able to "stand alone".

Scaffolding is valued in education for what Verenikina (2003) describes as its "conceptual significance and practical value" (p. 1). Scaffolding allows for differentiated learning through the provision of distinctive scaffolds that are put in place depending on the learner's current knowledge and ability to learn. Despite its underpinnings in social processes influencing the learning, this concept of scaffolding which is generally understood to be a social learning process has intimations of being products-focused due to its intended outcomes of providing cognitive development to produce individual and independent learners. This product-oriented outcome of the learning process does not have the same focus in the Communities of Practice approach. Communities of Practice are more focused on the *process* of learning, rather than the particular outcome; and the community is more integral than any particular scaffolds or any particular individual. It is participation in the community through which learning is achieved. As such, Communities of Practice are concerned with the collective group rather than the individual, and learning is deemed to have occurred when the individual forges their identity as a knowledgeable practitioner within the community (Fuller 2007).

A further distinction can be made between Communities of Practice and Wood et al.'s (1976) popular notion of scaffolding. Scaffolding learning often suggests that the teacher provides fragments of the concept being taught, so the learner is given step-by-step support to ultimately reach a full understanding of the concept (although, as Verenikina 2003 warns, this level of teacher control was not necessarily Wood et al.'s intent). In Communities of Practice, Lave (1991) emphasises the need for participation to occur through "broad exposure to ongoing practice" (p. 71). Lave's explanation of participation here suggests that the novice needs to have complete exposure to unabridged ideas and practices rather than exposure/experience to its subsidiary parts. Through this comprehensive exposure to the community's practice, newcomers gradually form their own identity as community members who are then able to participate more fully. Hence in Communities of Practice, the whole is evident from the outset.

The Community of Practice consisting of the novice "apprentice" and the "old-timers" contains a further qualification that makes it distinct from other applications of sociocultural learning theory. Communities of Practice explicate the potential for learning by *all* members in the community, not just the novice learner. Moreover, Communities of Practice are more explicit in acknowledging that the "expert" is not necessarily in the formal role of teacher (Fuller 2007). This elevates the role of peer-to-peer interaction and, in some ways, is more representative of Vygotsky's broader work in sociocultural theories of learning. Also, the collective responsibility for learning is emphasised in a Community of Practice, as it requires a commitment to participation in order to learn from and with others in the community. In a more traditional approach to teaching and learning, there is still a required commitment to participate, and the learning does have a social aspect; however, the responsibility for learning falls more heavily on the teacher, rather than all members of the community. Here again, we see evidence of the influences of Vygotsky's broader ideas regarding the social nature of learning.

One of the more clear distinctions between Communities of Practice and Vygotsky's sociocultural theory of learning is the latter's focus on cognitive development of the individual. Fuller (2007) describes the key difference in a

Community of Practice approach where the cognitive focus is removed to overcome what he describes as being "pre-occupied with the development of the individual's mind" (Fuller 2007, p. 19), to an emphasis on the collective's ability, and the knowledge that enhances the individual's participation within the community. Thus, it is the capacity of the community as a whole to achieve, rather than that of the individual that influences the process of learning. Wenger and Nuckles (2015) contrast these conceptions of teaching and learning as the "acquisition metaphor versus the participation metaphor" (p. 625).

The considerations outlined above help to demonstrate ways in which contemporary sociocultural theory through Communities of Practice continues to develop the early ideas of Vygotsky as well as highlight its nuanced differences. Even though these differences exist, it is important to note that Communities of Practice is still rooted in constructivist theory (Barab and Duffy 2012), within which there are varying perspectives of which sociocultural theory is one. Notions of constructivism have a basis in how the learner's personal and/or social experience influences knowledge formation or, rather, how the learner is situated personally, socially, culturally, historically and physically. Growth in thinking and awareness of these varying ways in which a learner experiences the world, and the relationship this has with learning and knowledge formation, is how the more recent terminology of *situated* learning has emerged.

3.4   Situated Learning Theory

Communities of Practice are founded in situated learning theory. In simple terms, situated learning theory, a phrase attributed to Lave and Wenger (1991), acknowledges that learning occurs through participation in the social environment (community) in which particular knowledge is used/applied. "Theories of situated activity do not separate action, thought, feeling, and value and their collective, cultural-historical forms of located, interested, conflictual, meaningful activity" states Lave (2009, p. 202). In other words, learning cannot occur through decontextualised instruction; it is situated in social, cultural and physical environments; it is often informal and unintentional; and according to Hughes (2007), it is not a construct of "how learning *ought to be* but, rather, ... an approach which could help reveal learning as it *actually is*" (p. 32, emphasis in original).

Situated learning originated from Lave and Wenger's (1991) studies of people in workplaces, namely, Yucatec midwives, Vai and Gola tailors, naval quartermasters, meat cutters and non-drinking alcoholics. Despite these origins, applications of situated learning have permeated various sectors and have become particularly prevalent in school settings. Barab and Duffy (2012) describe the implications of situated learning theory as requiring a shift "from the teaching of concepts to engaging the learner in authentic tasks that are likely to require the use of those concepts or skills" (p. 34). If the latter of these approaches is applied, the idea from anthropology, where situated learning has its roots, is that the learning of the requisite concepts and skills will occur naturally. This sort of "incidental learning" through exposure and participation is often thought of as informal learning. In a Community of Practice, however, the intentions are more defined, and the activities and experiences made available to promote exposure and participation are selected more deliberately.

The key elements of situated learning theory, as Barab and Duffy (2012) describe, "emphasize the reciprocal character of the interaction in which individuals, as well as cognition and meaning, are considered socially and culturally constructed" (p. 30). Essentially, this tries to capture the notion that "what is learned" cannot be separated "from how it is learned and used" (Brown et al. 1989, p. 32). This description sounds, and is, very similar to the premise of sociocultural constructivism. Where situated learning theory differs from constructivist theories is in its anthropological roots. Constructivism (which is explored in greater detail in Chap. 5 of this volume) is primarily concerned with knowledge acquisition. This acquisition of knowledge occurs in the individual's mind as they construct meaning (Land et al. 2012) from the information/experiences and social situations to which they are exposed. As noted earlier, this acquisition focus, even if it is through social means, still tends towards a product-focused view of learning.

The cognitive emphasis of learning in constructivism arises from its roots in educational psychology where it has predominantly been theorised, defined and presented by educational psychologists. Situated learning is anthropological in focus. It has been theorised, defined and presented with the heavy influence of anthropologist Jean Lave. Anthropology puts the whole person as the focus of study. It views learning as a "relational property of individuals in context and in interaction with one another" (Hoadley 2012, p. 287). The anthropological nature of situated learning means it is more concerned with the learning process, so it emphasises the social and cultural more than the cognitive.

Jarvis (2009) joins the many proponents of Communities of Practice in supporting a more anthropological view of learning. He states:

> Fundamental to our understanding of learning, therefore, is our understanding of the whole person in the social situation – it is a philosophical anthropology but also a sociology and psychology. Once we recognise that learning is not just psychological and that the exclusive claims of psychology detract from the fullness of our understanding of learning, we can look afresh at human learning. (Jarvis 2009, p. 31)

Barab and Duffy (2012) provide a useful comparison of the core differences between psychological and anthropological views of learning that further assist in describing both the underpinnings and the distinguishing features of each approach. They identify features of psychological versus anthropological perspectives in terms of:

- The focus of learning: cognition versus community relationships
- Who learns: students versus members of the community
- The unit of analysis: the activity versus the individual
- The outcomes: meaning alone versus meanings, identities and communities
- The location: schools versus the everyday world

- The learning goals: preparing for future tasks versus meeting immediate community/societal needs
- The implications for pedagogy: practice fields versus communities of practice (Adapted from Barab and Duffy 2012, p. 34)

Whilst this dichotomy is useful for understanding the underpinning principles informing practice in these two approaches to learning, the relationship between them must still be remembered. Constructivist views of learning are still important in addressing cognitive development. Situated learning expands on this and brings in additional factors influencing the learner. It is useful to consider the view of Jarvis (2009) who warns that:

> exclusive claims should not logically be made for any single theory… profound doubt is cast on many contemporary theories of learning as providing logical understanding of human learning, including behaviourism, information processing and all forms of cognitive theory. This is not to say that they are not valid in as far as they go, simply that they do not go far enough: they all have an incomplete theory of the person. (p. 32)

Indeed, achievement of a unifying theory of learning is elusive. Situated learning does, however, recognise the complexity of learning and its many contributing factors. It takes us into a different era of theorising, defining and presenting the notion of learning and its increasing mosaic of influential factors. However, in spite of its recent and pervasive ascendency in the discourses around learning theory and practice, it is not without its criticisms.

3.5   Critiques of Situated Learning and Communities of Practice

Criticisms of situated learning and its concomitant Communities of Practice are quite wide ranging. Lave and Wenger's (1991) situated learning theory was one of the first attempts to provide a theory of learning that shifted thinking away from psychological influences of learning to one that was more anthropological in basis. Although elements of their theory were present in learning discourses, such as social and cultural influences on learning, these antecedent discourses applied these terms to learning in regard to their influence on cognitive processes within an acquisition paradigm of learning. Lave and Wenger (1991) challenged this ubiquitous view and repositioned social and cultural factors as core to learning processes. However, as even they concede, their introduction to this new way of thinking was "left largely as an intuitive notion" (Lave and Wenger 1991, p. 42). Thus, criticisms quickly emerged concerning the lack of detail in how the shift in thinking was manifested in practice. Other criticisms have targeted the notion of "true" community when in reality, hierarchies and power relations exist in almost every organisation or group (community) of people. The emphasis on the collective has also drawn criticism as some argue that learning is ultimately something that occurs within the individual. These common criticisms of situated learning and

Communities of Practice are explored further in the following sections, and considered in particular, with regard to their relevance for education and schooling.

3.5.1   There's a Lack of Guidance to Translate the Theory into Practice

The most pervasive criticism of situated learning and Communities of Practice concerns the lack of specificity of how to put situated learning theory and Communities *of* Practice *into* practice. One author, for example, describes the original work of Lave and Wenger (1991) as "heuristic, controversial and provocative rather than exhaustive and definitive" (Hughes et al. 2007, p. 4). Subsequently, there have been a number of attempts to apply the theory across a multitude of contexts to experiment with this new approach to learning. As noted earlier, these contexts of application and study have often fallen outside of the workplace foci in which situated learning had its genesis.

Learning through Communities of Practice arose from Lave and Wenger's analysis of five case studies of workplace apprenticeships (Yucatec midwives, Vai and Gola tailors, naval quartermasters, meat cutters and non-drinking alcoholics). In saying this, however, Wenger (2000) does indicate that Communities of Practice are not a construct that he and Lave created; but rather:

Yucatec midwives; Vai and Gothe la tailors; naval quartermasters; meat cutters; and non-drinking alcoholic

> communities of practice have been around for as long as human beings have learned together. At home, at work, at school, in our hobbies, we all belong to communities of practice, a number of them usually. (Wenger 2011, p. 3)

Although Communities of Practice may be ubiquitous in the way Wenger (2011) describes, the analysis of the case studies he and Lave engaged in, and, indeed, early writings around situated learning, was based on workplaces, not classrooms of teachers and children. Hence, one distinctive example of the change in context arises from the application of Communities of Practice in approaches to learning and teaching in the formal school setting. Whilst both workplaces and classrooms can be likened in some ways, there are also substantial differences in a classroom or school "community" where the number of minors (children/students) far outweighs the number of teachers and where there is considerable difference in the age, in the accountability, and in the power relations between the two.

What this means is that there is little illustration of what situated learning theory and Communities of Practice look like in school education, and little to no guidance on how they can be implemented. This criticism is given to the use of the theory in its application to general organisational settings but possibly applies even more so to school settings. Lave and Wenger first conceptualised situated learning through the empirical data arising from their five different community organisations/group case studies. Technically, the rich description of these contexts gives some illustration of what situated learning looks like in practice. When it comes to the use of the theory in schools, however, it has been borrowed, interpreted and then applied to the classroom and school community. Certainly, there was no initial illustration of the practice in what is a substantially different setting where members of the community tend to be differentiated in terms of age, intended outcomes and the types of working relationships that can all exist in very different ways.

Despite the lack of guidance and the limited number of examples from which Lave and Wenger (1991) drew on to articulate their social theory of learning, situated learning and Communities of Practice have become prolific in a multitude of contexts. Many adaptations have occurred as different groups have borrowed and selected from what was initially a largely "intuitive notion". Today, this means we have a mosaic of examples of practice where a "one-size-fits-all" set of steps for implementation is unlikely to ever be appropriate or possible.

3.5.2   Power Relations and Communities of Practice

Related to this complication around applying situated learning theory in the fairly unique societal context of schools comes another key criticism of the approach. A number of authors have identified difficulty in the notion of "true" Communities of Practice due to the inherent nature of any groups of people to have some sort of hierarchy and power plays that influence the relationships and the nature of membership of people in a given group. Such a concern is detailed by Hughes et al. (2007):

> 'situated learning' and 'legitimate peripheral participation' can be framed in terms of access to, and sanctioned membership of, speech communities. Inequalities within communities of practice reflect socio-linguistically mediated practices of inclusion and exclusion. Positions of subordinate and superordinate authority – such as novice and old-timer – are coded and legitimated in and through the implicit and explicit use of language. Divisions between multiple communities of practice reflect hierarchies of cultural prestige and moral value that are embedded in modes of talk. (p. 9)

The primary concern of such a power play is that:

> a 'community of practice' might become a place where employees are 'indoctrinated' and where knowledge, ideas, innovations become 'appropriated' by those who hold the most power resources within that community. (Hughes 2007, p. 38)

Indeed, Wenger (2000) himself notes the "urgent need" that we have as newcomers to a particular group/community of expertise "to align our experience with the competence 'they' define" (p. 227). Given the age difference, relative expertise and the position of authority that teachers have compared to students in school and, for the most part, university settings, the construct of power is surely unable to be negotiated in ways that would represent "true" equality between members of the community. "Indoctrination", as Hughes et al. (2007) term it, is a likely outcome in these settings, especially in terms of behaviour, and in terms of the boundaries around what is offered for learning within the formal learning community and what is not. Engeström (2009) notes this spurious side of Communities of Practice in relation to hierarchical organisations, which schools and universities both qualify. He notes the difficulty of finding explicit guidance in how Communities of Practice can be implemented in what he refers to as "highly rationalised hierarchical mass-production organizations" (Engeström 2009, p. 43).

Lave and Wenger (1991) themselves note that power relations are not dealt with well in their original work and urge for increased analysis of how this aspect of Communities of Practice might operate. This call for more research does not mean that power relations are forgotten entirely in Lave and Wenger's work. As Contu and Willmot (2003) remind us, Lave and Wenger "incorporate considerations of power in respect to "the social organization of and control over resources" (Lave and Wenger 1991, p. 37)" (p. 285). Contu and Willmot also purport that notions of power are fundamentally tied to the meaning of "legitimate peripheral participation" and the notion of "newcomers" and "old-timers" – all cornerstones of Lave and Wenger's original work – although they also note that the ways in which learning is "embedded in relations of subordination" (p. 288) are lacking.

We would argue that the key question around this notion of power relations in formal learning communities is not so much about the appropriateness of hierarchy, subordination nor indoctrination but rather on how teachers work within this power relation to establish and promote a practice community where students feel a sense of belonging. It is, after all, the sense of belonging that primarily assists the forging of identity in the community, which in turn provides the impetus for participation and subsequently, development of competence. Wenger (2000) captures this saying "identity is a vehicle for participating in the social world" and that "a healthy identity is socially empowering" (p. 240).

3.6 Communities of Practice and Personalising Learning

The overview of situated learning and Communities of Practice provided here reinforces the notion of personalising learning that we are advocating: not as an individualised or individualistic approach, but rather, one that relies on the establishment and membership in a learning community. In personalising learning, individuals participate in a social environment through the social interactions they establish. This interaction and participation then lead to the scope for individuals to transform their ideas on the range of subject matter available in the learning environment. Learning approached in such a manner is what Wenger (2000) defines as:

> an interplay between the social competence and personal experience. It is a dynamic, two-way relationship between people and the social learning systems in which they participate. It combines personal transformation with the evolution of social structures. (Wenger 2000, p. 227)

It is in this interplay that the individual's learning needs, interests and preferences are catered for in the social setting of the classroom. Learning cannot be separated from that of other individuals sharing the learning space, and it cannot be decontextualised from real-life, real-world contexts. Indeed, Lave and Wenger (1991) purport that

> The organization of schooling as an educational form is predicated on claims that knowledge can be decontextualized, and yet schools themselves as social institutions and as places of learning constitute very specific contexts. (p. 40)

Personalising learning privileges the social construction of knowledge through participation in authentic, real-world contexts that learners can identify with and see relevance of in the broader world. It is a disposition towards learning that "engages the personal within the social frame" (Billet 2007, p. 60).

What we also recognise is that particular power plays and hierarchies are in some ways, an insurmountable barrier to forming what some call a "true" Community of Practice. The school and university classroom setting does not really allow for absolute equality between teachers and students; indeed such a move would be irresponsible in light of teachers' duty of care in these settings. It is this subtle movement away from the "newcomer" and "old-timer" notions in Communities of Practice that the more nuanced phrase of "Communities of Collaboration" is important. Whilst still borrowing heavily from the underpinning theory of social learning, Communities of Collaboration allow for this shift away from the more strict view of a Community of Practice and better acknowledge the working arrangements and relationships that predicate formal settings of education.

Situated learning remains an important underpinning theory in personalising learning. However, we also recognise the element of learning that does indeed occur as a cognitive function. Korthagen (2010) contends that "we seem to be faced with an intriguing and unsolved theoretical question, namely how the situated learning perspective and the perspective of traditional cognitive theory can be reconciled" (p. 99). Whether or not reconciliation between the two theories can be reached is a topic for discussion that falls outside the parameters of this book. Although, it is worth noting that in some ways, the debate around this lack of reconciliation reminds us of the contention that theory does not always translate easily into a set of steps to inform practice. However, theory can be used as a guide for informing particular pedagogical decisions, and we suggest that there is not a great need to align exclusively with theoretical notions stemming from anthropology or psychology. It is likely, in fact, that there are contexts where the two can work in a complementary fashion to maximise potential for learning. This is reflected in Jarvis' (2009) assertion that "it is impossible to have a theory that explains the learning process in every detail" (p. 31) and that openness to a "broader perspective will help us understand learning better" (p. 32).

We believe that personalising learning offers a framework for thinking about learning and teaching where such different perspectives on learning can come together and work in a complementary manner to enhance learning opportunities. Certainly, participation remains the key focus. Participation caters for the individual and the community, be it the small "sub" level community within a larger organisation or the larger organisation itself. What is important is the notion of participation of some kind.

> Placing the focus on participation has broad implications for what it takes to understand and support learning:
>
> - For individuals, it means that learning is an issue of engaging in and contributing to the practices of their communities.
> - For communities, it means that learning is an issue of refining their practice and ensuring new generations of members.
> - For organizations, it means that learning is an issue of sustaining the interconnected communities of practice through which an organization knows what it knows and thus becomes effective and valuable as an organization. (Wenger 2009, p. 213)

Ultimately, we see a key place for situated learning and Communities of Collaboration in schools and universities. We are aligned with Wenger's (2011) advice on what this means for teaching and learning, and although he was referring to schools in particular, we see it as equally applicable in the university setting. He states:

> The perspective of communities of practice affects educational practices along three dimensions:
>
> - Internally: How to organize educational experiences that ground school learning in practice through participation in communities around subject matters?
> - Externally: How to connect the experience of students to actual practice through peripheral forms of participation in broader communities beyond the walls of the school?
> - Over the lifetime of students: How to serve the lifelong learning needs of students by organizing communities of practice focused on topics of continuing interest to students beyond the initial schooling period?

From this perspective, the school is not the privileged locus of learning. It is not a self-contained, closed world in which students acquire knowledge to be applied outside, but a part of a broader learning system. The class is not the primary learning event. It is life itself that is the main learning event. Schools, classrooms, and training sessions still have a role to play in this vision, but they have to be in the service of the learning that happens in the world." (p. 5)

3.7 Conclusion

The importance of Communities of Collaboration as a key tenet in personalising learning is related to its defining elements that learning is process rather than product focused, participatory rather than acquisitional and collective rather than individual. This also helps to further the explanation provided in Chap. 2 as to how and why personalising learning is not analogous to individualised learning. Indeed, an individualised approach to learning would be antithetical to personalising learning, where Communities of Collaboration and its associated defining elements of process, participation and the collective are considered core.

Despite challenges, critics and, at times, a lack of clarity around what constitutes a Community of Collaboration and how it operates, we believe teachers and teacher educators are agents for establishing strong Communities of Collaboration that can enhance engagement, participation, motivation, identity formation and learning through everyday practices. We also acknowledge the notion that there is not one theory that can or should be applied to the way in which teaching and learning is approached. Teaching is a "complex and sophisticated business" (Loughran 2014, p. 275). Imagining that there is a unifying theory that addresses this complexity and sophistication does a disservice to the extraordinary difficulty that exists in creating a learning environment that is effective for everyone. Establishing a Community of Collaboration, based on ideas of Communities of Practice, is, we believe, one of the key elements in achieving this.

References

Barab, S., & Duffy, T. (2012). From practice fields to communities of practice. In D. Jonassen & S. Land (Eds.), *Theoretical foundations of learning environments* (2nd ed., pp. 29–65). New York: Routledge.

Billet, S. (2007). Including the missing subject: Placing the personal within the community. In J. Hughes, N. Jewson, & L. Unwin (Eds.), *Communities of practice: Critical perspectives* (pp. 55–67). Oxon: Routledge.

Brown, J., Collins, A., & Duguid, P. (1989). Situated cognition and the culture of learning. *Educational Researcher, 18*(1), 32–42.

Contu, A., & Willmott, H. (2003). Re-embedding situatedness: The importance of power relations in learning theory. *Organization Science, 14*, 283–290.

Dewey, J. (1916). *Democracy and education: An introduction to the philosophy of education.* New York: Macmillan.

Engeström, Y. (2009). From communities of practice to mycorrhizae. In J. Hughes, N. Jewson, & L. Unwin (Eds.), *Communities of practice: Critical perspectives* (pp. 41–54). Oxon: Routledge.

Fuller, A. (2007). Critiquing theories of learning and communities of practice. In J. Hughes, N. Jewson, & L. Unwin (Eds.), *Communities of practice: Critical perspectives* (pp. 17–29). Oxon: Routledge.

Haenen, J., Schrijnemakers, H., & Stufkens, J. (2003). Sociocultural theory and the practice of teaching historical concepts. In A. Kozulin, B. Gindis, V. Ageyev, & S. Miller (Eds.), *Vygotsky's educational theory in cultural context* (pp. 246–266). New York: Cambridge University Press.

Hoadley, C. (2012). What is a community of practice and how can we support it? In D. Jonassen & S. Land (Eds.), *Theoretical foundations of learning environments* (2nd ed., pp. 286–299). New York: Routledge.

Hughes, J. (2007). Lost in translation: Communities of practice – the journey from academic model to practitioner tool. In J. Hughes, N. Jewson, & L. Unwin (Eds.), *Communities of practice: Critical perspectives* (pp. 30–34). Oxon: Routledge.

Hughes, J., Jewson, N., & Unwin, L. (Eds.). (2007). *Communities of practice: Critical perspectives.* Oxon: Routledge.

Jarvis, P. (2009). Learning to be a person in society. Learning to be me. In K. Illiris (Ed.), *Contemporary theories of learning … Learning theorists in their own words* (pp. 21–34). Abingdon: Routledge.

Keamy, K., Nicholas, H., Mahar, S., & Herrrick, C. (2007). *Personalising education: From research to policy and practice*. Melbourne: Department of Education and Early Childhood Development.

Korthagen, F. (2010). Situated learning theory and the pedagogy of teacher education: Towards an integrative view of teacher behavior and teacher learning. *Teaching and Teacher Education, 26*, 98–106.

Land, S., Hannafin, M., & Oliver, K. (2012). Student-centered learning environments: Foundations, assumptions and design. In D. Jonassen & S. Land (Eds.), *Theoretical foundations of learning environments* (2nd ed., pp. 3–25). New York: Routledge.

Lave, J. (2009). The practice of learning. In K. Illeris (Ed.), *Contemporary theories of learning: Learning theorists ... in their own words* (pp. 200–208). Abingdon: Routledge.

Lave, J. (1991). Situating learning in communities of practice. *Perspectives on Socially Shared Cognition, 2*, 63–82.

Lave, J., & Wenger, E. (1991). *Situated learning: Legitimate peripheral participation (learning in doing: Social, cognitive and computational perspectives)*. Cambridge: Cambridge University Press.

Loughran, J. (2014). Professionally developing as a teacher educator. *Journal of Teacher Education, 65*(4), 271–283.

Verenikina, I. (2003). *Understanding scaffolding and the ZPD in educational research*. Proceedings of the International Education Research Conference (AARE – NZARE), 30 November–3 December 2003, Auckland, New Zealand. Retrieved from http://www.aare.edu.au/data/publications/2003/ver03682.pdf

Vygotsky, L. (1978). *Mind in society. The development of higher psychological perspectives*. Cambridge, MA: Harvard University Press.

Wenger, E. (1998). *Communities of practice: Learning, meaning and identity*. New York: Cambridge University Press.

Wenger, E. (2000). Communities of practice and social learning systems. *Organization, 7*(2), 225–246.

Wenger, E. (2009). A social theory of learning. In K. Illiris (Ed.), Contemporary theories of learning ... Learning theorists in their own words (pp. 209–218). Abingdon, Oxon: Routledge..

Wenger, E. (2011). *Communities of practice: A brief introduction*. Retrieved from http://hdl.handle.net/1794/11736

Wenger, E., & Nuckles, M. (2015). Knowledge acquisition or participation in communities of practice? Academics' metaphors of teaching and learning at the university. *Studies in Higher Education, 40*(4), 624–643.

Wood, D., Bruner, J., & Ross, G. (1976). The role of tutoring in problem solving. *Journal of Child Psychology and Psychiatry, 17*, 89–100.

Chapter 4
ICT for Learning: Technology and Pedagogy

Information and communications technologies (ICTs) are pervasive in twenty-first-century society, something that subsequently warrants their importance in twenty-first-century education. Whilst the use of ICTs in education is fairly ubiquitous, the ways in which they are utilised are, however, quite varied. A range of factors influence the ways in which ICTs are used in education including those related to access, socio-economic status, ethics, cyber safety and teacher confidence and competence. These influential factors have contributed to technology use in schools becoming an important topic for consideration, particularly in regard to the what, where and how of ICT for learning. Fitting with the theme of this manuscript, the considerations privileged in this chapter are those concerned with the relationship between ICT, pedagogy and personalising learning. We explore ICT's potential to be a vehicle for personalising learning and argue that the achievement of such potential lies in understanding the perspectives of, and relationships with, pedagogy in deeper thinking about technology and learning that teachers and teacher educators need to undertake.

4.1 Introduction

Recognising the prevalence of ICT in society and its potential for enhancing twenty-first-century teaching and learning, Keamy et al. (2007) identify it as one of their four key tenets. Aligned with their overarching view of teaching and learning, Keamy et al. describe ICT as an enabler of personalising learning that:

- allows each pupil greater diversity for learning
- enhances interactivity between individual students and individual teachers
- provides a space for personalised, flexible learning beyond the classroom walls
- allows students to live locally whilst learning globally – through the use of external resources accessed via the world wide web. (Keamy et al. 2007, p. 2)

© Springer Nature Singapore Pte Ltd. 2018   41
M. Jones, K. McLean, *Personalising Learning in Teacher Education*,
https://doi.org/10.1007/978-981-10-7930-6_4

In order for this tenet to be realised in personalising learning, it is important to understand the complex relationship between ICT, learning, theory and pedagogy in education. Each component in the relationship between ICT and learning, and in particular technological, theoretical and pedagogical components, has a significant history of development and contribution to learning in its own right. It is no surprise, therefore, that for the full potential of ICT to be realised in personalising learning, teacher educators, practising teachers and pre-service teachers need to understand some of the complexity of this relationship. Romeo (2015) describes teachers as being "confused and conflicted about the value of technology for learning and teaching" (p. 23) and notes that the transformational effects of technology, and in particular ICT, continue to be highly contested. In this chapter, we consider ICT in relation to its historical roots in the broader use of the term "technologies" to describe tools or equipment used in processes (Yallop et al. 2005). Our use of the term ICT embraces this process focus and aligns in particular with Jonassen et al.'s (2008) idea of technology for processes of communication.

A brief exploration of the three major components of the technology-theory-pedagogy relationship highlights the interwoven contributions of each to ICT as an enabler of learning in personalisation approaches. Factors influencing the uses of ICTs in education are briefly considered including those related to use and function, access, socio-economic status, ethics, cyber safety, information integrity and teacher confidence and competence. Before this exploration, however, it is important to note the ways in which certain terms and ideas have been conceived in the writing of this chapter. The term "learning" has been used in this chapter to describe the individual acquisition of knowledge skills and understanding. The term "education" is used as a descriptor of the formal, institutional or organisational entity that embodies community's or society's policies and practices for facilitating learning. It is also important to note that we acknowledge that information and communications technologies and education and learning have all been in existence since before the notions of "teaching", "learning", "education" and "school" entered the lexicon of general language. This chapter discusses these notions within a more contemporary understanding of what these terms have come to mean.

4.2   Technology and ICT

4.2.1   ICT Use and Function

The characteristics and aspects of technology which might be considered in harnessing the technological perspective in personalising learning can be made using as an illustration of the functionality of the well-known and usually much-loved device – the mobile or "smart" phone. The relatively simple interface and sophisticated integration of numerous functions and applications of a smart phone would hardly be considered complex to use by its "skilled" operators. Smart phone users may not know "how it all works together", but generally users do know how to "press the buttons" or "select the apps", to achieve the connectivity that is desired. The operation of mobile or smart phones is relatively simple and yet increasingly sophisticated. Communicating by smart phone, using text, video or audio, is, in most cases, relatively simple too. Accessing and storing data on a smart phone is also a relatively straightforward operation for most people. Further, the information databases that can be accessed using a smart phone are seemingly endless, adding unprecedented information options to communication. In other words, without much conscious thinking, a great deal of the world's information is literally "at the fingertips" of the mobile user.

The functionality, diversity of information and mobility of ICT devices in the public realm are those capabilities that Keamy et al. (2007) allude to as giving the promise of flexibility and access that can be harnessed in personalising learning. It may also be that the capabilities "behind the face" of the device provide even more potential. These capabilities do, however, come with the need for increased knowledge and skill, especially in teacher education, and perhaps most critically, in developing an approach that engages personalising learning. For example, whilst the inclusion of graphics in teaching materials is widely accepted as a positive addition in design, knowing where to place and how to best utilise a graphic image, or even to portray the intended message through an appropriate visual image, is not always simple or easy to achieve. Perhaps even more crucial here are the teaching considerations, such as those raised by McLaren (2012), who asks how teachers might consider ethics and emotions in the technology space. Dealing with controversial issues of ICT usage requires even greater perception and response in the technological learning space than that normally associated with the more familiar classroom pedagogies in which the teacher and teacher educator can almost immediately gauge the nuances of the learner responses. In personalising learning approaches, using ICT with such features may not be readily available in the technological learning space. This suggests a need for teachers and teacher educators to develop a different awareness of the nuances of the technology space, to counter the fact that these may not otherwise be seen or heard immediately. Rather, sensitivity to other cues in the learning environment may be needed to form a part of the pedagogy for teaching and learning with ICT.

4.2.2 The Integrity of Information

Another challenge that teachers of contemporary ICT-enhanced learning spaces encounter relates to the notion of information integrity. Although powerful search engines may, in a fraction of a second, generate a vast array of seemingly related information to given search terms, a second consideration in personalising learning with technology is the extent to which identified information is actually useful to the user. Although the simplicity of clicking and texting opens doors to an abundance of information, the value of the information is dependent on the knowledge, understanding and skills of the user in determining its worth (Ng 2015). Information per se might be called a "neutral commodity", but it is the relationship of the information to the characteristics of the "problem", "inquiry" or learning it addresses that characterise its value. For example, a weather observation and prediction "It looks like storms" says very little. A weather prediction comment "It looks like storms" made by a child looking at the sky is often a keen observation, but not information on which weather warnings for industry or business would be made. A weather prediction "It looks like storms" made by experts from the Department of Meteorology and transmitted over numerous synchronous devices will be taken seriously by those needing to prepare for such eventualities. Thus, the user (and by default the teacher of such users) must be able to critically examine not just the information itself that they access but also the authority and reliability of its source.

A similar notion emerging in more recent times is that of "fake news". Fake news is that which is broadcast globally, from known or unknown sources, and which gains the attention of media and individuals across the world and is often difficult to distinguish from "real news" (Shellenbarger 2016). In a study exploring teenagers' views of news (Marchi 2012), it was found that teenagers prefer news in the form of opinion pieces rather than objective reporting of issues and events. Marchi's study also unpacked a number of definitions of fake news such as that being parodied in comical or satirical television shows and a close link between humour, interest and learning. Teenagers often learned more about current affairs from comedic presentations and jokes, as these captured their interest and encouraged further explanations of the topic or event. The fast pace and superficial information in traditional news broadcasts (radio or television) were inferior to those programmes that did not simply relay objective information but rather provided further commentary. The warning here, as Marchi indicates, is that:

> Bloggers and talk show hosts are riveting sources of opinion, but many do not fact check or show concern for reliability. While this problem is not limited to youth, it underscores the critical importance of media literacy and journalism training for high school students. (Marchi 2012, p. 257)

It is at the discretion of the receiver to ascertain the integrity of the information. Solving problems such as these, that is, recognising the reliability and real value of information, is rapidly becoming a pre-cursor skill to the use of information. Ng (2015) and others term such skills as digital literacy and describe these skills as involving:

> … the understanding of multimodality and its use for learning as well as in the workplace. The ability to use digital technologies to solve problems, innovate, collaborate and communicate responsibly in the workplace is a central tenet of twenty-first century skills. (Ng 2015, p. 6)

Pre-service teachers, practising teachers and teacher educators need to be able to ascertain the integrity of information that both they themselves and their students might encounter, especially as so much information is now sourced from global networks. Given the placement and nature of ICT in the "real world", its capabilities can be readily applied in "real-life problem-solving situations", for both teachers and students. Further, the global and dynamic nature of information necessitates both connectivity and collaboration in acquiring and fine-tuning knowledge, skills and understanding of truthfulness and integrity. Personalising learning with technology, through bringing together the local and the global (Keamy et al. 2007), provides a unique opportunity to address this area of critical thinking. As an example, McLaren (2012) suggests that engagement in the active exploration of such topics and issues as systems, values, environment, design and evaluation can assist in the development of critical thinking skills (p. 239).

4.2.3   Issues and Concerns Relating to ICT in Education

The global context of ICT and social media use presents a range of issues for education pertaining to the "rules and regulations", or "cyber safety" as it has come to be known, associated with the use and manipulation of information in the global network. With increasing societal use of social networking sites (Ofcam 2015; Perrin 2015; Sensis 2015), the education system is challenged to use ICT in ways that connect with these digital life – worlds without exposure to risks associated with "ubiquitous connectivity" (Masters 2015, p. 35) such as privacy and the suitability of different types of information in the public forum. Keamy (2009) notes that personalising learning is characterised by ICT allowing:

> ... each pupil greater diversity for learning to allow for enhanced interactivity between individual students and individual teachers and a more immediate presence inside the classroom of resources from outside the classroom. (Keamy 2009, p. 248)

Keamy (2009) further emphasises that personalisation requires a "deep personalisation model" (p. 248). In realising the potential of personalisation, this suggests a conscious process for the enactment of ICT as a tenet of personalising learning. Greenfield (2014) provides the example of the concept of Facebook changing the protocols for privacy to suit company needs. This change meant that users from then on needed to divulge much more of their personal information in the space than ever before in order to become or continue as a user of the software. Greenfield (2014) notes the implications of this decision in relation to users forfeiting their privacy to secure the benefits of the "friends" and connections that social media such as Facebook provide. More recently, Google changed its search tracking parameters in order to force users to accept marketing strategies it chose to implement in more directly targeting advertising at the user (Cadwalladr 2016; Angwin 2016). These examples highlight the complexities associated with the "greater diversity for learning" (Keamy et al. 2007, p. 2) that ICT provides. Deep personalisation in the "real-world" domain of ICT allows the learner and the teacher equal voice in decision-making and developing their own approaches to such issues in their own lives. Ng (2015), in discussing the benefits of online learning, notes that students found the learning environment more equal and democratic and that "all voices were heard" (p. 12). Given the importance of collaboration associated with personalising learning, the use of both synchronous video technology and asynchronous discussions could encourage both reflection and, as Ng (2015) suggested, deeper learning.

Schools and universities are inevitable users of and subscribers to a range of ICT platforms and models including Bring your Own Device (BYOD) models that are increasingly used in schools (McLean 2016). The ease with which platforms in particular can be adapted for educational use is very much a positive in the education realm (Ng 2015). Moreover, in personalising learning, the concept of associating the needs of learners with automation in preferences, individual supporting materials, activities and perhaps even tailored assessment and remedial action where necessary has the potential to contribute to a personalised learning experience. However, the extent to which this is a reality in education is open to debate. Similarly, at the touch of a device (e.g. smart phone, tablet or laptop), students can collaborate synchronously or asynchronously with peers, lecturers or others who may reside anywhere in the world to enable deep personalisation. This presents rich opportunities to "enhance interactivity" (Keamy et al. 2007, p. 2) and enable learning, provided consideration is given to use of the multitude of different sources and individual's access to appropriate ICTs that will perform the sorts of functions that enable their participation and access to relevant storage devices and software. Whilst offering a rich opportunity for communication forms that are likely to assist in preparing children, adolescents and adults for their place in a largely unknown future (Manyika 2016; Manyika et al. 2017) and in a swiftly changing and globalised world, these considerations also have the potential to isolate individuals and risks leaving them behind their fellow learners if circumstances leading to a paucity of access are not addressed.

4.3   ICT in Education: Theory and Pedagogy

The complexities that the integration of ICT presents for educators and learners means that careful consideration must be given to the ways in which it is used and embedded. As such, learning theories and subsequent pedagogies need to be examined with regard to the new and different challenges and opportunities that ICT offers.

4.4   Learning Theory and ICT

Over the history of teaching and learning, a vast wealth of understanding has been accumulated in the form of theories of learning. We now know that one theory cannot explain all of the complexity of human learning. Theories have been modified, adapted, expanded, created and re-embraced as knowledge and understanding of learning and teaching, and as the numerous strategies and approaches needed in teaching and learning, have increased. Learning theories can be used to explain how people learn, how the learning space can be designed and how teaching approaches and strategies might be tailored for different learning and learner needs. Historically, as a profession, and as knowledge of learning and teaching expanded, there has been a movement away from theories with a "one-size-fits-all" scientific focus on outcomes in the form of behaviour (behaviourism) to a greater understanding of how information is processed in the brain (cognitivism), to exploring the nature of different types of learning (constructivism) and to what learners might require in information processing. More recently, the nature of learning as a social undertaking (social constructivism and situated learning theory) has become prevalent, as has the encompassing of far wider recognition and consideration of the environment, in all its facets, and how this may affect learning (ecological systems theory) (Romeo 2015). Stemming from these and alongside new thinking, theoretical positions in relation to technology are currently being developed and explored.

Selwyn (2012) argues that critical understanding of digital technologies including ICT is essential in education against the current backdrop of globalisation. Papert (1993) too challenged educators to work more creatively with computers in ways that encourage the development of thinking. This critical approach is also inherent in the personalising learning tenet of ICT where "learning globally" requires critical understanding to determine the validity of information accessed via various technology platforms, including the World Wide Web. For example, the trustworthiness of information in "current affairs" is dependent on the relationship between a number of factors, not all of which can be easily determined in the short timespan in which media generally operates, nor can it often be verified from a 30 s "news grab" distributed for public consumption. Yet such is the kind of information that is predominating in the global space of ICT and to which children and the general public are being so regularly exposed. The relationship between information and its portrayal within the protocols of broadcast commercial or government entities is being designed to meet the technical parameters of the technology that distributes it. The knowledge, skills and understanding of the recipient who encounters information portrayed in such ways determine both its integrity and usefulness. Learning theories that encourage the critical thinking required to examine such integrity and usefulness are the current challenge in education.

With digital technology being "an utterly integral but wholly unremarkable component of educational conditions and arrangement around the world" as Selwyn (2012, p. 5) describes, the need for critically and theoretically informed approaches for determining how ICT is utilised in education is of critical importance. Teachers' use of ICT in education is informed by beliefs and understandings about how people learn (Newhouse 2015; Selwyn 2012), which, in turn, stem from the suite of prevailing theories of learning. This *critical* focus is needed to challenge assumptions, power relationships, issues of access and practices inherent in current theoretical positions.

The contemporary learning theories guiding personalising learning are those of sociocultural theory, social constructivism, situated learning and ecological systems theory. These theories enable ICT to be utilised such that the dual service of allowing teachers to collaborate as well as to gain peer and expert assistance in this complex environment may be realised. Such collaborative use of ICT with peers enables teachers to expand and critique their own knowledge in assessing information and using ICT for learning. Moreover, personalising learning offers an approach through which teachers can also ensure that their students develop their own individual critical understanding for the same or similar decision-making.

4.5 ICT Pedagogy

Application of learning theories that support the use of ICT raises the question of aligned and effective pedagogies. Bransford et al. (2000) indicate that an integrated approach to ICT in education, guided by effective pedagogy, can support learning with ICT. Pedagogy, according to Eisner (1983), is the "art and craft of teaching" (p. 4). Today, it has also taken on the mantle of the "art, craft and *science* of teaching" (e.g. Crawford 2014), whereby the work of the teacher in designing learning most often encompasses, integrates and/or interweaves ICT into an approach that also utilises social and contextual factors. These social and contextual factors include the architecture of the learning space or the landscape of the learning environment. Implementation of design, assessment and evaluation are associated practices, along with the more humanistic roles of "loco parentis", guide, counsellor and "all-round" mentor and advisor to students (and sometimes parents). As we learn more about individual, preferences, differences and abilities in learning, along with characteristics such as personality and the maturation of learners, the task of the teacher in addressing the individual needs of each learner becomes more complicated. As both social and educational knowledge and practices advance, the transference of the responsibility for learning from teacher to learner becomes tantamount to successful learning.

Pedagogy for effective use of ICT in education places emphasis on its meaningful use embracing concepts such as student-centred (Newhouse 2015), lifelong learning (Selwyn 2012) and collaboration (Kruse 2013; Walta and McLean 2014). These concepts also characterise personalising learning. Newhouse and Clarkson (2008) describe 11 attributes of effective learning environments for promoting meaningful use of ICT, which again resonate with the tenets of personalising learning, through a pedagogical focus on collaboration, knowledge construction, individual learning styles, authentic learning and active engagement of learners. These pedagogies are all informed by the theory of social constructivism learning theory noted in the previous section, which privileges the nature of learning as a social undertaking.

A further framework that is increasingly used in education is technological pedagogical content knowledge (TPACK) (Koehler and Mishra 2009). TPACK brings together three areas of knowledge (content, pedagogical and technology) for the effective integration of ICT in the classroom. This framework recognises the importance of teachers' knowledge in each of these three key areas and the relationships or interactions between them. One of the challenges associated with using TPACK in teacher education continues to be the lack of "a natural knowledge base upon which to build" (Koehler et al. 2014). Koehler et al. (2014) suggest that this challenge can be addressed through pre-service teachers engaging with all three knowledge areas (content, pedagogical and technological) in an "integrated manner" (p. 109). It is further argued by Koehler et al. (2014) that TPACK is not so much about the content that needs to be covered when teaching with ICT but more so the creativity and collaboration with which it is used. To achieve this strategy, they suggest a need for stronger alignment of ICT use with broader educational outcomes, rather than a narrow curriculum focus. These concerns of alignment, integration, integrity, creativity, collaboration and broad outcomes are also evident in the tenets of personalising learning.

As indicated earlier, ICT characteristics and technological capabilities on their own do not produce learning. As an example, the familiar "research project" that is a widely used task in education today can be particularly enhanced by the myriad of information and data that is so easily found on (and often regurgitated from) the Internet. We have already discussed from an information or technology perspective the need for gauging the authenticity of information accessed from such accessible platforms. Ensuring that students have the skills to verify and authenticate their information depends on the methods adopted within the pedagogical design of the research project. Factors inherent in the task, both physical and cognitive, need to be addressed in the design such that learners have to *use* the information they access, rather than just locate it and re-present it in their own words. Support for different levels of skill and expertise, and the gathering of resources and refinement of subjects, topics, expectations and quality of investigations, might all be components of the pedagogy applied.

A similar case of "apparent ease" (at least technologically speaking) to the use of a smart phone noted earlier is the incorporation of online discussions and forums which are particularly popular in higher education. Interactions in online discussion can either be very powerful, affirming and motivating or simply another superficial "tick-a-box" type of exercise seen as a component of a task to be signed off. The key to achieving the former more powerful and meaningful learning lies in the pedagogical approach used. The pedagogy adopted in the design of online forums provides a framework for the discussion that takes place. This framework manifests in the quantity and quality of online interactions between students and with teacher educators. For example, the use of questioning versus providing information/answers, and the nature of questioning to promote higher-order, critical thinking, alters both the pedagogy and the outcomes for students (e.g. see Jones and Ryan 2017).

In a personalising learning approach with ICT, the opportunity to allow the learner to "lead" in their learning can be easily facilitated with ICT. The essence of ownership and leadership of the learning, however, requires the design of the interaction to be one in which the human qualities of comfort, support, motivation, perhaps excitement, challenge and affirmation all play a part. The role of the teacher, peers and others as supporters, resources and "players" in the learning does not occur without the application of appropriate pedagogical design. Indeed, pedagogy, informed by theory, may well be called the key to unlocking the full potential of the relationship between ICT and personalising learning.

4.6   The Current State of ICT in Higher Education

ICT use in higher education has predominantly been based on transmission models of teaching involving passive levels of student engagement, such as viewing online recorded lectures or listening to podcasts (Herrington et al. 2009, 2014; Johnson et al. 2013). The uptake of ICT in innovative ways has been slow as tertiary educators grapple with barriers unique to university teaching (Schneckenberg 2009), particularly compared to its more widely embraced usage in other educational settings (e.g. collaborative and interactive use of mobile devices for learning in primary schools). It is perhaps through a focus on personalising learning in higher education that meaningful, authentic active approaches to engagement in learning can be realised. Howland et al. (2012) describe meaningful use of ICT as occurring when the use of ICT is "intentional, active, constructive, cooperative and authentic" (p. 3). These characteristics are also inherent in the tenet of ICT as an enabler that allows "diversity for learning" (Keamy et al. 2007, p. 2).

The dynamic, holistic (cognitive, aesthetic and psychomotor) and rapidly changing nature of ICT in the education landscape makes assessment of its effectiveness difficult to address. Moreover, the diversity of undertakings in which ICT is now integral across discipline and curriculum areas, and overtaking even the physical "written word" and mental "addition and subtraction" in some instances, defies the notions of traditional evaluation and measurement regimes of comparative and interventionist approaches. Even the TPACK framework that has attracted widespread use is still subject to further assessment (Koehler et al. 2014).

The merging of theory, pedagogy and ICT provides an unprecedented opportunity for learning. Whilst it is a complex relationship, there are ways of addressing and perceiving of the complexity that enable learning. Norman (2011) argues that complexity in technology itself is not the problem. Rather he maintains that "understandability" and "understanding" are the keys to eradicating confusion and ensuring things are not complicated. These concepts of understandability and understanding can be applied to exploring the relationship between technology, theory and pedagogy for learning too. Norman maintains that "conceptual models, which reside in people's minds" (p. 37), help to transform what might be "complex" into workable, understandable mental concepts. Further, he suggests that complexity can be "tamed" through proper design. Personalising learning in teacher education allows each individual pre-service teacher to become comfortable with both the understandability of the technology and their understanding of the nuances, possibilities and points to be addressed in designing ICT for learning. As an example, whilst texting and communication via text have become everyday occurrences, research is now noting the increasing incidence of misinterpretation of messages and the negative consequences that often ensue. Without the visual and aural nuances of vision and voice, the text does not always deliver the intended message. Designing messages that cannot be misinterpreted is a part of teachers' communication skills. Designing them in, with and through technology adds a further layer to these skills.

ICT and personalising learning are natural partners. Applying relevant theories and pedagogy will allow the dual roles of ICT to be realised. These dual roles include the use of ICT for facilitating the learning of pre-service teachers, practising teachers and teacher educators and as a tool for the design and generation of new ways of learning.

4.7 Conclusion

The very terminology of technology and, in education, the use of the phrase *information and communication technology* reflect the symbiotic nature of technology and education for learning (McLean 2013). Moreover, as we learn more about the *nature and processes* and *the how and why* of learning in a world where communication, collaboration and creativity are becoming the fundamental characteristics of human, social, economic and environmental undertakings, it is no surprise that technology in general, and ICT in particular, is considered a pivotal tenet in, or theme of, personalising learning in education.

ICT in education is not a simple, nor straightforward enterprise. Rather, the *effective* use of ICT for learning in education embraces considerations of individual attributes, context, task, economics and environment. ICT's multiplicity of profiles in the public space, as illustrated by the chameleon mobile phone, and the very complexity of its conceptual nature, perhaps best illustrated by that of *connectivity*, belie a phenomenon which continues to pose a duality of possibility, potential and problem for the educator and learner alike. Moreover, in the same way that recognition and acknowledgement of the "village's" involvement in the raising of a child are encouraged, the traditional voices and expertise of teaching and learning, and even of an educational system, as they have been known in the past two centuries are being considerably challenged.

ICT in education reflects the precedents and priorities of a society and the concerns and considerations of the social contract. Science and medicine continue to abound in new technological ways to address illness and disease of humankind, animal kind and the planet itself, at the same time taking technologically driven exploration further seaward into the depths of our oceans and skyward into the outer realms of the universe. It is essential that teaching and learning, particularly in teacher education, change to reflect this societal use. This requires a shift from thinking about the integration of ICT as a *tool* for learning to that of a *vehicle* for learning (Jones and McLean 2012). Although subtle, such a shift signals an important change in thinking about ICT in education that is more holistic and reflective of societal use. Romeo (2008) notes that ICT offers a way to bring the real world into the classroom by solving real problems through connecting with local and the global issues and resources. As a vehicle for learning, the often wondrous and mesmerising possibilities that ICT forecasts are predictions of an exciting future where ICT is integral to and integrated in all areas of education as lifelong learning.

Providing an educational framework for learning that caters for the individual and society at large to understand, use, accommodate and adapt to the ever-increasing technological-driven world, however, is no simple undertaking. Providing students with the knowledge and skills to make critical and often life-changing decisions about such technological pursuits remains the multidimensional task of education and, in particular, the teacher. Hence, it is important that personalising learning has a place in teacher education. Just as in other areas of education, similar and sometimes inaccurate assumptions of the levels of students' understanding of, access to and capabilities with technology in tertiary education are often made. The myth of "digital natives" (Prensky 2001) persists in some sectors, but in fact not all students coming into higher education or tertiary education have equal capabilities in technology (Johnson 2015; Vichie 2017). Approaches to addressing the problems of different levels of ICT access, skills, knowledge and understanding are required in school systems, in those courses preparing future teachers, as well as in the professional learning of practising teachers. In many ways, personalising learning can contribute such an approach to learning in and with ICT (although issues of access may still persist).

The nature of communications on the global network, even at times the "anonymity" with which users can work, can minimise both social and generational differences and enhance interactivity, not only between teacher and student but between members of a wider community of learners. The information and communications nature of ICT readily provides a space for personalising learning and greater opportunity for more flexible learning as it can encompass individual learning, small or large groups, and communication in synchronous or asynchronous modes, through text, audio, video or multimodal forms.

Undoubtedly, work and the social fabric of communities are changing rapidly alongside increasing technological capacity. The nature of employment and the kinds of tasks employees of the future will be undertaking will be vastly different to those undertaken by workers today. Personalising learning, especially in teacher education, would seem a logical and critically needed approach to equipping pre-service teachers with the knowledge, skills, understandings and mindsets they will need in order to adequately address the needs of learners in the immediate and more distant future. Further, as technology becomes an increasingly pervasive part of our everyday lives, concerns about ICT issues held by the media and the general public will both impact on pre-service teacher education and future teachers, as they will be expected to be able to apprise learners of not only the potential and the benefits of ICT and the skills to use them but also with the foresight to see even further into the future.

References

Angwin, J. (2016). Google has quietly dropped ban on personally identifiable web tracking. *ProPublica: Journalism in the public interest.* 21 October, 2016. Retrieved from https://www.propublica.org/article/google-has-quietly-dropped-ban-on-personally-identifiable-web-tracking

Bransford, J. D., Brown, A. L., & Cocking, R. R. (Eds.). (2000). *How people learn: Brain, mind experience and school.* Washington, DC: National Academy Press.

Cadwalladr, C. (2016). Google, democracy and the truth about internet search. *The Guardian.* Sunday 4 December, 2016.

Crawford, R. (2014). A pedagogic trinity–Exploring the art, craft and science of teaching. *Journal of Pedagogic Development, 4*(2), 77–84.

Eisner, E. (1983). The art and craft of teaching. *Educational Leadership, 40*(4), 4–13.

Greenfield, P. (2014). *Mind and media: The effects of television, video games, and computers.* New York: Psychology Press.

Herrington, J., Herrington, A., Mantei, J., Olney, I., & Ferry, B. (2009). *New technologies, new pedagogies: Mobile learning in higher education.* Wollongong: University of Wollongong.

Herrington, J., Ostashewski, N., Reid, D., & Flintoff, K. (2014). Mobile technologies in teacher education: Preparing pre-service teachers and teacher educators for mobile learning. In M. Jones & J. Ryan (Eds.), *Successful teacher education: Partnerships, reflective practice and the place of technology* (pp. 137–151). Rotterdam: Sense Publishers.

Howland, J., Jonassen, D., & Marra, R. M. (2012). *Meaningful learning with technology* (4th ed.). Boston: Pearson.

Johnson, N. (2015). Digital natives and other myths. In M. Henderson & G. Rome (Eds.), *Teaching and digital technologies: Big issues and critical questions* (pp. 11–21). Melbourne: Cambridge University Press.

Johnson, L., Adams Becker, S., Cummins, M., Freeman, A., Ifenthaler, D., & Vardaxis, N. (2013). *Technology outlook for Australian tertiary education 2013–2018: An NMC horizon project regional analysis.* Austin: The New Media Consortium.

Jonassen, D., Howland, J., Marra, R. M., & Crismond, D. (2008). *Meaningful learning with technology* (3rd ed.). Boston: Pearson.

Jones, M., & McLean, K. (2012). Personalising learning in teacher education through the use of technology. *Australian Journal of Teacher Education, 37*(1), 75–92.

Jones, M., & Ryan, J. (2017). The online space: Developing strong pedagogy for online reflective practice. In R. Brandenburg, K. Glasswell, M. Jones, & J. Ryan (Eds.), *Reflective theory and practice in teacher education* (pp. 205–222). Singapore: Springer.

Keamy, K. (2009). Lining up the ducks: Personalising education and the challenges it poses for a school's leadership. *The International Journal of Learning, 16*(2), 245–255.

Keamy, K., Nicholas, H., Mahar, S., & Herrrick, C. (2007). *Personalising education: From research to policy and practice.* Melbourne: Department of Education and Early Childhood Development.

Koehler, M. J., & Mishra, P. (2009). What is technological content knowledge? *Contemporary Issues in Teacher Education, 9*(1), 60–70.

Koehler, M. J., Mishra, P., Kereluik, K., Shin, T. S., & Graham, C. R. (2014). The technological pedagogical content knowledge framework. In J. M. Spector (Ed.), *Handbook of research on educational communications and technology* (pp. 101–111). New York: Springer.

Kruse, J. W. (2013). Implications of the nature of technology for teaching and teacher education. In M. P. Clough, J. K. Olson, & S. Niederhauser (Eds.), *The nature of technology: Implications for learning and teaching* (pp. 345–370). Rotterdam: Sense Publishers.

Manyika, J. (2016). *Technology, jobs and the future of work.* Briefing Note prepared for the Fortune Vatican Forum December 2016. McKinsey Global Institute.

Manyika, J., Chui, M., Mehdi, M., Miremadi, M., Bughin, J., George, K., Willmott, P., & Dewhurst, M., (2017). *A future that works: Automation, employment and productivity.* McKinsey Global Institute.

Marchi, R. (2012). With Facebook, blogs and fake news, teens reject journalistic objectivity. *Journal of Communication Inquiry, 36*(3), 246–262.

Masters, J. (2015). Balancing risks and growth in a digital world. In M. Henderson & G. Romeo (Eds.), *Teaching and digital technologies: Big issues and critical questions* (pp. 34–45). Melbourne: Cambridge University Press.

McLaren, S. (2012). Considering some big issues and the role of technology education in transformational change. In P. J. Williams (Ed.), *Technology education for teachers* (pp. 231–260). Rotterdam: Sense Publishers.

McLean, K. (2013). Literacy and technology in the early years of education: Looking to the familiar to inform educator practice. *Australasian Journal of Early Childhood, 38*(4), 30–41.

McLean, K. (2016). The implementation of bring your own device (BYOD) in primary [elementary] schools. *Frontiers in Psychology, 7*(1739), 1–3. https://doi.org/10.3389/fpsyg.2016.01739.

Newhouse, C. P. (2015). When does technology improve learning? In M. Henderson & G. Romeo (Eds.), *Teaching and digital technologies: Big issues and critical questions* (pp. 197–213). Melbourne: Cambridge University Press.

Newhouse, C. P., & Clarkson, B. (2008). Using learning environment attributes to evaluate the impact of ICT on learning in schools. *Research and Practice in Technology Enhanced Learning, 3*(2), 139–158.

Ng, W. (2015). *New digital technology in education. Conceptualizing professional learning for educators*. Cham: Springer International Publishing.

Norman, D. (2011). *Living with complexity*. Cambridge, MA: The MIT Press.

Ofcom. (2015). *Adults' media use and attitudes*. Retrieved from http://stakeholders.ofcom.org.uk/market-data-research/other/research-publications/adults/media-lit-10years/

Papert, S. (1993). *The children's machine: Rethinking school in the age of the computer*. New York: Basic Books.

Perrin, P. (2015). *Social networking usage: 2005–2015*. Pew Research Center. Retrieved from http://www.pewinternet.org/2015/10/08/2015/Social-Networking-Usage-2005-2015/

Prensky, M. (2001). Digital natives, digital immigrants. *On the Horizon, 9*(5), 1–15.

Romeo, G. (2008). Information and communication technologies in education: Curriculum and pedagogy issues. In N. Yelland, G. Neal, & E. Davich (Eds.), *Researching pedagogies, practices and learning with information and communication technologies (ICT) in education* (pp. 19–42). Rotterdam: Sense Publishing.

Romeo, G. (2015). Learning, teaching, technology: Confusing, complicated and contested. In M. Henderson & G. Romeo (Eds.), *Teaching and digital technologies: Big issues and critical questions* (pp. 22–34). Melbourne: Cambridge University Press.

Schneckenberg, D. (2009). Understanding the real barriers to technology-enhanced innovation in higher education. *Educational Research, 51*(4), 411–424.

Selwyn, N. (2012). *Education in a digital world*. London: Routledge.

Sensis. (2015). *Sensis social media report: How Australian people and businesses are using social media*. Retrieved from https://www.sensis.com.au/assets/PDFdirectory/Sensis_Social_Media_Report_2015.pdf

Shellenbarger, S. (2016). Most students don't know when news is fake, Stanford study finds; teens absorb social media news without considering the source: Parents can teach research skills and skepticism. *Wall Street Journal (Online)*, 21 Nov 2016.

Vichie, K. (2017). Higher education and digital media in regional Australia: The current situation for youth. *Australian and International Journal of Rural Education, 27*(1), 29–42.

Walta, C. J., & McLean, A. S. (2014). Structuring an online pre-service education program. In M. Jones & J. Ryan (Eds.), *Successful teacher education* (pp. 65–81). Rotterdam: Sense Publishers.

Yallop, C., Bernard, J. R. L., Blair, D., Butler, S., Delbridge, A., Peters, P., & Witton, N. (2005). *Macquarie dictionary* (4th ed.). Sydney: Macquarie University/The Macquaire Library Pty Ltd.

Chapter 5
Personal *Means* Learner as Central

This chapter explores student-centred learning as a core practice for personalising learning. Keamy et al. (2007) identify this core practice as a key tenet for personalising learning, which they termed "Learner as Central". As a notion that has been fundamental to more contemporary ideas about effective teaching and learning in recent decades, much of this chapter looks to present an overview of what is already known about student-centred learning and how it has been developed, critiqued and refined in its relatively short history in education. In providing this summary, we are able to clearly explicate the ways in which this particular tenet is essential to personalising learning in the higher education context and more broadly. We also challenge the generally accepted dichotomy that is often presented between student-centred and teacher-centred learning, purporting instead that a strong duality between these approaches is needed to personalise learning in an effective manner.

5.1 Introduction

Placing the learner as central in the process of learning is not a new concept in education. Commonly referred to as either student or learner-centered, it is a notion that has gained increasing attention since Dewey's early work in the late 1800s leading up to the progressive education movement. The personalising learning tenet of Learners as Central mirrors these early ideas of student-centred learning and deals with education that involves:

- a highly-structured approach that places the needs, interests and learning styles of students at the centre
- engaged learners who are informed and empowered through student voice and choice
- assessment that is related to meaningful tasks and includes assessment for and from students

© Springer Nature Singapore Pte Ltd. 2018
M. Jones, K. McLean, *Personalising Learning in Teacher Education*,
https://doi.org/10.1007/978-981-10-7930-6_5

- a focus on improving student outcomes for all and a commitment to reducing the achievement gap (Keamy et al. 2007, p. 2)

These ideas are easily recognisable from a range of other educational theories and approaches spanning back decades. For example, Dewey (1897) in stating his pedagogical creed said that "Education, therefore, must begin with a psychological insight into the child's capacities, interests, and habits" (p. 77). Dewey's sentiment links closely to Keamy et al.'s (2007) first point above in placing Learners as Central. Moreover, in considering theory and pedagogy around inclusive education, Florian (2009) refers to the reforms that "stress accountability, choice, achievement and excellence [that] coexist with other reforms that encourage the development of inclusive education" (p. 43), which also resonates with the notions above of needs, interests, learning styles and choice. Choice has long been acknowledged as a key factor for engendering intrinsic motivation (Deci and Ryan 1985; Wigfield et al. 2012). Deci and Ryan (1985) indicate that this choice does not even need to be substantive, stating "even a modest opportunity to be self-determining in relation to one's learning appears to enhance intrinsic motivation and facilitate learning" (p. 257). The basic fact, as so elquently expressed by Doyle (2011), is that "the one who does the work does the learning" (p. 7), something Doyle states is conclusively demonstrated in the research around nueroscience, biology and cognitive psychology.

In these ways we can see that the notion of Learners as Central has been a part of the education psyche of many theorists and pioneers in education reformations to promote increased flexibility and improved learning. Student-centred learning responds to the growing body of research evidence that indicates that "learning is not the result of teaching, rather it is the result of what children do with the new information they are presented with" (Sewell 2002, p. 24). Whilst it is not new in and of itself, it has still had limited uptake, particularly in the higher education sector (Doyle 2011; Wanner and Palmer 2015).

In this chapter we look at what is meant by Learners as Central by considering research that both supports and critiques ideas around this student-centred approach to learning. These views are examined and ultimately used to construct an argument for why student-centred learning is important and why teacher education should be adopting these approaches to model effective teaching and to provide optimum learning experiences for students.

5.2 What Is Student-Centred Learning?

Student-centred learning is widely described by various authors in the field of psychology and education. It has emerged over a period of decades in which there has been a fundamental shift from learning underpinned by individual theories of learning such as behaviourism and cognitivism (e.g. Skinner; Piaget) to the progressive education movement initiated by Dewey, which provided the beginnings of the more interdependent underpinnings of social constructivism (Vygotsky 1978) and Communities of Practice (Lave and Wegner 1991). It is a term used synonymously throughout the literature with "learner-centered" and whilst there are copious explanations and definitions provided by a multitude of authors writing in this field, most contain a similar core message about what it is to have a student-centred approach to learning.

In general, student-centred learning is underpinned by theory around social constructivism (Elen et al. 2007; Jonassen and Land 2012; Smit et al. 2014). To understand what this looks like in practice, most authors describe the "features of student-centred learning environments by contrasting them with other types of instruction" (Elen et al. 2007, p. 106). This has been the case from the very beginnings of writing about constructivism as a way to differentiate it from the more widely known and practiced transmission approach to teaching (Jonassen and Land 2012). Such comparisons, which will undoubtedly be familiar to readers, often present a dichotomous view of teacher-centred versus student-centred learning. Some of these, for example, are:

- Traditional versus contemporary
- Transmission versus discovery
- Passive versus active
- Content-focused versus process-focused
- De-contextualised versus authentic
- Summative versus formative (in terms of assessment)
- Objective versus subjective
- Identical versus differentiated
- Fixed versus open
- Controlled versus self-regulated
- Imposed versus negotiated

In more recent thinking, this perceived dichotomy has been seen as more of a continuum rather than oppositional representations. In other words, teachers and students adopt teaching and learning practices that are neither fully teacher nor fully student-centred, but, rather, an amalgam of the two (Smit et al. 2014). Smit et al. go on to describe, from their reading of the literature, "five tangible characteristics" (p. 696) that help to distinguish student-centred learning environments. These are (1) tasks, (2) student activities, (3) teacher activities, (4) sources of information, and (5) assessment. We have represented these characteristics and their defining components in Fig. 5.1.

These five categories are helpful in thinking about the different aspects of education and thus how each might be enacted to achieve instruction that is more or less student or teacher directed. However, some research suggests that even this continuum is a flawed way of thinking about effective education. Indeed, there is evidence that considers these traditionally adversarial approaches to teaching and learning as needing to be seen as more complementary – that is, that both need to

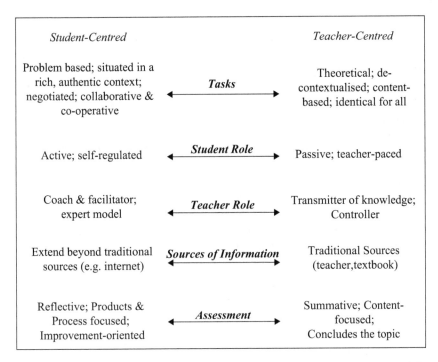

Fig. 5.1 Practice across the continuum of student- and teacher-centred learning (Adapted from Smit et al. 2014)

be embedded throughout all teaching situations to maximize the potential for learning (Elen et al. 2007).

5.3   Critiques of Student-Centred Learning

There is an inherent danger in adopting a dichotomous view of teacher- and student-centred learning, as though the two were mutually exclusive or even on some continuum. Indeed many criticisms of the different representations of constructivism in the classroom (e.g. discovery/problem-based/inquiry learning) stem from such a distinct separation of these two approaches. As noted earlier, student-centred learning is inherently associated with constructivism. At its polar opposite, approaches of explicit, direct teaching, often termed instructionism, are generally aligned with transmissive, teacher-centred approaches.

Criticisms of constructivist approaches to learning include claims/assertions such as:

• Constructivism is a theory of learning, not a theory of teaching.

- Students constructing their own meaning are likely to misconstruct ideas at least some of the time.
- There is no empirical evidence that constructivist approaches to teaching lead to improved learning outcomes.

Most of these criticisms (and by default approbations of instructionist approaches) are concerned with what is broadly considered as a lack of rigor. This lack of rigor is said to be manifested in pedagogies that give students too much choice, too much focus on constructing their own meaning and too much pressure to understand the application of ideas before adequately grasping what these ideas even are. Such concerns are highlighted in Kirschner et al.'s (2006) contentious paper *Why minimal guidance during instruction does not work: An analysis of the failure of constructivist, discovery, problem-based, experiential, and inquiry based teaching* where they claim that there is substantial evidence to demonstrate the superiority of direct instruction for successful learning. Others (e.g. Mayer 2004, 2009; Richardson 1996) also argue that direct instruction is a more effective teaching strategy compared to other, less guided, student-centred approaches.

Upon its publication, a number of critiques of Kirschner et al.'s (2006) paper ensued (e.g. Herman and Gomez 2009; Hmelo-Silver et al. 2007; Schmidt et al. 2007). These responses to the claim that "direct works best" highlight that problem-based learning and inquiry, at the very least, draw heavily on scaffolded instruction to ensure learning is structured, supported, guided and achievable. Even Mayer (2004) acknowledges in his paper that there is *guided* discovery learning that can be effective in education. Moreover, it has actually been argued that even in transmission-style approaches to teaching, learners will construct their own meaning (Jonassen and Land 2012); it is just that student-centred learning environments acknowledge and work with this more overtly.

The evidence drawn upon to promote the "success" of fully guided approaches have been critiqued in methodology (Hmelo-Silver et al. 2007; Wise and O'Neill 2009) and conceptualisation (Gresalfi and Lester 2009). Other studies have also shown that student-centred learning can lead to gains in student achievement (Hmelo-Silver et al. 2007) or show that there is no difference in grade outcomes between the two approaches at all (Smit et al. 2014). Another response to Kirschner et al.'s (2006) critique (Schmidt et al. 2007) queried their use of the Atkinson-Shiffrin model of Human Cognitive Architecture to explain the theory underpinning their stance against student-centred learning approaches.

Cognitive learning theory's *Human Cognitive Architecture* explains that the cognitive load associated with "minimally guided" learning experiences is too great for the human brain to hold the information in short-term (working) memory for the time required for processing and transfer to long-term memory (Kirschner et al. 2006). In response to this criticism about student-centred learning, and problem-based learning in particular, Schmidt et al. (2007), who also draw on the Atkinson-Shiffrin model of memory, argue that problem-based learning is in fact entirely compatible with Human Cognitive Architecture. They claim that Kirschner et al.

equate student-centred learning to approaches with minimally guided instruction and remind us that this is not the case.

Most student-centred learning approaches provide substantial structure and guidance. The notion of guidance is, in fact, fundamental to Vygotsky's notion of the zone of proximal development (ZPD), where students reach their learning potential through the guided assistance of a more-able peer or expert facilitator. The notion of ZPD is, in turn, fundamental to the theory of social constructivism (Vygotsky 1978). It is interesting to note that not one of the papers critiquing student-centred learning and constructivism even mentions this core aspect of underpinning theory.

The difference in student-centred learning is that the tasks are more open and flexible; students are better able to progress through a task at their own pace, often adopting different preferred styles, and thus are better catered for in terms of their learning needs and differences. The role of the teacher is still fundamental in selecting possible tasks and activities to challenge learners and to monitor and guide them through these activities to ensure learning is successful. Guidance should not be interpreted as transmission, and it is unfortunate that those advocating for fully guided instruction tend to create the impression (or even state it outright in some cases) that "guided" means explicit, direct, transmissive approaches to teaching, when it does not need to mean this at all. It is also timely at this point to remind ourselves of Verenikina's (2003) discussion around the multiple interpretations and applications of ZPD and scaffolding and that these ideas were not necessarily conceptualised to be teacher-controlled approaches but, rather, are open to negotiation and collaboration between teacher facilitators and learners.

Wise and O'Neill (2009) describe constructivist and *instructionist* positions as "two sides ... talking past one another" (p. 82). They indicate key differences in their underpinning values, with one focused on learning for life and future learning (constructivism) and the other on acquisition of knowledge and skills (instructivism). This discrepancy in the core values informing each approach permeates all practices from how the teaching and learning occurs to ways in which evidence of learning is collected and regarded. Duffy (2009) surmises this regrettable dichotomous view of teaching by admonishing what he sees as the failure in communication between constructivist and instructionist researchers. Constructivists, says Duffy, appear to ignore that information processing plays an important role in the learning process and that "instructionists" ignore that structure and guidance are generally embedded in student-centred/constructivist learning environments.

Research conducted by Elen et al. (2007) reveals findings that support this idea. They explored pre-service teacher conceptions of the relationship between teacher- and student-centred learning environments and how these two approaches affected their learning at university. Their findings show that rather than advocating for an either/or approach, or even a continuum between the two, pre-service teachers recognised the benefit and need for both student- and teacher-centred approaches to be utilised *concurrently* to best ensure effective learning. This presents a new idea about how these approaches to teaching and learning can be seen, "not conflicting but mutually reinforcing features of a learning environment" (Elen et al. 2007, p. 115).

5.4   Why Student-Centred Learning Is Important

The primary claim of those supporting a student-centred learning environment is that it is one that allows for appropriate motivation and engagement in learning due to its capacity to be tailored to students' differing needs, abilities and interests and meaning making (e.g. Land et al. 2012; Smit et al. 2014). In a student-centred learning environment, learning tasks are designed within rich, authentic contexts that students can relate to. This assists students' level of understanding and sense of competence in a task (Smit et al. 2014), something important in likely perseverance in the face of challenge (Bandura 1986; Mega et al. 2014). Students also have some modicum of control (or choice) over the learning goals and processes in a student-centred learning environment (Smit et al. 2014), which, as noted earlier, assists in enhancing intrinsic motivation, a key factor in determining subsequent learning achievement (Deci and Ryan 1985; Mega et al. 2014; Sogunro 2015). Active construction of meaning occurs through appropriate scaffolding that assists learners to "productively engage [in] the complexity, authenticity, and open-endedness of the environment" (Land et al. 2012, p. 15). Again, these factors are important for engaging and motivating students in their learning, and they have implications for self-efficacy and learning achievement (Bandura 1986; Mega et al. 2014). Finally, the negotiated and social construction of knowledge that typifies student-centred learning environments (Smit et al. 2014) is also important for students' identity formation as a member of the learning community (Lave and Wegner 1991) and for knowledge formation as a result of interactive communication and facilitated collaboration (Hill 2012).

Student-centred learning environments acknowledge and leverage the fact that humans are social beings whose ideas, opinions and values are shaped by social, cultural and historical circumstances. It is for this reason that student-centred learning privileges learning activities and approaches where "meaning is personally, rather than universally defined" (Land et al. 2012, p. 4). Drawing on the work of Bransford et al. (2000), Land et al. (2012) state:

> Learners hold powerful, often naïve and incomplete, beliefs that are deeply rooted in their everyday experience. While individual models tend to be tacit and sometimes at odds with accepted notions, they provide the basis through which learners interpret and explain new concepts. Such beliefs tend to persist even in the face of contradictory evidence; simply telling children that not all heavy objects sink or that the earth is round often fails. Instead, teachers and designers must use methods of eliciting pre-existing beliefs and actively building upon them. (p. 12)

Given the tenacity with which people tend to hold onto their beliefs (Loughran 2010), *even in the face of contradictory evidence* as Land et al. (2012) state, it becomes important to consider how belief systems are formed and altered if learning is to be achieved.

5.5   Changing Beliefs

It is worth briefly noting the importance of beliefs when we are considering how learning occurs, even though the notion of beliefs is not the primary focus of this book or chapter. Beliefs have important implications for teaching and learning given they can both aid and impede the reception of new ideas. Beliefs that tend to be formed when information comes from trusted sources (Mercier and Sperber 2011), and/or in a child's early years (birth to 8 or birth to 12 depending on the school of thought), are the most formative (Pirnay-Dummer et al. 2012). Pirnay-Dummer et al. also indicate that those beliefs formed and held for the longest period of time are also the most stable and thus less susceptible to easy influence. This relationship between cognitive development and belief formation makes it easy to see why children entering schooling do so with already strongly held ideas and beliefs.

It has been widely documented that students' beliefs are difficult to change. This notion has influenced the development of conceptual change theory (Posner et al. 1982) in science education and the notion of identifying and working with prior knowledge in learning more generally (Pirnay-Dummer et al. 2012). Resistance to altering ideas and beliefs is pervasive. Individuals will employ strategies such as "confirmation bias" (Mercier and Sperber 2011, p. 63). Confirmation bias, Mercier and Sperber explain, is where a person will readily accept information that aligns with already formed ideas and reject information that does not and that they do this despite the level of logic and rationale behind conflicting reasoning presented. Indeed, to influence changes in established ideas and beliefs, teachers need to create cognitive conflicts within learners such that they become "dissatisfied with their current concepts" and thus more readily look for "plausible alternatives" (Posner et al. 1982, p. 223). It is for this reason mainly that purely transmissive approaches to teaching will never work in promoting deep understanding.

The range of "ideas, information, beliefs and attitudes that learners bring with them to the classroom are some of the elements that comprise what could be termed as their prior knowledge" (Loughran 2010, p. 57). Working with prior knowledge is one of the key premises on which constructivist and student-centred learning is based.

5.6   Prior Knowledge

Student-centred learning recognises that learning occurs through the integration of new and existing (prior) knowledge and experience of the learner. Land et al. (2012) remind us that these prior experiences "provide a uniquely personal framework"

(p. 12) through which individual students operate their learning. "Prior knowledge involves learner feelings and attitudes, which can have a strong bearing on how students learn" (Loughran 2010, p. 59). Student-centred learning environments that effectively seek out and build upon students' prior knowledge are better able to achieve effective teaching and learning. High levels of existing knowledge will also impact the extent of learning and the speed at which it is attained (Schwartz et al. 2009). The implications of this for teaching are linked to the level of guidance that different students may require in the learning process. Herman and Gomez (2009) indicate that required levels of guidance are dependent on the extent of the learners' prior knowledge, where students with higher levels of prior knowledge generally require less scaffolding and guidance than those who have low prior knowledge. This is important for the teacher's planning because, as Loughran (2010) highlights:

> Students learn much more effectively when they are placed in positions where they are building on what they already know because they can link the new information to their existing information. In so doing, it is more likely that their curiosity will be aroused and that they will be encouraged to create and build their knowledge in ways that might help them to better understand the topic being studied. (p. 61)

To ensure individual students are best able to reach their learning potential, teachers need to ensure their planning caters for both the amount of learning that might be achieved as well as the speed at which it takes place, and these factors need to be considered for *individuals* in the classroom, rather than the group as a whole. Awareness of students' prior knowledge also influences how student groupings might be determined and which students the teacher will spend more or less time with to provide one-on-one support. Identification of prior knowledge is also essential in a number of discipline-based areas of learning. Actively seeking what students already know (or think that they know) can assist teachers in identifying possible mis- (or alternative) conceptions that might need to be addressed through the selection of activities to provide the required cognitive dissonance that allows for shifts in ideas and beliefs (Pirnay-Dummer et al. 2012).

The repercussions of not planning appropriately for these factors will increase the potential for the teacher to create one of two undesirable states: that they run out of meaningful learning experiences for the set learning period and students become bored, or there is so much learning material set at an inappropriate pace that students are left confused. Both of these situations result in a disservice and an injustice to the students and undermine their potential to learn.

5.7 Guidance and Scaffolding

The notion of guidance is one of the most hotly debated aspects of the student-centred learning environment. As noted earlier, it is the perceived lack or minimal levels of guidance in student-centred learning that draw the most criticism. There are a number of reasons for this, including those discussed previously in this chapter concerning the tendency of early proponents of student-centred learning to contrast it with teacher-centred approaches to help explain how they operate, the ongoing tendency for many authors in the field to present student- and teacher-centred learning as an "either/or" dichotomy, the tendency of critics to assume that all student-centred approaches lack appropriate levels of guidance and research evidence that purportedly demonstrates the superiority of guidance in student achievement. Much about these criticisms has been discussed in detail above, so it will not be repeated again here. Rather, this section outlines what guidance and scaffolding looks like in the student-centred learning environment, why it is important and when and how it is administered for optimal success.

One of the underlying issues concerning the debates around guidance is the lack of consistency in which the notion of guidance is applied and understood (Tobias and Duffy 2009). Verenikina (2003) argues that there is a similar lack of consistency in the interpretation and use of scaffolding. In addressing these concerns, we firstly draw attention to the problematic use of the terms "guidance" and "scaffolding" as being interchangeable. Guidance was the term used by Vygotsky (1978) to describe the way in which a teacher responds to the learning environment and learning needs of her students when facilitating learning. We see this facilitation as being intentional as well as incidental, responsive rather than prepared and informal in its enactment. Guidance, in this way, is how the teacher anticipates potential directions and challenges that might be encountered by different learners, as well as her readiness to follow unanticipated directions and challenges that the students present in the moment. Scaffolding reinforces guidance rather than being the same thing. Scaffolding is also intentional, but less incidental than guidance. Scaffolding refers to the planned structures that the teacher puts in place. They are prepared ahead of time, in an informed manner, to anticipate the types of activities and challenges different learners will need to be successful in the intended learning. This makes scaffolding a more formal approach to the teaching and learning than guidance. Both are important to the success of social constructivism, and despite some claims (or perhaps assumptions), both are usually inherent in the student-centred approaches that support constructivist approaches to teaching and learning.

5.8 Guidance and Scaffolding in Constructivist Approaches to Learning

Many proponents of student-centred and constructivist learning attest to the extensive guidance and scaffolding that is embedded in their approaches (e.g. Gresalfi and Lester 2009; Hmelo-Silver et al. 2007; Schmidt et al. 2007). Indeed, participation in the sorts of rich, authentic tasks that characterise student-centred learning "cannot be operationalised successfully without scaffolding" (Land et al. 2012, p. 11). Thus, in constructivist approaches, the question is not so much related to *how much* scaffolding or guidance is offered, but rather what *form* it should take and when and how much of it should be provided (Gresalfi and Lester 2009).

This notion of *forms* of guidance, and what they look like in the student-centred learning environment, seems to be a significant point of difference in instructionist and constructivist discourses. The former tends to represent guidance as explicit instruction given through direct teaching (Sweller et al. 2007), whilst the latter sees guidance as the teacher questioning, probing, redirecting and explaining – but only when it is deemed appropriate, at a point of need in the student's learning and understanding (Gresalfi and Lester 2009).

Tobias and Duffy (2009) stress that in a student-centred learning environment "guidance is provided only when learners are unable to proceed. That is, it scaffolds or helps learners move beyond what they can do without assistance" (p. 5). Hmelo-Silver et al. (2007) indicate that this scaffolding is what ensures that learners can be engaged in:

> complex tasks that would otherwise be beyond their current capabilities. Scaffolding makes the learning more tractable for students by changing complex and difficult tasks in ways that make these tasks accessible, manageable, and within the student's zone of proximal development. (p. 100)

Thus, direct instruction is a part of the student-centred learning environment, but it is "provided on a just-in-time basis and generally once students experience a need to know the information" (Hmelo-Silver et al. 2007, p. 100). It is also provided in a manner that does not explicitly provide students with answers (Hmelo-Silver et al. 2007), but rather directs them towards finding answers for themselves. It is in this way that teachers are then viewed as a coach or facilitator of learning (Smit et al. 2014).

Coaching and facilitation of learning is a far more complex and difficult task for teachers compared to the direct instruction of communicating a body of information about which they are considered expert (at least in comparison to the learners). As facilitators of learning, teachers need to not only judge the amount of guidance that might be required but also determine the "kind of guidance that most matters for learners, when and how guidance should be provided to learners, and which learners benefit from guidance in specific learning tasks" (Herman and Gomez 2009, p. 68).

Land et al. (2012) have identified four forms of guidance that teachers utilize to scaffold learning. They are:

1. Conceptual guidance on concepts related to the problem;
2. Metacognitive guidance on how to reflect, plan, and monitor;
3. Procedural guidance on how to use the environment's features and proceed through the environment; and
4. Strategic guidance on how to approach the task or refine strategies. (Land et al. 2012, p. 15)

These four types of guidance demonstrate the need for teachers to design learning such that the task itself is scaffolded with questions and resources that link to the learning outcomes and then to provide guidance by being responsive to the directions students take in completing these tasks to supplement and/or redirect attention and focus as needed. This extensive planning and responsiveness to student learning is what helps to ensure the "stopping [of] mindless progress through the task, thus redirecting students' attention to important learning goals" (Hmelo-Silver et al. 2007, p. 101). It is also essential to note that scaffolding is "gradually withdrawn or faded as the learner develops competence" (Tobias and Duffy 2009, p. 5). This point is also indicative of learning having taken place and that the student is ready to discuss and apply the learning outcomes independently as needed. Knowing when and how to best scaffold and/or guide students' learning, and, indeed, knowing when *not* to, is what makes teaching such a complex and sophisticated task.

5.9 Student-Centred Approaches to Assessment

Creating a student-centred learning environment is pointless if it does not include student-centred approaches to assessment. One of the underpinning issues with the critiques about student-centred learning and constructivism is that it is often judged on "an analogous mismatch attempting to assess constructivist-inspired pedagogies by using non-constructivist assessments" (Schwartz et al. 2009, p. 38). Students' achievement results on tasks that are more aligned with transmissive teaching, surface thinking and recall, rather than problem-solving and deep thinking, do not "give credit to the knowledge and skills students learn [in student-centred learning environments]" (Smit et al. 2014, p. 709).

Assessment can be influential in motivating deep approaches to pre-cursor learning. Maeten et al. (2010) report on studies that show that a student's favourable perception of an assessment's relevance and authenticity engenders deeper approaches to learning than that for those who do not perceive such relevance and authenticity. As Schwartz et al. (2009) remind us, "when evaluating instruction it is important to use outcome measures that capture what we want students to achieve" (p. 38). In a constructivist, student-centred learning environment, this means using assessment that allows for the examination of "students' abilities and dispositions to construct new knowledge, not just execute old knowledge" (Schwartz et al. 2009, p. 35).

In general, constructivist approaches see assessment as embedded in the learning process. This means there is usually initial assessment (linked to the aforementioned importance of prior knowledge), formative assessment and summative assessment. These different forms of assessment are important for helping students to construct meaning and achievement from a point of current understanding. The importance of this embedded assessment is explained by Vale et al. (2010):

> assessment for learning in the form of pre-testing and ongoing assessment are essential for plotting students' developmental pathways and planning sequential and differentiated lessons. They are aiming to design programs that match each student's zone of proximal development. (Vale et al. 2010, p. 575)

Another feature of assessment in constructivist-informed learning environments is that students have an opportunity to learn throughout the assessment process itself

(Schwartz et al. 2009). Examples of this might include engaging students in peer or self-assessment. It could also be achieved by providing an assessment experience in which acquired skills and knowledge could be expanded beyond the level of acquisition present upon entering the task. This, Schwartz et al. say, demonstrates the student's capacity for future learning.

Rust et al. (2005) outline a "social constructivist assessment process model" (p. 231) that they believe recognises that "knowledge and understanding of assessment processes, criteria and standards needs the same kind of active engagement and participation as learning about anything else" (p. 232). Their model, based on assumptions of constructive alignment (Biggs and Tang 2011) and explicit assessment criteria, involves three key stages:

1. Engaging with criteria – involving students in self- or peer assessment using the criteria and involving tutors in discussion about the meaning of criteria
2. Creating criteria – involving students and/or tutors in the selection and writing of assessment criteria
3. Engaging with feedback – designing instruction such that students have to actively engage with assessment feedback in some way, e.g. responding to feedback on a draft piece of work; examining a benchmark piece of work and assessing their own work against this; providing written comments and tasking students with estimating their grade based on what has been written; etc.

Of these, the notion of responding to feedback is purported to be "the most important part in its potential to affect future learning and student achievement" (Rust et al. 2005, p. 234).

Implementing assessment in the constructivist learning environment ultimately has a lot to do with the types of assessment performed, the timing of these assessments and the ways in which students and teachers engage with criteria and feedback on assessment. All are important in helping to ensure that constructivist-informed learning activities are assessed in authentic and appropriate ways.

5.10   Conclusion

"Students as central" is the premise of personalising learning that has been considered in this chapter, and this is taken to mean that social-constructivist, student-centred approaches to learning, teaching and assessment are taking place. This premise is based on sociocultural learning theory that promotes deep and complex learning in authentic and relevant learning environments. Knowledge and skills in this environment are not treated "as isolated content to be processed, elaborated, and retrieved" but rather "authentic practices that situate knowledge-in-use" (Land et al. 2012, p. 11 citing Sawyer 2006).

In achieving this authentic practice and situated knowledge in use, we contend that the rhetoric around the teacher-centred versus student-centred dichotomy of teaching and learning approaches is far from useful. Rather, we support the notion extended by Illeris (2009) that:

> All learning implies the integration of two very different process, namely an external interaction process between the leaner and his or her social, cultural or material environment, and an internal psychological process of elaboration and acquisition. (p. 8)

In achieving both these external and internal processes successfully, both teacher-directed and student-directed learning are required. Our version of teacher-directed learning looks very much like the sorts of strategies outlined in this chapter where "guidance" and "scaffolding" are applied as they are needed, in concurrent and complementary ways.

We wonder, along with Tobias and Duffy (2009), whether "the idea of providing guidance *only as needed* may be the basis for the misinterpretation that constructivists do not provide guidance (p. 5, emphasis added). Alternatively, perhaps the acknowledged lack of a single unifying theory "to guide the design of student-centred learning environments which creates challenges for research, scalability, and generalisability" (Land et al. 2012, p. 4) is more the issue for those who argue against such approaches to learning.

Ultimately, we purport that making students central in personalising their learning aligns closely to Land et al.'s (2012) description of student-centred learning environments that:

> support learners as they negotiate multiple rather than singular points of view, reconcile competing and conflicting perspectives and beliefs, and construct personally-relevant meaning accordingly. (Land et al. 2012, pp. 6–7)

We expand on this stance in Chap. 7 where we consider the implications of such a view for the teacher education context.

References

Bandura, A. (1986). *Social foundations of thought and action: A social cognitive theory.* Englewood Cliffs: Prentice-Hall.

Biggs, J., & Tang, C. (2011). *Teaching for quality learning at university* (4th ed.). New York: Open University Press.

Bransford, J. D., Brown, A. L., & Cocking, R. R. (Eds.). (2000). *How people learn: Brain, mind, experience, and school.* Washington, DC: National Academy Press.

Deci, E., & Ryan, R. (1985). *Intrinsic motivation and self-determination in human behaviour.* New York: Plenum Press.

Dewey, J. (1897). My pedagogic creed. *School Journal, 54*, 77–80.

Doyle, T. (2011). *Learner centered teaching: Putting the research on learning into practice.* Virginia: Stylus Publishing.

Duffy, T. (2009). Building lines of communication and a research agenda. In S. Tobias & T. Duffy (Eds.), *Constructivist instruction: Success or failure?* (pp. 351–367). New York: Routledge.

Elen, J., Clarebout, G., Lèonard, R., & Lowyck, J. (2007). Student-centred and teacher-centred learning environments: What students think. *Teaching in Higher Education, 12*(1), 105–117.

Florian, L. (2009). Towards an inclusive pedagogy. In P. Hick, R. Kershner, & P. Farrell (Eds.), *Psychology for inclusive education* (pp. 38–51). Oxon: Routledge.

Gresalfi, M., & Lester, F. (2009). What's worth knowing in mathematics? In S. Tobias & T. Duffy (Eds.), *Constructivist instruction: Success or failure?* (pp. 264–290). New York: Routledge.

Herman, P., & Gomez, L. (2009). Taking guided learning theory to school: Reconciling the cognitive, motivational, and social contexts of instruction. In S. Tobias & T. Duffy (Eds.), *Constructivist instruction: Success or failure?* (pp. 62–81). New York: Routledge.

Hill, J. (2012). Learning communities: Theoretical foundations for making connections. In D. Jonassen & S. Land (Eds.), *Theoretical foundations of learning environments* (2nd ed., pp. 268–285). New York: Routledge.

Hmelo-Silver, C., Duncan, R. G., & Chinn, C. (2007). Scaffolding and achievement in problem-based and inquiry learning: A response to Kirschner, Sweller, and Clark (2006). *Educational Psychologist, 42*(2), 99–107.

Illeris, K. (2009). A comprehensive understanding of human learning. In K. Illeris (Ed.), *Contemporary theories of learning: Learning theorists…in their own words* (pp. 7–20). Abingdon: Routledge.

Jonassen, D., & Land, S. (Eds.). (2012). *Theoretical foundations of learning environments* (2nd ed.). New York: Routledge.

Keamy, R. K., Nicholas, H., Mahar, S., & Herrick, C. (2007). *Personalising education: From research to policy and practice* (Paper No. 11. Office of Education Policy and Innovation). Melbourne: Department of Education and Early Childhood Development.

Kirschner, P., Sweller, J., & Clark, R. (2006). Why minimal guidance during instruction does not work: An analysis of the failure of constructivist, discovery, problem-based, experiential, and inquiry-based teaching. *Educational Psychologist, 4*, 75–86.

Land, S., Hannafin, M., & Oliver, K. (2012). Student-centred learning environments: Foundations, assumptions and design. In D. Jonassen & S. Land (Eds.), *Theoretical foundations of learning environments* (2nd ed., pp. 3–25). New York: Routledge.

Lave, J., & Wegner, E. (1991). *Situated learning: Legitimate peripheral participation*. Cambridge: Cambridge University Press.

Loughran, J. (2010). *What expert teachers do. Enhancing professional knowledge for classroom practice*. Abingdon: Routledge.

Maeten, M., Kyndt, E., Struyven, K., & Dochy, F. (2010). Using student-centred learning environments to stimulate deep approaches to learning: Factors encouraging or discouraging their effectiveness. *Educational Research Review, 5*(3), 243–260.

Mayer, R. (2004). Should there be a three-strikes rule against pure discovery learning? The case for guided methods instruction. *American Psychologist, 59*(1), 14–19.

Mayer, R. (2009). Constructivism as a theory of learning versus constructivism as a prescription for instruction. In S. Tobias & T. Duffy (Eds.), *Constructivist instruction: Success or failure?* (pp. 184–200). New York: Routledge.

Mega, C., Ronconi, L., & De Beni, R. (2014). What makes a good student? How emotions, self-regulated learning, and motivation contribute to academic achievement. *Journal of Educational Psychology, 106*(1), 121–131.

Mercier, H., & Sperber, D. (2011). Why do humans reason? Arguments for an argumentative theory. *Behavioural and Brain Science, 34*(2), 57–74.

Pirnay-Dummer, P., Ifenthaler, D., & Seel, N. (2012). Designing model-based learning environments to support mental models for learning. In D. Jonassen & S. Land (Eds.), *Theoretical foundations of learning environments* (2nd ed., pp. 66–94). New York: Routledge.

Posner, G., Strike, K., Hewson, P., & Gertzog, W. (1982). Accommodation of a scientific conception: Toward a theory of conceptual change. *Science Education, 66*(2), 211–227.

Richardson, V. (1996). The role of attitudes and beliefs in learning to teach. In J. Sikula (Ed.), *Handbook of research on teacher education* (2nd ed., pp. 102–119). New York: Macmillan.

Rust, C., O'Donovan, B., & Price, M. (2005). A social constructivist assessment process model: How the research literature shows us this could be best practice. *Assessment and Evaluation in Higher Education, 30*(3), 231–240.

Sawyer, R. K. (2006). Introduction: The new science of learning. In R. K. Sawyer (Ed.), *The Cambridge handbook of the learning sciences* (pp. 1–18). Cambridge, MA: Cambridge University Press.

Schmidt, H., Loyens, S., van Gog, T., & Paas, F. (2007). Problem-based learning is compatible with human cognitive architecture: Commentary on Kirschner, Sweller, and Clark (2006). *Educational Psychologist, 42*(2), 91–97.

Schwartz, D., Lindgren, R., & Lewis, S. (2009). Constructivism in an age of non-constructivist assessments. In S. Tobias & T. Duffy (Eds.), *Constructivist instruction: Success or failure?* (pp. 34–61). New York: Routledge.

Sewell, A. (2002). Constructivism and student misconceptions: Why every teacher needs to know about them. *Australian Science Teachers Journal, 48*(4), 24–28.

Smit, K., de Brabander, C., & Martens, R. (2014). Student-centred and teacher-centred learning environment in pre-vocational secondary education: Psychological needs, and motivation. *Scandinavian Journal of Educational Research, 58*(6), 695–712.

Sogunro, O. (2015). Motivating factors for adult learners in higher education. *International Journal of Higher Education, 4*(1), 22–37.

Sweller, J., Kirschner, P., & Clark, R. (2007). Why minimally guided teaching techniques do not work: A reply to commentaries. *Educational Psychologist, 42*(2), 115–121.

Tobias, S., & Duffy, T. (2009). The success or failure of constructivist instruction. An introduction. In S. Tobias & T. Duffy (Eds.), *Constructivist instruction: Success or failure?* (pp. 3–10). New York: Routledge.

Vale, C., Weaven, M., Davies, A., & Hooley, N. (2010). Student centred approaches: Teachers' learning and practice. In L. Sparrow, B. Kissane, & C. Hurst (Eds.), *Shaping the future of mathematics education: Proceedings of the 33rd annual conference of the Mathematics Education Research Group of Australasia*. Fremantle: MERGA.

Verenikina, I. (2003). Understanding scaffolding and the ZPD in educational research. In *Proceedings of the International Education Research Conference (AARE – NZARE)*, 30 November–3 December 2003, Auckland, New Zealand. Retrieved from http://www.aare.edu.au/data/publications/2003/ver03682.pdf

Vygotsky, L. (1978). *Mind in society: The development of higher psychological processes.* Cambridge, MA: Harvard University Press.

Wanner, T., & Palmer, E. (2015). Personalising learning: Exploring student and teacher perceptions about flexible learning and assessment in a flipped university course. *Computers & Education, 88*, 354–369.

Wigfield, A., Cambria, J., & Eccles, J. (2012). Motivation in education. In R. Ryan (Ed.), *The Oxford handbook of human motivation*. New York: Oxford University Press.

Wise, A., & O'Neill, K. (2009). Beyond more versus less: A reframing of the debate on instructional guidance. In S. Tobias & T. Duffy (Eds.), *Constructivist instruction: Success or failure?* (pp. 82–105). New York: Routledge.

Chapter 6
Mindsets for Lifelong Learning

This chapter explores the concept of Lifelong Learning, which has been identified as one of the four tenets or themes in personalising learning. Now more than ever before in history does the work and lifestyle changes experienced by individuals warrant consideration of the lifespan of learning acquisition and the requirements for learners. Subsequently, in their teaching, teachers need to encompass flexibility, variable pathways and longer-term "mindsets" and understandings of learning and its implications for life and living. This chapter discusses the importance of Lifelong Learning in the twenty-first century where we are faced with a rapidly and ever-changing world. The importance of the notion of Lifelong Learning for teachers, and teacher educators in particular, is highlighted along with its links to personalising learning in pre-service teacher education to demonstrate how it is only as lifelong learners ourselves that we can continue to provide effective and relevant education to the following and future generations of children, youth and adults.

6.1 Introduction

Keamy, Nicholas, Mahar and Herrick (2007) suggest that teachers should adopt a Lifelong Learning mindset because of the characteristics they associate with it as a concept, especially its flexibility and the range of pathways it embraces to meet the needs of all students. Lifelong learning is held by some to be a simple structural entity, especially in relation to work and work practices. Others view Lifelong Learning as a more holistic life-related concept. The implications of these different perspectives are critical in teacher education as teachers and teacher educators undertake the dual roles of learner and teacher in the dynamic environment of education – perhaps in all stages of life. In teaching, to encourage Lifelong Learning, teacher educators and teachers (both pre-service and practising) must decide for themselves, what definition of Lifelong Learning they subscribe to and what position they take on the contested nature of Lifelong Learning.

© Springer Nature Singapore Pte Ltd. 2018
M. Jones, K. McLean, *Personalising Learning in Teacher Education*,
https://doi.org/10.1007/978-981-10-7930-6_6

In the discussion in this chapter, we will explore the dimensions of Lifelong Learning and some of the contested nature of the concept. We will look at the impact of the different Lifelong Learning perspectives on education and society in differing communities' policies and practices for social and economic prosperity. We will also explore the relationship between Lifelong Learning and the personalising of learning in pre-service teacher education, for teacher educators and for practising teachers.

6.2   Theories and Practices of Lifelong Learning and Their Relationship to Personalising Learning

As with many of the constructs in education, there is no single definition of the concept of Lifelong Learning, but rather, several ways of defining the concept and explaining how it is achieved and understood. Acknowledging this, Aspin and Chapman (2012), in their discussion of the philosophy of Lifelong Learning, noted five areas of concern framing the nature and definition of Lifelong Learning. These areas of concern are:

- The ways in which Lifelong Learning is defined, characterised and understood;
- The kinds of knowledge, understanding and skill people want and/or need;
- The ways in which Lifelong Learning can be brought about;
- The ways in which people might be able to learn, understand and progress in their Lifelong Learning endeavours;
- The grounds upon which Lifelong Learning programmes can be justified and adopted. (Adapted from Aspin and Chapman 2012, p. 4)

Some of these concerns pose particular considerations that are worth noting in relation to the place of Lifelong Learning as a tenet of personalising learning and are explored in this chapter.

6.2.1   What Is Lifelong Learning?

As its name suggests, Lifelong Learning is concerned with the different forms of learning, both formal and informal, that take place over the course of a person's life. The advent of Lifelong Learning as a particular field of education emphasises the deliberate act of learning across one's lifetime, although it has also been considered as the incidental learning that one cannot help but acquire through participation in life and society. In considering Lifelong Learning within the framework of intentionality, a number of authors have attempted to define and describe this somewhat abstract concept. Some of these definitions and descriptions are considered below.

Gerthard Fischer (2000) highlighted some of the dimensions of Lifelong Learning:

> Lifelong learning is an essential challenge for inventing the future of our societies. It is a necessity rather than a luxury to be considered. It is a mindset and habit for people to acquire. It creates the challenge to understand, explore and support new, essential

dimensions of learning such as self-directed learning; learning on demand, informal learning and collaborative and organisational learning. (p. 265)

Fischer (2000) emphasised the dimension of internal, individual or personal nature of Lifelong Learning as a "habit of mind" and then put forward a more structural interpretation of Lifelong Learning as a suite of approaches to learning.

The term lifelong education has often been used as synonymous with Lifelong Learning. Halttunen, Koivisto and Billet (2014) suggest though, that the ideas of lifelong education and Lifelong Learning are in fact two quite different concepts. Lifelong education was the term used for more formal approaches to professional and post-secondary education courses run largely by educational institutions and/or professional associations and accrediting bodies. Today, as noted above, Lifelong Learning encompasses much more than formal courses. Halttunen et al. (2014) define Lifelong Learning as "a personal fact that arises through engagement and negotiations with what is experienced and how we mature over time" (p. 21). Their suggested framework for Lifelong Learning incorporates acknowledgement of the individual's learning as being central, with considerations of the continuity of learning and recognition of the places of learning, in conjunction with acknowledgement and certification of not only formal learning, but of often diverse and more informal learning circumstances. Finally, they contend that any conceptualisation of a framework for Lifelong Learning should be encouraged and disseminated through a wide variety of settings in which learners participate.

Drawing on Knapper and Cropley (2000), Saribas (2015) described lifelong learners as:

active learners who plan and assess their own learning; learn in both formal and informal settings; learn from peers, teachers and mentors; integrate knowledge from various disciplines and use different learning strategies in different situations. (p. 83)

This holistic definition can be related more to the personal/individual nature of Lifelong Learning across the lifespan, than to one more closely aligned only with professional life, economics and/or workplace practices. Teachers and teacher education are pivotal in all of the facets of Lifelong Learning, as it is they who will primarily be the designers of the learning spaces, environment architecture, landscapes and activities that will facilitate such learning. Moreover, it is likely that teachers and teacher educators will be the people responsible for instilling (or not) a love of learning and for equipping learners with the skills and capabilities to pursue their own learning both within and outside of the formal education setting. It is the engendering of such a love for learning that we believe is crucial for any hope of Lifelong Learning to be adopted by individuals across their lifespan.

6.2.2 Lifelong Learning and Bronfenbrenner's System of Social Ecology

The second area of concern expressed by Aspin and Chapman (2012) refers to the kinds of knowledge, understanding and skills people want and/or need. The relationship between personalising learning and Lifelong Learning lies not only in the kinds of skills knowledge and understanding – the learning – but in the foundations of that learning which are informed by particular learning theories. We have chosen the work of Urie Bronfenbrenner as an illustration of this relationship due to its similar holistic view of the person that we believe both personalising learning and Lifelong Learning encompass.

In education today, theories of learning such as Bronfenbrenner's bioecological systems theory (Bronfenbrenner and Ceci 1994; Bronfenbrenner and Evans 2000; Bronfenbrenner 2005) inform current learning considerations and the practices of teachers. It is also linked to the Lifelong Learning tenet of personalising learning, as well as many other areas of education. Bronfenbrenner brought to learning the idea that the environmental context in which a learner develops is highly influential on their learning and ought to be studied as related but distinct from the individual's actual development. Bronfenbrenner perceived of his theory as a set of concentric circles, with the individual at the core and progressively nested circular entities representing five levels of environmental factors, radiating outwards, whose interactions impact the development of the person (Fig. 6.1).

The influences of the various systems making up Bronfenbrenner's model, and their interactions, can present as risk or protective factors in the development of an individual. Awareness of these factors, as they pertain to the individual, have significance for teachers and teacher educators as the variety of influences can manifest in ways that serve to support or inhibit the person's capacity to learn at a given point in time. Awareness can assist the educator in identifying the broader environmental context from which the individual comes, and subsequently take a more holistic approach to shaping the individual's learning environment. A brief overview of the layers comprising Bronfenbrenner's model of ecological systems theory of development follows.

The individual is situated at the centre, innermost layer of the model, nested within the microsystem. The system influences represented in the model need to be considered in light of the individual and what it is that identifies him/her at a given point in time. That is, the gender, age, health status, ethnicity, religion, etc. all contribute to the individual's identity, and arguably, all of these factors are subject to change over the individual's lifetime.

The microsystem is the innermost system layer of Bronfenbrenner's model and encompasses those factors in which the person is directly involved. Examples of these factors may include the individual's family, school, classroom, sports team, etc. The events occurring in the person's microsystem have immediacy due to the person's direct, proximal relationship with these contexts.

The mesosystem is the second inner system layer and represents the influences on an individual that stem from the ways in which the various components of the microsystem interact. For example, the ways in which the home and school settings are mutually supportive or oppositional can impact the person's attitude and/or capacity to learn. Bronfenbrenner (1994) describes the mesosystem layer of the model as "a system of microsystems" (p. 40).

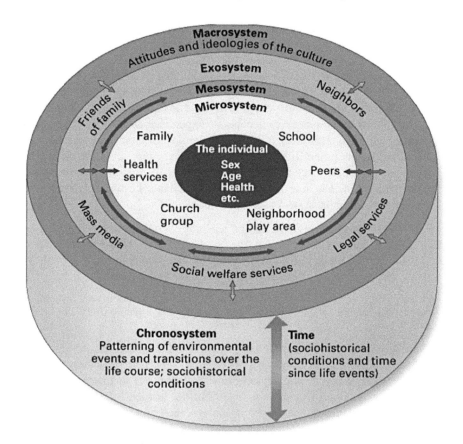

Fig. 6.1 Bronfenbrenner's model of ecological systems theory of development (Image used with permission from *Child Development* by John Santrock, ©2014 McGraw-Hill Education)

The exosystem is the third system level of Bronfenbrenner's model. This layer identifies the factors affecting an individual that do not directly involve them, but rather occur in the broader social context and have a ripple effect such that the learner is ultimately impacted in some way. A fairly straightforward example of an exosystem factor is the influence of a parent's workplace on the home environment and home life of a student. If the workplace is impacting the parent in a particular way, this will often shape the emotional atmosphere of the household. It is this atmosphere that then affects the individual at the centre of the model.

The macrosystem is the second to last system layer of the model and is referred to as "the societal blueprint for a particular culture or sub-culture" (Bronfenbrenner 1994, p. 40). Within this system, facets of society in which the person is situated such as cultural and political systems are brought together. The influence of beliefs, ways of knowing, customs and material possessions (among others) are embedded and acknowledged through the macrosystem.

The chronosystem is the outermost and third dimensional layer of Bronfenbrenner's ecological systems theory. The chronosystem represents the events and changes in a person's life over the passage of time. The effects of these interactions form patterns that could be social, human, historical or other alterations in the inner layers of the system that impact longitudinal development. Examples might include a change in the family structure due to a death or a divorce. It might be a significant alteration in the socio-economic experience due to long-term loss of income or a significant change in the broader social fabric such as beginning school or leaving home. Broadly, the chronosystem represents the events that occur and are subject to change in the person's life. It represents the chronology of the person's life and how they are shaped and changed by the experiences and interactions within the system over their lifetime.

In an interview about his thoughts on teaching, Bronfenbrenner (2005) spoke about having students "experience the adventure, and hard-won harvest of disciplined creative thought that goes beyond any one discipline" (p. 1). Whilst he acknowledged that transmitting knowledge was important, he believed that:

> the greatest gift one can give to the young is to enable them to deal critically and creatively with the new answers, and the new questions which the future brings. (Bronfenbrenner 2005, p. 1)

These words align with the notion of Lifelong Learning – the creating of a mindset and a capacity to learn what is required *when* it is required or desired. Bronfenbrenner's social ecology system theory also relates to Lifelong Learning through its recognition of the holistic nature of the learner. It is specific factors related directly and indirectly to a person, and how these factors interact at different points in time, that influence the identity formation, learning capacity and societal interaction of all individuals. By taking these holistic factors and their interactions into consideration, educators can better determine the appropriate levels of challenge, support and interaction to present to the individual. Such a notion clearly embraces the idea of personalising learning and helps to demonstrate the significance of Lifelong Learning as a tenet of personalising learning.

Personalising learning within a context of Lifelong Learning may well enable the embracing of the broad spectrum of the ecology of human development that Bronfenbrenner elaborated. It may provide a mechanism for adapting to the kinds of questions and answers of knowledge, understanding and skills that teachers have faced in the past and that continue to challenge them today. With greater recognition, this adaptation may be enhanced as they continue to present as enablers and impediments for individuals' learning in the future.

6.3 Lifelong Learning and Society

Two further areas of concern posed by Aspin and Chapman (2012) perhaps reflect the social dimension of Lifelong Learning. In particular, they draw attention to the ways in which people might be able to learn, understand and progress in their

Lifelong Learning endeavours and the ways in which Lifelong Learning can be brought about. Consideration of these two concerns allows for discussion of the relationship between personalising learning and the social nature of Lifelong Learning. The two concerns reflect the growing impetus of both economic and social moves towards recognition of, and greater determination of, Lifelong Learning in everyday life.

Perhaps pivotal to these areas of concern is the growing influence that technology has in the workforce. The impact technology has in examples such as manufacturing, where automation taking the paid jobs of low-skilled manual labourers creates redundancies, increases the impetus for consideration of Lifelong Learning and the need for personalising learning. We are in an age where the changing workforce requires continual reskilling and learning from its workers.

In a report relating to technology and the future of work, Manyika (2016) forecasts the continuing rise of digitally based independent work in contrast to manual work and suggested that:

> the disruption to the world of work that digital technologies are likely to entail could pose significant challenges to both policy makers and business leaders, as well as workers. (Manyika 2016, p. 4)

Manyika (2016) recommends that education systems need to adapt in order to accommodate such changes. In education, according to Manyika, there needs to be an emphasis on creativity, critical and systems thinking, as well as on basic science, technology, engineering, and mathematics (STEM) skills. In a further, more detailed report, which looked at the impact of automation on employment and productivity, Manyika and his colleagues noted the uncertainty of the future for policy makers and for work practices (Manyika et al. 2017). They contend that the rapid pace of advances and implementation of such developments as automation and robotics "is a prospect that raises more questions than it answers" (p. 4).

6.3.1 The Future Workforce

In 2016, in Australia, the Foundation for Young Australians (FYA) commissioned a report on the skills Australian youth will need for work both now and in the future. As lower skill level positions of labourer, administrator, technician, trades person and machinery operator are lost through automation and advanced mechanical and computerised data processing, jobs in community and personal services, professionals and management are estimated to rise rapidly. This shift in workforce requirements is said to demand a new vision of the types of skills that need to be imparted through education, skills that promote higher-order thinking and transferrable skills and practices and skills that teachers will be expected to facilitate.

Termed "enterprise skills" (FYA 2016, p. 4) the transferrable skills necessitated by the "new" workforce include "problem solving, financial literacy, digital literacy, teamwork, communications, critical thinking, creativity and presentation skills and are different from technical skills which are specific to a particular task, role or industry" (FYA 2016, p. 4). Whilst by no means the domain of education alone, the attainment of these skills by learners in general will be largely acquired through the practices of the teachers who teach them and through the approaches to learning used in primary (elementary), secondary (high school) and tertiary education. Moreover, in order to "teach" these skills, teachers themselves will need not only to be familiar with them, but to have an advanced understanding of them, and to be able to demonstrate them in practice. Perhaps the most critical aspect of this report is not that such skills will be required in the future, but rather that they are required now, especially in those teachers preparing the youth of today to take their place in the workforce in the next few years. Further, and somewhat alarmingly, the investigation reports that only one in ten teachers has recently participated in professional learning designed to help them assist students in gaining generic, transferable skills for future work. Moreover, a sizeable percentage of teachers (10%) believed that they had considerable need for their own learning in relation to new technologies and the workplace (FYA 2016, p. 18).

The authors of the FYA report call for curriculum change in providing the substance of skilling for the twenty-first century; different teaching pedagogies and approaches "including cross curricular and team teaching and greater use of inquiry and project based learning, especially in real-world environments" (FYA 2016, p. 20). The report acknowledges the complexities of developing these skills in teachers, referring to the work of Barron and Darling-Hammond (2010), who note that both sustained time and ongoing support from a community of learners are required to engender proficiency at such skills and to generate understanding rather than just process acquisition. Whilst understandably more focused on secondary (high school) and tertiary (university and vocational) teaching and learning, there are also calls for a national enterprise skills strategy beginning in primary schools which would:

- Begin early in primary school and build consistently, year on year, throughout high school
- Be provided in ways that young people want to learn; through experience, immersion and with peers
- Provide accurate information and exposure about where future jobs will exist and the skills to craft and navigate multiple careers
- Engage students, schools, industry and parents in co-designing opportunities in and outside the classroom. (Owen 2016, p. 3)

Whilst the FYA report was contextualised to the Australian environment, the Organisation for Economic Co-operation and Development (OECD) reports and policy briefs (2007, 2013, 2014) suggest that similar concerns and promulgations regarding the place of transferrable skills in education are being considered in the European Union and other individual nations.

6.3.2 The Future Workforce and Lifelong Learning

Certainly, as we have seen, the structural dimension of Lifelong Learning is inherently a social one. Given the nature of changes in skill and knowledge requirements for work in the future (and perhaps even the here and now), the "mindset" and skills to learn, as principles of Lifelong Learning, become paramount in the emphasis education has as we delve into the era that is the mid-twenty-first century. With the rapid rate of technological advancement (Manyika 2016), it is unlikely that the content of what is taught in tertiary education, let alone primary or secondary, will be current by the time each cohort of tertiary students enter the workforce. The content certainly will not be seeing them through their working years. With technology infiltrating personal life every bit as much as working life, skills that are focused on *how* to learn need to have far greater emphasis in education than on *what* to learn. It is in this context that Lifelong Learning becomes such a critical part of how we reconceive teaching, learning and teacher education. Personalising learning would seem a practical and appropriate approach to providing those (teachers) who will provide to learners the ways and means by which they can acquire such skills, knowledge and understandings. Moreover, the real-life experiences and contexts that are also emphasised in personalising learning in teacher education will enable pre-service teachers to both practice Lifelong Learning and to imbue such practices in the learning approaches of their students and, thus, the workforce of the future.

Whilst the reports noted above are focused on the not too distant future of workforce requirements, it is also worth noting at this point that several authors, such as Zarifis and Gravani (2014), believe the broader nature and imperative of Lifelong Learning has been overtaken by an overemphasis on work, employment, economics and technology. Policy and planning, however, such as the work by the European Commission (2007, 2015) on teacher education including Lifelong Learning, provide impetus for the exploration and development of Lifelong Learning for personal and social reasons as much as for reasons rooted in workforce needs and thus for personalising learning in education.

6.4 Lifelong Learning in Education

The kinds of skills that will be needed in both the workplace of the future, and in life in general, are but one perspective of the lifelong nature of learning. Futurists have predicted since the beginning of this century (e.g. Handy 2001) that, unlike their forefathers, who commonly held one position of employment for their lifetime, twenty-first century workers are likely to have at least three different career-focused occupations over their working lives, if not more. In his recent publication, Lovegrove (2017) describes what he terms the Mosaic Principle. He argues that rather than seeking the specialisation that seems to have predominated the world of work, individuals need to seek broader directions and take a broader approach to both life and their careers. Whilst he does not eliminate the idea of specialisation altogether, Lovegrove does place it within the context of a broader approach to life, learning and career. Using the metaphor of the mosaic, in which smaller pieces become part of a much bigger "picture", he suggests that individuals "can build a remarkable life and career of eclectic breadth and diversity" (p. 2) allowing much greater adaptability and broadmindedness and a somewhat different approach to both life and career than their predecessors. It is unfortunate that such a view of the possibilities is generally at odds with current political, organisational and management approaches to education, learning and specialisation in which money is the pivotal and decisive factor.

Lovegrove's (2017) mosaic mirrors the call for education to assist individuals in having a different future knowledge and skill base to that of the traditional discipline and content approaches of current contemporary mainstream education. It adds the perspective of a broader "life view" rather than a selective, narrow, specialised one; and it echoes a Lifelong Learning approach to learning, career and life. Lovegrove (2017) elaborates six dimensions of the mosaic principle, one of which is that of the transferable skills also associated with the work-focused research above. His additional five dimensions, moral compass, intellectual thread, extended networks, contextual intelligence and a prepared mind, each pertain to the broadening of an approach to life. The moral compass refers to the ways in which individuals deal with conflicting life decisions. The dimension of intellectual thread is the notion of having what Lovegrove calls a "T-shaped approach" to expertise, with one particular area of expertise that can be adapted and applied across a range of interests and intertwined with learning from broader experiences. For educators and teachers this might mean specialising in the discipline of teaching and learning, but applying the discipline knowledge, understanding and wisdom to a myriad of problem-solving situations. It might also mean developing and applying a multiplicity of approaches to teaching and learning at a variety of levels, from pre-school to seniors, the aged or mature, experienced older learners.

This adaptation and application to different contexts is referred to as "contextual intelligence" and related to the level of competence and efficiency in successfully making these adaptations across different contexts. Much like the earlier concepts of emotional intelligence (Goleman 1997), spiritual intelligence (Zohar and Marshall 2000) and even in line with the notion of multiple intelligences (Gardner 1993), Lovegrove (2017) suggests that contextual intelligence allows individuals to quickly adapt to different contexts. The final dimension, a prepared mind, suggests that whilst choice and opportunity are often key instigators for directions taken in life, preparation – "emotionally, intellectually and financially" (p. 29) – usually underpins successful harnessing of opportunities in a broader life. Each of these has implications for education.

What have these perspectives to do with pre-service teacher education, Lifelong Learning and personalising learning? Whilst work is not the only focus of education by any means, it is an important area of concern. It will be the teachers, in the immediate and more distant future, who are tasked with the responsibility of ensuring the nation's youth have the required skills, knowledge and understanding, not only for work, but for active citizenship and full participation in life. It will no doubt be the responsibility of teachers across the globe to provide similar, if not the same, skill sets as their own for their students. What is of concern is the lack of political recognition and consideration of the changing nature of learning and work as a part of teacher education and the appropriate preparation of teachers now and into the future. Many governments simply seem unable to deal with the implications for teaching, and teacher education in particular, of the rapid nature of these changes.

In the recent Teacher Education Ministerial Advisory Group [TEMAG] (2014) review of teacher education commissioned by the Australian federal government, 38 recommendations were made, none of which mentioned the changing nature of learning and/or work, nor the expectations of teachers in relation to the provision of ongoing skills, knowledge and understanding for learners in a changing world. Furthermore, the report did not make any mention, or even inference, to the notion of Lifelong Learning, a significant omission given the impracticality of education to otherwise equip current and future generations of learners for such a rapidly changing and uncertain future. In fact, rather than a focus on need, change and creativity in education, TEMAG's 2014 recommendations focused on a narrow band of literacy and numeracy and (somewhat in contrast to Lovegrove's 2017 idea of a need to broaden our scope of knowledge and skills) suggested that primary teachers should have one particular area of specialisation, such as science. Personalising learning in teacher education might allow for a Lifelong Learning approach which will encompass specialisation, numeracy, literacy and all of the other disciplines that constitute work and society in the world of today and will allow teachers to address the needs of constant change in knowledge skills and understandings for the future.

6.5 Lifelong Learning in Teacher Education

The last area of concern raised by Aspin and Chapman (2012) is that regarding the grounds upon which Lifelong Learning programmes can be justified and adopted, which they say alludes the question of funding, planning, responsibility for and implementation at all levels – from personal to organisational structures. A number of writers have explored different aspects of the positioning of Lifelong Learning in teacher education. The work of Saribas (2015) and Kuzu et al. (2015), focusing on the place of Lifelong Learning in pre-service teachers in Turkey, explores the relationship between tendencies towards Lifelong Learning and what was termed scientific literacy, environmental literacy and other variables in the work of teachers. The studies investigated the strength of teachers' scientific and environmental literacy alongside other variables, in seeking to determine how teachers' knowledge of these influenced their tendency towards Lifelong Learning. From the findings of these quantitative studies which used a Lifelong Learning tendency scale (Coşkun and Demirel 2010), it was recommended that an interdisciplinary approach to science teaching and learning be implemented in pre-service teacher education and that pre-service teacher education courses should be organised to encourage and develop the lifelong abilities and skills of pre-service teachers.

In contrast to the quantitative nature of these investigations, Kok (2014) used a qualitative, phenomenological, in-depth interview approach to investigate the social and cultural motivating factors of experienced teachers in Malaysia that may have contributed to their experiences and perceptions of Lifelong Learning. The findings of Kok's study identified a number of complex interactions between individuals and their environment that impacted on perceptions of Lifelong Learning. The model of Lifelong Learning that was identified for school teachers incorporated the following stages of development:

- *Reflection and Evaluation* in which individuals reflected on their life and evaluated their life experiences.
- *Opportunity and Decision-Making* in which the reflection stage motivated individuals to take action and avail themselves of opportunities for further study.
- *Supports and Overcoming Obstacles*, the stage in which the logistics, management, support and organisation needed for teachers in the profession to actually take up further study are addressed. Many teachers had family commitments which necessitated the support of spouses, and sometimes parents and others, in order that the teacher find both time for and resolve issues such as travel and other practicalities in order to actually participate in further study. The facilitation of organisations such as education departments and employers in providing time, funding and supporting individuals in their work life, to both encourage and support further study were also considered in this stage.
- *Ongoing Growth* was the fourth and final stage. In the context of this study, participants who had now completed a university degree, while they were teaching, saw the rewards in terms of work status, salary and future earnings, as well as in the personal gains of knowledge, skills and transformation of their relationship with their profession.

Undoubtedly, it can be suggested that some of the findings of this study have a universal application across different cultures and environments. In Ireland, Dolan (2012) writes about reforming teacher education in the context of Lifelong Learning and in particular focuses on the Bachelor of Education programme. Writing from a European Union (EU) perspective, Dolan (2012) presents a rationale for the adoption of Lifelong Learning as one of the theoretical paradigms or frameworks for reforming teacher education. She acknowledges the "increasingly complex nature of teaching and teacher education" (p. 463) and the recognition that initial teacher education is insufficient to equip teachers for a rapidly changing technological world where the future roles and challenges of teaching and learning are largely unknown. Whilst 4-year teacher education programmes have a long history in countries such as Australia, in Ireland the change from 3 years to 4 is a relatively recent undertaking. Considering, in particular, primary teacher education, Dolan argues that with a foundation of Lifelong Learning, current programmes and, indeed, teacher education itself can be "reconceptualised" creatively and innovatively in order to prepare and equip teachers with appropriate knowledge, skills and understandings to help them address the challenges of both the local (Irish) and global environment in an "informed manner" (p. 464).

In contrast to the previous studies described in this section where there was a focus on the individual's learning, Dolan (2012) privileges the shape, design and form of courses, that is, the external environment of the individual pre-service primary teacher. She begins with one of the online courses in teacher education offered in Ireland as an example of the changing architecture of teacher education. Describing the context of the European Commission's moves towards improving teacher education in the EU, she traces the development of contemporary primary teacher education in Ireland, exploring in particular policy development. She notes that the Irish curriculum has, for some time, identified the need for school children to learn to be lifelong learners. In essence, Dolan's suggestions for developing primary teachers as lifelong learners intuitively adopt an approach implicit in personalising learning. Dolan (2012) suggests for Ireland:

- Introducing Lifelong Learning as a compulsory component of the teacher education curriculum
- Devising a curriculum for teacher educators
- Incorporating teachers as active partners
- Promoting the co-construction of knowledge
- Reflective practice
- Establishing a broader role for teacher education
- Fostering collaboration between partners

These suggestions might well characterise how Lifelong Learning may be implemented in the international arena of teacher education, not just in Ireland. Feldman (1997) identifies similar characteristics that encapsulate how personalising learning in teacher education may symbiotically "fit" with Lifelong Learning in his description of "teaching as a way of being" (p. 757).

In exploring the different perspectives of personalising learning and its relationship to Lifelong Learning, perhaps the work of Palmer (2007) should also be considered. In his seminal publication, *The Courage to Teach* Palmer lays the foundations for that which authors such as Lovegrove (2017) and others suggest as the broad spectrum of Lifelong Learning. Palmer speaks of the fragmentation of learning and suggests that teachers should look to the works of Einstein and Bohr rather than Newton and Descartes, as the latter works focus on mechanisms, while the former emphasise relationships and dynamic processes. Palmer believes that teaching and learning should be concerned with educating the mind and the heart. Personalising learning, within a framework or system of Lifelong Learning, would seem appropriate for reaching both of these goals.

6.6 Conclusion

This chapter has explored a relationship between personalising learning and Lifelong Learning. It has endeavoured to "unpack" and illustrate the various dimensions of the concept of Lifelong Learning with a view to providing the reader with considerations about which they will hopefully make their own decisions as to what will help them build a lifetime of teaching and learning. We have briefly examined some of the defining characteristics of Lifelong Learning, from a personal nature and approach to learning, to a fully constructed formal systems and programme approach, designed and operated beyond the "ownership" of the individual. We have looked at the movement towards a more holistic perception of learning, its facilitation, and in particular, its needs, formation and potential uses in work and in life in the future. Finally, we have drawn on some of the visionary writings of a number of educators in establishing the communal and individual considerations of Lifelong Learning, that again, hopefully, will encourage teachers and teacher educators to broaden their horizons and those of their students in personalising their learning and promoting such a pursuit throughout their lifetimes.

References

Aspin, D., & Chapman, J. (2012). Towards a philosophy of lifelong learning. In D. Aspin, J. Chapman, K. Evans, & R. Bagnall (Eds.), *Second international handbook of lifelong learning* (Vol. 26, pp. 3–35). Dordrecht: Springer.

Barron, B., & Darling-Hammond, L. (2010). Prospects and challenges for inquiry-based approaches to learning. In H. Dumont, D. Istance, & F. Benavides (Eds.), *The nature of learning: Using research to inspire practice, Educational Research and Innovation* (pp. 199–255). Paris: OECD Publishing.

Bronfenbrenner, U. (1994). Ecological models of human development. In T. Postlethwaite & T. Husen (Eds.), *International encyclopedia of education volume 3* (2nd ed., pp. 37–43). Oxford: Elsevier.

Bronfenbrenner, U. (2005). Thoughts on teaching. *Human Ecology, 33*(3), 26.

Bronfenbrenner, U., & Ceci, S. J. (1994). Nature-nurture reconceptualized in developmental perspective: A bioecological model. *Psychological Review, 101*, 568–586.

Bronfenbrenner, U., & Evans, G. W. (2000). Developmental science in the 21st century: Emerging questions, theoretical models, research designs and empirical findings. *Social Development, 9*, 115–125.

Coşkun, Y., & Demirel, M. (2010). Lifelong learning tendency scale: The study of validity and reliability. *Procedia Social and Behavioural Sciences, 5*, 2343–2350.

Dolan, A. (2012). Reforming teacher education in the context of lifelong learning: The case of the BEd degree programme in Ireland. *European Journal of Teacher Education, 35*(4), 463–479.

European Commission. (2007). *Communication from the commission to the council and the European parliament: Improving the quality of teacher education.* European Commission. Retrieved from http://eur-lex.europa.eu/legal-content/en/txt/pdf/?uri=celex:52007dc0392&from=en

European Commission. (2015). *Shaping career-long perspectives on teaching: A guide on policies to improve initial teacher education. Education and training 2020: Schools policy.* Retrieved from http://ec.europa.eu/dgs/education_culture/repository/education/library/reports/initial-teacher-education_en.pdf

Feldman, A. (1997). Varieties of wisdom in the practices of teachers. *Teaching and Teacher Education, 13*(7), 757–773.

Fischer, G. (2000). Lifelong learning – More than training. *Journal of Interactive Learning Research, 11*(3/4), 265–294.

Foundation for Young Australians (FYA). (2016). *The new basics: Big data reveals the skills young people need for the new work order.* Report prepared for FYA by AlphaBeta. Retrieved from https://www.fya.org.au/wp-content/uploads/2016/04/The-New-Basics_Update_Web.pdf

Gardner, H. (1993). *Multiple intelligences: The theory in practice.* New York: Basic Books.

Goleman, D. (1997). *Emotional intelligence.* New York: Bantam Books.

Halttunen, T., Koivisto, M., & Billet, S. (Eds.). (2014). *Promoting, assessing, recognizing and certifying lifelong learning. International perspectives and practices.* Dordrecht: Springer.

Handy, C. (2001). *The elephant and the flea.* London: Random House.

Keamy, K., Nicholas, H., Mahar, S., & Herrick, C. (2007). *Personalising education: From research to policy and practice.* Melbourne: Department of Education and Early Childhood Development.

Knapper, C., & Cropley, A. J. (2000). *Lifelong learning in higher education.* London: Kogan Page.

Kok, J. (2014). Lifelong learning: The experiences of Malaysian school teachers. *Social Sciences and Humanities, 22*(1), 147–163.

Kuzu, S., Demir, S., & Canpolat, M. (2015). Evaluation of life-long learning tendencies of pre-service teachers in terms of some variables. *Journal of Theory and Practice in Education, 11*(4), 1089–1105.

Lovegrove, N. (2017). *The mosaic principle.* London: Profile Books.

Manyika, J. (2016). *Technology, jobs and the future of work.* Briefing Note prepared for the Fortune Vatican Forum December 2016. McKinsey Global Institute.

Manyika, J., Chui, M., Mehdi, M., Miremadi, M., Bughin, J., George, K., Willmott, P., & Dewhurst, M. (2017). *A future that works: Automation, employment and productivity.* McKinsey Global Institute.

OECD. (2007). *Lifelong learning and human capital: Policy brief.* Retrieved from www.oecd.org/publications/Policybriefs

OECD. (2013). Lifelong learning and adults. In *Education today 2013* (pp. 71–80). OECD Publishing.

OECD. (2014). Indicator D6: What does it take to become a teacher? In *Education at a glance 2014: OECD indicators* (pp. 496–514). OECD Publishing.

Owen, J. (2016). Foreward. In *Foundation for Young Australians (FYA), The New Basics: Big data reveals the skills young people need for the new work order* (p. 3). Foundation for Young Australians.

Palmer, P. (2007). *The courage to teach* (2nd ed.). San Francisco: Jossey Bass.

Saribas, D. (2015). Investigating the relationship between pre-service teachers' scientific literacy, environmental literacy and life-long learning tendency. *Science Education International, 26*(1), 80–100.

Teacher Education Ministerial Advisory Group (TEMAG). (2014). *Action now: Classroom ready teachers.* Retrieved from http://www.studentsfirst.gov.au/teacher-education-ministerial-advisory-group

Zarifis, G., & Gravani, M. (Eds.). (2014). *Challenging the 'European area of lifelong learning'. A critical response.* Dordrecht: Springer.

Zohar, D., & Marshall, I. (2000). *SQ: Spiritual intelligence: The ultimate intelligence.* London: Bloomsbury.

Chapter 7
Personalising Learning: The Teacher Education Context

In this chapter the teacher education context is examined more closely by looking at effective teacher education, the current teaching and teacher education policy climate in Australia and how personalising learning can assist in addressing the existing policy concerns whilst also providing a quality and effective teacher education experience for its students. The four key tenets of Learners as Central, Information and Communications Technologies (ICT), Communities of Collaboration and Lifelong Learning explored in the previous chapters will be drawn together and considered in light of their strengths and weaknesses and for their capacity to address priorities in teacher education.

7.1 Introduction

The notion of personalising learning in the teacher education context is considered in this chapter as new and imperative for the way in which teacher education needs to evolve. This evolution is needed to address a range of concerns about the design and delivery of teacher education, policy priorities in the current teacher education climate as well as holding true to the informing theories and approaches to effective teaching and learning that cut across educational contexts and sectors.

Around the world teacher education is portrayed as being in crisis and that teachers are not "classroom ready" upon graduation from their initial teacher education courses. This creates what is often viewed as an "urgent" need to improve the quality of teacher preparation (Teacher Education Ministerial Advisory Group [TEMAG] 2014), something exacerbated by the low status that teacher education suffers as a profession. "Everyone picks on it" says Larabee (2010):

> professors, reformers, policymakers, and teachers; right wing think tanks and left wing think tanks; even the professors, students, and graduates of teacher education programs themselves. (p. 297)

© Springer Nature Singapore Pte Ltd. 2018
M. Jones, K. McLean, *Personalising Learning in Teacher Education*,
https://doi.org/10.1007/978-981-10-7930-6_7

There are a number of reasons for these criticisms and for the low status of teaching in broader society. Some of these reasons are linked to historical contexts that influence how teacher education has occurred in both the past and present; and others are to do with social and cultural influences. For example, there are criticisms stemming from the level of exposure the general population has to teaching – Lortie's (1975) "apprenticeship of observation" that explains the uncritical thinking that "everyone's been to school, so everyone knows how to teach". In addition, as Larabee (2010) notes, "teaching is an extraordinarily difficult job that looks easy, which is a devastating combination for its professional standing" (p. 298). This deceptive simplicity is something that Darling-Hammond and Bransford (2005) liken to the role of a conductor in an orchestra:

> In the same way that conducting looks like hand-waving to the uninitiated, teaching looks simple from the perspective of students who see a person talking and listening, handing out papers, and giving assignments. Invisible in both of these performances are the many kinds of knowledge, unseen plans, and backstage moves – the skunkworks, if you will, that allow a teacher to purposefully move a group of students from one set of understandings and skills to quite another over the space of many months. (Darling-Hammond and Bransford 2005, p. 1)

Others also note the "complex and sophisticated business" (Loughran 2014, p. 275) of teaching, including Reid (2014) who expresses the tacit knowledge of teaching, indicating that to be effective, teachers need to understand:

> how and why an expert teacher moves, arranges her body in relation to the material elements of her teaching space. …how, when and why an expert teacher speaks and is silent, says things and listens, comments and responds to learners; how and why she sequences and arranges ideas and activities to assist the learners; and how she connects and interacts in relation to them as individuals and as a group. (p. 127)

These tacit understandings of effective teaching are neither innate nor accidental in an expert teacher's practice. They are deliberate and informed behaviours that are changing and responsive to a given student or group of students and selected from a broad repertoire of knowledges and skills to maximise learning potential. They are acquired through the scholarship of teaching, a craft that is trialled, analysed, discussed and practiced. It is nuanced and complex and remains largely invisible to those looking on from the outside.

Despite widespread knowledge of the complexity of learning how to teach, and indeed teaching about teaching, this "invisibility" contributes to a general lack of confidence among the wider public in regard to current teacher preparation programmes, teacher educators, teachers and teacher candidates and varied opinion on how improvements should be made. Whilst there is evidence that aspects of teaching and teacher education do need to improve, and these discourses are prevalent in teacher education worldwide (e.g. Darling-Hammond 2015; Loughran and Hamilton 2016; Macbeath 2012; Zeichner 2010), this chapter focuses primarily on the Australian context. The chapter begins with a brief consideration of the history of teacher education in Australia, which illustrates the enduring nature of the "quality" debate that has plagued teacher education since its inception and involves issues around perception, location, effectiveness and balance between theory and practice.

Recent research and commentary around the need for a pedagogy that is more specific to teacher education, and what this entails, is then introduced. Finally, ideas of
personalising learning are considered for their potential to address criticisms, align
with some of the narrative around teacher education-specific pedagogy, embrace
research about quality and, subsequently, speak to various stakeholders and policy
imperatives about enhancing the state and the status of teacher education.

7.2   A Brief Timeline of Teacher Education and Its Concomitant Issues

Over the decades, since formal teacher education became a requirement for entry
into the profession, there have been various models of its delivery. Aspland (2006)
depicts the historical development of teacher education in Australia, which is summarised in Fig. 7.1, giving a brief overview of the timeline for the development of

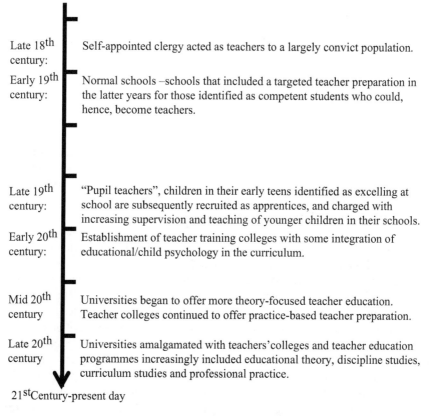

Late 18th
century: Self-appointed clergy acted as teachers to a largely convict population.

Early 19th
century: Normal schools –schools that included a targeted teacher preparation in
                    the latter years for those identified as competent students who could,
                    hence, become teachers.

Late 19th
century: "Pupil teachers", children in their early teens identified as excelling at
                    school are subsequently recruited as apprentices, and charged with
                    increasing supervision and teaching of younger children in their schools.

Early 20th
century: Establishment of teacher training colleges with some integration of
                    educational/child psychology in the curriculum.

Mid 20th
century   Universities began to offer more theory-focused teacher education.
                    Teacher colleges continued to offer practice-based teacher preparation.

Late 20th
century   Universities amalgamated with teachers'colleges and teacher education
                    programmes increasingly included educational theory, discipline studies,
                    curriculum studies and professional practice.

21stCentury-present day

Fig. 7.1 Timeline of teacher education development in Australia (Adapted from Aspland 2006)

teacher education in Australia, spanning from white settlement and colonisation in the eighteenth century to the present day.

In the early twenty-first century, present-day teacher preparation has altered little since its half-century-old location into universities. Furthermore, whilst the points in time may differ slightly from those of other countries, the phases of moving into an academic teacher education in Australia are not dissimilar from those in other regions of the world. Many countries, for example, saw education and subsequently teacher education rise out of the religious missionaries who took up the education agenda as a form of evangelisation during times of colonisation. Furthermore, "normal schools" were popular across the globe: throughout England, Europe, the United States, Chile and many Asian countries as well. Most countries then formed teacher colleges as an initial step in formalising teacher education before moving to university-based delivery. These similarities demonstrate the pattern of teacher education development, making Australia far from unique in its current positioning. Nor is Australia unique in the level of criticism levelled at teacher education. Where Louden (2008) wrote of *101 damnations of initial teacher education in Australia*, to report on over 100 investigations and inquiries into Australian teacher education over a 30-year period, others in their own countries have reported similar onslaughts. As Cochran-Smith (2004) notes: ever "since the time teacher education emerged as an identifiable activity there have been few periods when it was not being critiqued" (p. 295).

7.2.1 Concerns with Quality

Issues concerning teacher education have largely been, and remain, around quality. There was little to no formal education required for teachers throughout the nineteenth and early twentieth century. Rather, teachers were selected based on their position in society (e.g. clergy) or their own performance in school (e.g. pupil teachers). For a long time, a "modest familiarity with the subject matter" (Larabee 2010, p. 291) was considered adequate for entry into the field.

In the face of increasing recognition that a better quality of teacher preparation required more explicit teaching about *how* to teach, teacher education eventually became professionalised, and a 1–2-year, and eventually the current (in Australia) 4-year, university qualification, with a minimum of 2 years dedicated to teaching-specific study, became a requirement for entry into the profession. This perceived need for formalised, academic preparation stemmed from acknowledgement that knowledge of content does not necessarily translate into knowledge of practice nor, subsequently, knowledge of how someone learns. Thus, being a "good" student oneself does not necessarily make one a "good" teacher. These early models of teacher education, which were primarily conducted through the "pupil teachers" of normal schools, were reliant on what Lortie (1975) termed the "apprenticeship of observation", that is, learning to teach from memories of what is observed or experienced throughout the 10–12 years of being in schools as a student. Such an "apprenticeship" model of learning to teach was particularly seen for its shortcomings. As Korthagen (2016) notes:

> teaching about teaching requires specific pedagogical approaches that are fundamentally different from those guiding teaching in schools. (p. 311)

Alongside the formalisation of teacher qualifications in teacher colleges and universities came the increasing inclusion of theory about child development and education and learning. Content and curriculum knowledge were also addressed alongside the professional practice in schools (Aspland 2006). With the advent of these theory-based inclusions, criticisms gradually turned from teacher preparation providing too much in the way of practical teaching knowledge and skills to providing too much theory, and exacerbating this, theory that was provided in the college/university setting which was seen to be disconnected and decontextualised from classroom practice.

From these early practice-focused, apprenticeship forms of teacher education to more recent theory-informed approaches emerged the concept of the theory-practice divide that has bedevilled teacher education since its subsumption in colleges and universities. Finding a balance between these two equally critical aspects of teacher education is possibly one of the most elusive, questioned and researched areas of teacher education in the Common Era. One of the key aspects of achieving such a balance is thought to rely on the nature of the professional practice experience or practicum.

7.3   The Practicum

Since the introduction of theory into teacher education, concerns that it is overly theoretical and that does not adequately prepare graduates for the classroom have persisted. This argument has been embedded, in particular, in the debate around the "theory-practice divide", and current trends in teacher education discourses are how this divide can be bridged to ensure high-quality teachers are recruited and retained in the teaching profession. The professional practicum component of modern-day teacher education is espoused to be the place in which pre-service teachers apply and reflect on theoretical notions of teaching and, thus, address this so-called theory-practice divide.

There exists a multitude of ways in which practicum is achieved in different teacher education programmes in Australia, demonstrating the lack of unity in ideas on the best way to administer this universally accepted critical component of teacher preparation. One of the key approaches growing in recent years and which does appear to cut across programmes is the use of informal and formal partnerships between universities and schools. Indeed, partnerships, as a currency of quality, are so highly regarded that, as shown in the next section, it has infiltrated policy directions in teacher education in a number of countries.

7.4 Partnerships: The Policy Imperative

There has been an increasing shift towards the use of university-school partnerships as a means of achieving integrated teacher education in Australia and other countries of the world. Whilst universities themselves have taken initiatives to establish both formal and informal partnerships with their stakeholder partners, in more recent years, this work has become a higher education policy imperative for governments worldwide. This is particularly the case in England's *School Direct Programme* (McNamara and Murray 2013) where teacher education has moved out of university and back into school settings almost entirely. Other examples include the United States' *Professional Development Schools* (Darling-Hammond 2012) and *Teaching Academies of Professional Practice* in Australia's state of Victoria (Department of Education Victoria 2017). Other small and large partnership initiatives (see Jones and Ryan 2014a for examples across Australia) also continue to be administered by local university schools and faculties.

The small-scale nature of individual schools' and faculties' efforts to engage in partnerships, whilst undoubtedly being instrumental in laying the evidentiary foundations for the importance of partnerships for teacher education, has also been recognised as a concern due to the lack of broad system-based approaches (TEMAG 2014). This concern was also noted some years earlier in Kruger et al.'s (2009) report regarding the need for university-school partnerships to move "beyond determined efforts of inspired individuals". The basis for most of these partnership initiatives has been to enhance the linking of theory and practice in teacher education. They have been promoted and trialled in a range of forms over a number of years (e.g. Catelli 1995; Darling-Hammond 2012; Jones et al. 2016; Kenny 2009; Korthagen 2001; Pegg et al. 2007). It is this imperative to address the integration of theory and practice that drives advice stemming from Australia's recent TEMAG (2014) report where the integration of theory and practice was presented as one of its most important recommendations.

TEMAG (2014), along with many others (e.g. Darling-Hammond 2014; Zeichner et al. 2015), presents the professional experience component of teacher education as the space in which this theory-practice integration can and must occur. Research has been unanimous in reporting that effective teacher education occurs when its theoretical and practical components are tightly entwined (Darling-Hammond 2012, 2014; Jones et al. 2016; Kosnick and Beck 2009; Loughran and Hamilton 2016; Zeichner et al. 2015). Recognition of this has led to a call for universities and schools to develop much stronger relationships and to work in close, collaborative partnership (e.g. Darling-Hammond 2014; TEMAG 2014; Ure et al. 2009).

Whilst we also support the place of strong, collaborative, integrated approaches to teacher education, we are also cautious about how partnerships are considered in this space. Partnerships are often presented as a panacea to the ails afflicting teacher education, as it is in this context that learning about teaching is viewed to be authentic and better able to reflect the realities of classroom teaching. However, there are important considerations to be made before any form of a partnership approach is enacted.

7.4.1 Back to the Apprenticeship Approach

Practising and pre-service teachers alike see the practical learning in the classroom as the learning that counts most towards their teacher education. The school is generally viewed as the setting in which pre-service teachers can put theoretical ideas about teaching and learning into practice. This has led to recent discourses around whether the university should have a place in the preparation of teachers and whether it is better to perhaps move back to school-based "training" approaches, something that indeed England has recently done. We would argue, however, that as Korthagen et al. (2006) and Zeichner and Liston (2014) warn, it is *reflection on practice* that is important and *not practice on its own* that leads to meaningful learning about teaching. Importantly, it is the time spent *away* from the classroom that teachers find the "space and time for exploration and critical thinking away from the fray" (Gewirtz 2013, p. 12).

The caution required in treating partnerships as providing the space for "real" learning about teaching is that we risk reinforcing the apprenticeship of observation model of teacher education. There are three primary concerns about this overemphasis on the practice-based component of teacher education. Firstly, history demonstrates that an overemphasis on classroom-based learning about teaching is inadequate without some consideration of theoretical underpinnings. As Kosnik et al. (2016) warn, "reducing university involvement in teacher education can lead to loss of status for teaching (which is already quite low in Australia) and reduction in the important research component" (p. 209). It is ongoing research into practice and policy that, after all, brings about reform and leads to improved practices over time. Secondly, there is no guarantee that pre-service teachers will have access to quality teaching in this approach as there is wide variation in the quality of teaching and learning occurring in classrooms. TEMAG received a number of submissions to express concerns around this and the general lack of insight in how to provide effective supervision:

> Submissions to the Advisory group highlighted a lack of quality assurance and a lack of structured training for supervising and mentor teachers to ensure they have the necessary skills to supervise, provide support and feedback, and assess professional experience placements. Stakeholders reported that supervising teachers are often selected to supervise professional experience placements based on the length of their teaching service. The Highly Accomplished and Lead levels of the Professional Standards offer a clear framework for identifying the teachers who are most skilled to fulfil the role, but there is scope for AITSL to further elaborate how the Professional Standards can inform selection and training of supervising teachers. (TEMAG 2014, p. 32)

Finally, if learning about teaching only occurs by observing and mimicking those approaches already established in the classroom, we risk consolidating status quo practices and never challenging or progressing ideas about effective pedagogies (Kosnik et al. 2016). This is reflected by Korthagen's (2016) comment in which he notes the risk of workplace learning and cautions:

> that it can easily become a process of socialization into established patterns and may lead to a reproduction of traditional habits and norms. Without additional measures it may hardly serve as an opportunity for powerful professional learning (Wideen et al. 1998).

Hence, increased time in practice does not necessarily imply deep learning and can even obstruct teachers' reflections and inquiry into what is really effective in teaching and learning (Gelfuso and Dennis 2014). In other words, practical experience is not equal to professional development. (Korthagen 2016, p. 321)

7.4.2 Not All Partnerships Are Created Equal

Another caution relating to the uncritical acceptance of using partnerships in teacher education concerns the *nature* of partnerships and how they are enacted. Whilst partnerships between schools and universities are a logical and natural component of effective teacher preparation, not all partnerships are created equal. There are many variations on the ways in which partnerships are conceived and enacted. In fact, Boyle-Baise and McIntyre (2010) remind us of Teitel's (2003) assertion that "the words 'collaboration' and 'partnership' are two of the most over-used and *mis-used* words in the late twentieth and early twenty-first centuries" (p. 317, emphasis added).

Those partnerships that have been found to be most effective have close alignment in intended goals and strong involvement from all partners. This is important for ensuring that knowledge of university and school programme outcomes that can otherwise be quite disparate are negotiated, aligned and addressed. Other examples of *arrangements* that are termed partnerships can, however, be quite superficial and meaningless in providing effective learning for pre-service teachers and other partner stakeholders, mainly because of the disconnect between stakeholder outcomes.

Kruger et al. (2009) indicate that more effective partnerships are ones of collaboration and that these types of partnerships have a focus on the learning of children in the class rather than the learning of pre-service teachers. In these child-focused partnerships, Kruger et al. claim that the learning for everyone is more effective. Lesser partnerships they describe are those that do not have this child-centred learning focus and fall somewhere on a declining continuum from collaborative to complementary.

Jones et al. (2016) also discuss partnership typology, but in less value-laden terms. They suggest that effective partnerships can be connective, generative or transformative in type and highlight that there can be beneficial learning in each, even though connective partnerships tend to be more short term than generative or transformative partnerships. For example, one of the potential benefits of connective partnerships is in their seeding potential for more generative partnerships in which longer-term and/or changed practices might occur. A large number of partnerships will commence as connective (which are similar to what Kruger et al. (2009) refer to as complementary), because they allow for the initial trust-building that is often required when new partnerships are being established (Jones et al. 2016).

What is important, regardless of the type of the partnership, is that the intended purpose and outcomes of the particular partnership are both clearly defined and subsequently met through the enactment of the partnership. When this occurs, the partnership can be viewed as effective and is then more likely to contribute to "growth in confidence, praxis, identity and relationships" (Jones et al. 2016, p. 115).

As Jones et al. (2016) also acknowledge, the *extent* of growth can be dependent on the level of collaboration between various stakeholders including universities and schools, pre-service teachers themselves, and pre-service and classroom teachers. Co-ordination to provide alignment between the school's and the university's programmes and ongoing communication between partners before, during and after the partnership period is essential for success.

Alongside the strong focus on partnerships, a number of additional policy directions have emerged in Australia in recent times with the aim of improving teaching and teacher education. Examples of these include a focus on entrance requirements into teaching programmes, closer scrutiny of literacy and numeracy skills and changes to assessment practices to better reflect teacher professional standards (see TEMAG 2014). Among these, though, partnerships, and what they might constitute, are purported to be the essential and most important focus for the way in which teacher education is evolved in the coming years.

7.5   Teacher Education Pedagogy

With the persistent criticism and investigation into teacher education quality, it comes as no surprise that research into teacher education pedagogies has become increasingly prevalent in the past few decades. Interestingly, a lot of this research points to a lack of evidence for claims made around the ineffectiveness of teacher education (Aspland 2006), but the claims persist regardless. An optimist might acknowledge, however, that this persistence has served as something of an impetus for the increased research in the field, which is beneficial to the overall growth and enhancement of teacher education practices. Important insights are emerging from both higher education and teacher education research in regard to what is and is not effective in the complex endeavour of teaching about teaching. Perhaps some of the most prominent of these works is that of John Biggs' deep learning through constructive alignment from the 1990s and early 2000s and, more recently, the work of Grossman, Hammerness and McDonald (2009) and Reid (2014) regarding *core practices*. Also, Boyd (2014), Korthagen (2011), Loughran (2014), Kosnick and Beck (2009) and others identify the critical importance of reflection, congruent teaching and modelling and other approaches specific to teacher education pedagogy. These pedagogies of higher and teacher education are outlined below and are linked to the notions of personalising learning that have been explored in the preceding chapters of this book.

7.5.1   Constructive Alignment

The notion of constructive alignment is not specific to teacher education per se but gains its relevance due to its positioning in the scholarship associated with effective higher education in general. Biggs (1996) describes constructive alignment as the marriage of instructional design with constructivist approaches to teaching and learning. Constructive alignment occurs when constructivism:

> guides decision making at all stages in instructional design: in deriving curriculum objectives in terms of performances that represent a suitably high cognitive level, in deciding teaching/learning activities judged to elicit those performances, and to assess and summatively report student performance. (Biggs 1996, p. 347)

Constructive alignment requires systematic alignment between learning outcomes, teaching and learning activities and assessment tasks (Biggs and Tang 2011). It is the inclusion of alignment between teaching and learning activities with both assessment and learning outcomes that Biggs and Tang claim makes constructive alignment distinctive from most other outcome-focused approaches. The implication of this for teacher education is the challenge to move beyond the traditional passive, content heavy, lecture-style approaches to teaching and learning that do not align with the types of outcomes generally espoused in teacher education courses such as capable, skilled, responsive and high-performing teachers.

According to Biggs and Tang, constructive alignment leads to deep learning and tends to instil intrinsic motivation in students. Promoting deep learning means that students are more likely to have positive learning experiences, be interested in the main ideas and themes of course work and experience a sense of needing and wanting to know. Achieving deep learning requires a focus on teaching and learning that:

- elicits active responses from students rather than passive reception of information;
- builds on students' prior knowledge;
- challenges students' misconceptions;
- assesses for meaning rather than recall;
- promotes learning from mistakes; and
- focuses on depth rather than breadth of learning. (Adapted from Biggs and Tang 2011, p. 27)

The principles of personal constructivism are clearly evident in this overview of what is required of the teacher in engendering deep learning. Notions such as building on prior knowledge, challenging misconceptions and eliciting active responses are all characteristic of constructivism. Chance (2014) surmises the qualities of a deep learning environment as ones that are experiential and highly engaging. These ideas can be clearly linked to personalising learning's tenet regarding the Learner as Central.

The emphasis on the personal in this overview of constructive alignment should not be taken as the only consideration required for achieving quality and meaningful learning. As Biggs and Tang (2011) note, current conceptualisations of constructivism can vary from personal to the social, cognitive-focused and postmodern views. All views share the commonality of placing the learner as an active participant at the centre of the learning experience, whereby they can construct meaning drawing on prior knowledge and current experience and where teachers are guides and facilitators rather than wellsprings of knowledge.

Another general approach advocated to assist in achieving meaningful and effective learning, particularly in professional courses, of which teacher education is one, is that of work integrated learning or *WIL* (Patrick et al. 2008). WIL, which requires some practical learning situated in a relevant workplace, is said to better tie the theory and practice of professional course work. This supports the general notion of Kosnik and Beck (2009), who indicate in their book *Priorities in Teacher Education* that the expansive information about teaching and learning is often crammed into teacher preparation courses such that "breadth of coverage militates against breadth of understanding" (p. 3). The impact of this, they argue, is that upon entering the profession, teachers do not have sufficient understanding of key ideas about teaching and learning in order to select from and operationalise the suite of choices they have about how to approach their practice in the most effective ways. WIL and other ideas regarding more teacher education-specific pedagogies might better ensure that teacher educators "show exemplary pedagogical behaviour" (Korthagen 2016, p. 312) where theory and practice together support the increased understanding that Kosnick and Beck call for. The most prevalent of these teacher education-specific pedagogies are reflective practice (see Brandenburg et al. 2017; Loughran and Hamilton 2016), modelling (Boyd 2014; Loughran et al. 2016) which has also been described as "congruent teaching" (Swennen et al. 2008) and the study of core practices (see Grossman et al. 2009; Reid 2014). These established and emerging paradigms offer a way to reconceptualise teacher education practice, particularly when aligned with personalising learning. Before continuing to explain the way in which this alignment can occur, a brief outline of WIL and these other teacher education-specific pedagogies is provided.

7.5.2   Work Integrated Learning (WIL)

WIL is "an umbrella term for a range of approaches and strategies that integrate theory with the practice of work within a purposefully designed curriculum" (Patrick et al. 2008, p. iv). Its core requirement is that students experience at least some of their learning situated in the workplace for which they are preparing to enter. In teacher education, this relates to the university-based learning about teaching and the classroom-based practice of teaching. As noted earlier, the incorporation of classroom teaching practice as a key element of teacher education has gradually emerged after both practice-based and theory-based preparation alone were recognised for their respective shortcomings. Hence, the combination of both university, theory-based and school, practice-based experiences have been a part of teacher education for some time. Implemented with what might arguably be quite varied levels of success, the place of theory and practice in teacher education is both a sanctioned and stable part of nearly all teacher education courses in the world. The focus in more recent times is not so much on whether it should it occur, but rather on how. There is a multitude of research and literature focused on how the work integrated learning practice of school placements can be leveraged for their effectiveness in the preparation of new teachers, some of which has been explored in the discussion around *partnerships* earlier in this chapter. Indeed, it is quite possibly from WIL practices that other university-based aspects of teacher education have been considered more carefully.

Teacher educators cannot really control what happens in the classroom setting of the school-based practice outside of setting particular tasks that they ask their students to complete. However, what is done with the practical experience once the student returns to university has great potential for informing and enhancing teacher educator practice. Early in the practice of work integrated learning in teacher education, pre-service teachers were usually required to take the theoretical aspects of their learning from university and implement them in the practice-based environment of the classroom. Criticisms of this quickly identified the "gap" between this theory-practice model where pre-service teachers were generally left to make sense of the theory they experienced at university and that which they had in the classroom with minimal support from anyone who had knowledge or understanding of these two quite unique environments (Darling-Hammond 2006; Zeichner 2002). This realisation has informed substantial research into what it means to really integrate work practices to achieve learning. Models suggesting concurrent university-school experiences, or more recently termed, university-school partnerships (e.g. TEMAG 2014), as well as ways of using classroom experience as the context for discussion, analysis and reflection practice back in the university setting, dominate current discourses around teacher education. As such, partnerships and models of analysis and reflection have become increasingly prevalent in the literature and research around pedagogies of teacher education.

7.5.3   Modelling and Congruent Teaching

One of the key ways in which analysis and discussion of teaching practice has been approached is through modelling. Loughran (2006) defines modelling as "a means for demonstrating practice" (p. 39) and something that teacher educators employ when they want to teach about teaching. Coupled with this notion is that of "pedagogical reasoning" (Shulman 1987), whereby the teacher educator makes the decisions about teaching actions explicit to students to ensure that both *the what and the why* of practice are made clear (Wood and Geddis as cited in Korthagen 2016).

Modelling is considered important in demonstrating effective teaching practice; however, as Loughran (2006) warns, not all modelling is in fact exemplary, and hence on its own, it is insufficient for learning about effective teaching. It is for this reason that pedagogical reasoning becomes an important part of learning about teaching. Modelling coupled with pedagogical reasoning provides an opportunity for analysis, discussion and reflection. It also enables modelling of both poor and exemplary teaching practice as the analytical discussion can isolate why something may or may not be effective and in what ways different contexts might influence the outcome. Such a process, alongside the linking of theory to the discussion, analysis and reflection, provides a three-part process referred to as "explicit modelling"

(Lunenberg et al. as cited in Korthagen 2016, p. 331) or "congruent teaching" (Swennen et al. 2008, p. 531).

Examples of congruent teaching identified by Swennen et al. (2008) include practices such as thinking aloud, stepping out, reflection breaks, co-teaching, linking modelling and theory and the role of values. Common across these practices is the notion of "meta-commentary" (Wood and Geddis as cited in Swennen et al. 2008, p. 532). Similar to the practice of pedagogical reasoning (Shulman 1987), meta-commentary is where teacher educators make explicit the reasons they employ particular actions in their teaching rather than hoping that students will notice them from the modelling alone. This notion of being explicit about practice also underpins the relatively recent movement in teacher education pedagogy, which has been termed "the practice turn".

7.5.4 The Practice Turn

The practice turn describes a relatively recent movement in the pedagogy of teacher education that encourages a shift in curriculum organisation away from disciplines of knowledge (foundation studies, content, methods) and towards "approximations of practice", that is, teaching around a set of core practices that "attend to the clinical aspects" of teaching (Grossman et al. 2009). Grossman et al. (2009) argue that this "turn" towards practice-based elements of learning about how to teach enables the teacher educator to "attend to both the conceptual and the practical aspects associated with any given practice" (p. 278) and thus reduces, or even eliminates, the artificial divide between theory and practice. Supporting this, Reid (2011) indicates that such a "(re)turn" to practice would "allow us to start to relate and *integrate* the experience that our students have of our courses" (p. 294, emphasis in original).

Core practices identified by Grossman et al. (2009) include those that occur with high frequency, are cross-disciplinary, are accessible to novices for mastery practice, reveal more about students and teaching, preserve the complexity of teaching and are research-informed. They argue that to achieve such a curriculum, "pedagogies of enactment" (Grossman et al. 2009, p. 283) are needed, whereby pre-service teachers have "opportunities to rehearse and enact discrete components of complex practice in settings of reduced complexity" (p. 283). Ways in which such teaching can be achieved include analysing and discussing videos of classroom teaching, analysing case studies, taking a particular practice (e.g. story-reading) and problematising it (e.g. when to pause, whisper, shrink back, sit up, etc.) to tell the story and allowing multiple opportunities to rehearse (to one another, to a child, to a teacher). The study of core practices allows pre-service teachers to reflect on what makes practice exceptional and what makes it mediocre, in order to build mastery.

7.5.5 *Reflection*

Common across pedagogies of teacher education is the notion of reflection. Reflection has long been associated with teacher education but perhaps only in the past two decades has it been theorised and emphasised as *essential* in what it brings to learning about teaching. Indeed, Jones and Ryan (2014b) propose that reflection is emerging as "the contemporary paradigm of teacher education" (p. 178).

The importance of reflection is linked to other discourses around learning that emphasise the importance of thinking. Thinking back on experiences and effective thinking in the middle of experiences are two important characteristics of effective teacher practice. Whilst there have been cautions against making a direct association between thinking and reflection (e.g. Coia and Taylor 2017) less we risk an uncritical process that lacks the rigour that effective reflection requires, there is without doubt an important place for thinking in the process of reflecting. Whilst reflection is not in its entirety equivalent to thinking, it is a precondition for reflection to occur. Being able to think back on experiences and think of future possibilities are aspects of reflection. Similarly, thinking "on one's feet" in the classroom to maximise learning and circumvent averse episodes is equally important. These forms of reflection are described by Schön (1983) as reflection *on* and *in* action, respectively.

What sets effective reflection apart from thinking, however, is the deliberate sourcing of relevant and widespread information to inform the associated thinking. It is broadly informed thinking that makes reflection *critical* in its nature, as opposed to descriptive. Critical reflection examines assumptions by sourcing information from one's students and colleagues. It is also informed by research literature. These elements alongside one's own thoughts and reactions to particular experiences make up Brookfield's (1995) four lenses of critical reflection. Descriptive reflection, on the other hand, tends to provide a recount of events and fails to examine particular experiences for deeper and/or alternative understandings.

Historically, reflection on action has been reasonably prevalent in teacher education practice, although not necessarily taught or enacted well. Teaching for reflection *in* action, however, has been more elusive, and perhaps because of this, it is not attended to as much in how teacher educators encourage their students to reflect. Russell and Martin (2017) contend that "reflection and reflective practice are rarely modelled or taught in ways that give it special meaning in the context of teaching and learning" (p. 28). Scholars of teacher education almost unanimously call for a pedagogy of teacher education that makes reflection a formal, critical and scaffolded part of teacher education (e.g. Loughran 2006; Russell and Martin 2017; Zeichner and Liston 2014).

Reflection is inherent to each of the above-mentioned pedagogies of teacher education. With regard to work integrated learning, reflection on the experience in the classroom is where the learning is most likely to take place. This is represented by Korthagen et al.'s (2006) proposition that learning occurs from reflection on experience rather than from experience alone. In modelling, encouraging analysis of modelled practice is tantamount to encouraging critical reflection, as is the analysis and rehearsal of core practices. Reflection goes hand in hand with all forms of effective teacher pedagogy and is the mechanism through which learning about effective teaching occurs.

7.6   Personalising Learning as Teacher Education Pedagogy

7.6.1   Learners as Central

As noted earlier, Biggs and Tang (2011) discuss that various conceptualisations of constructivism share the common feature of learner being an active participant at the centre of the learning experience. This defining characteristic of constructivism, and indeed, constructive alignment, is also fundamental to the notion of Learners as Central, one of the key tenets of personalising learning. Thus working with the general practice of constructive alignment in teacher education also assists in achieving one of the four key ways of personalising learning.

The study of core practices, modelling and reflective practice as new paradigms for teacher education lend themselves to the ideas behind constructive alignment and Learners as Central, because they are all concerned with learning processes as much as learning outcomes. They achieve this emphasis by demanding the *active* participation of students. Biggs and Tang (2011) state that this requires the action verb associated with the intended learning to be present in all three of the learning outcome, the teaching and learning activities and the assessment. When this occurs, students are more likely to be engaged in active, deep learning where:

> the students themselves do the real work, the teacher simply acts as 'broker' between the student and a learning environment that supports the appropriate learning activities. (Biggs and Tang 2011, p. 100)

7.6.2   Communities of Collaboration

The notion of "students doing the real work" and "teachers as brokers" described by Biggs and Tang (2011) within a constructively aligned, deep approach to teaching and learning also resonates with ideas of Lave and Wenger's (1991) description of Communities of Practice. Biggs and Tang (2011) note that working collaboratively with both teachers and peers is one of four essential aspects of working towards change in the way we understand and see the world, which is essentially how they present the notion of learning. Personalising learning borrows this notion and expands it into the realm of situated learning in which Communities of Practice, or from Keamy, Nicholas, Mahar and Herrick's (2007) perspective, Communities of Collaboration, work individually and collectively to experience learning. Still, here, learning occurs through participation in the community. It is the merging of Learners as Central with a Community of Collaboration in which learning is enhanced.

Many other researchers in the field of teacher education point to the importance of the community in which the learning takes place (e.g. Darling-Hammond 2012; Loughran 2006; Zeichner 2010). Without the Community of Collaboration, learning can only have a cognitive, passive focus. Situated learning theory, alongside underpinning conceptions of social constructivism, is clear in demonstrating the increased capacity for learning that occurs through the social aspect. In social constructivism, this is represented through the Zone of Proximal Development (Vygotsky 1978) in which a more able adult or peer can elevate the level of learning that might otherwise be achieved; and in situated learning, the focus is removed from the cognitive and placed on the learning that occurs through immersive, participatory experiences situated in relevant contexts.

In teacher education, both cognitive and participatory situated learning need to be privileged. The university setting provides both the theoretical underpinnings of learning and the establishment of effective learning environments. The school setting provides contextual meaning and opportunities for practical applications. Thus, Communities of Practice support notions of work integrated learning. In discussing theory and practice, Korthagen (2001) notes that the understanding of one of these is reliant on understanding the other – they are symbiotic in their mutual contribution to effective teacher education. It is in recognition of this that the meta-commentary (Wood and Geddis 1999) or pedagogical reasoning (Shulman 1987) of explicit modelling (Loughran 2006) and congruent teaching (Swennen et al. 2008) are important in teacher education pedagogy, as it is not the exposure to practice, be it through modelling or in the school context, that the learning about teaching occurs, but rather in the reasons for particular teaching actions. Thus, it is together that the university and the school settings can provide the relevant experiences for the integration of theory and practice as one provides the experiences for reflection and the other the deconstruction and focus on reasons for particular practices at particular times and in particular contexts. Such an integrated view of teacher education is essential if we are to overcome the ersatz dichotomy that has been cultivated in teacher education since its stationing in universities. As Loughran and Hamilton note:

> Constructing theory and practice as a dichotomy has been an issue for teacher education that has typically been played out in less than productive ways. Schools have been seen as the 'home' of practice and universities as the 'ivory towers' of theory thus creating a divide to be bridged rather than as different sites in which the development of knowledge and practice of teaching is different but complimentary. (Loughran and Hamilton 2016, p. 6)

The merging of constructivism with situated learning and the privileging of each of teacher education's equally important settings (i.e. universities and schools) help to grow a Community of Collaboration to better enable constructive alignment of intended outcomes in teacher education. The university provides the space for reflection and deconstruction of practice, such that, with expert facilitation, key insights, or core practices, can be identified and reinforced. The classroom experience provides the material for this reflection, the "fodder" for assisting developing teachers to experience deep, meaningful learning about their teaching. In other words, learning about teaching occurs in the consideration of practice within a community of peers and expert facilitators who assist with the linking of theory and practice, through work integrated learning and critical reflection, congruent teaching and the rehearsal and study of core practices.

It is undoubtedly the recognition of the inextricable nature of theory and practice, and universities and schools, that underpins the current partnership agenda in teacher education. After decades of being based in one and embedding the other, there appears to at last be a realisation that it is through equal recognition and emphasis, the interweaving of theory and practice, that constructive alignment of learning activity, assessment and outcomes will best be achieved. Communities of Collaboration are core to the enactment of practices that support such outcomes.

7.6.3 ICT as a Key Enabler

ICT, especially in the form of computers and their various applications and evolutions, has been relentless in its infiltration since its advent in education settings in the late twentieth century. From its beginnings in predominantly military applications, ICT has been invasive to the point that even children under 10 years of age generally carry some sort of mobile device that provides them with connectivity to phone and the Internet 24 h a day. As educators, we have no choice but to embrace this "technolution" of the lives of people in modern society. The ease of access to technology has to change the nature in which we assume children, and people in general, access information. Indeed, in the weeks recently preceding the writing of this chapter, the 7-year-old niece of one of the authors told her father on the eve of Easter Sunday that she knew the "Easter Bunny wasn't real" and, she added, "neither is Santa or the tooth fairy". Bemused, her father queried, "Oh, and how do you know this?" "I *Googled* it!" she announced, as if this should have been completely obvious.

The experience of this father and of his daughter's confident assertion, and indeed, the fact that at such a young age, the author's niece has both the access and the nous to investigate the answers to her wonderings through technology, demonstrates the imperative for the meaningful use of technology to be incorporated into education. To not embrace this enabling access to information in the design and delivery of education, which is now at the fingertips of almost everyone in the western world, and at a level that was unimaginable even just a decade ago, would be nothing short of irresponsible. There can be no argument; ICT simply is a key enabler of learning.

The only questions educators should be asking themselves are: in what form and how best can ICT be exploited for its learning potentiality? And "exploited" is the operative term in these considerations. Given the pervasiveness of ICT in everyday life and living of modern society, and the fact that most people, including children of a primary-school age, carry a mobile device with a range of connectivity capabilities, means we need to leverage its use in teaching and learning. To prepare for such a technology-rich learning environment, learning to utilise ICT for learning in teacher education is absolutely paramount.

Addressing students' needs in an ever-changing technologically rich environment and using technological tools to enhance learning are both a complex and evolving issue facing all educators (Cox 2010; Fluck 2010). It requires an ongoing commitment from teachers and teacher educators to remain abreast of rapid changes, broadening devices and seemingly endless applications. Selecting appropriately from this plethora of devices and applications is an arduous and often time-consuming endeavour. A strong emphasis on curriculum renewal and on encouraging the use of a variety of eLearning and other ICT strategies to engage both postgraduate and undergraduate pre-service teachers in the skills, knowledge and values that will prepare them for teaching in the twenty-first century is at a critical point.

Despite the prevalence of applications and devices available (or perhaps because of it), research indicates that "most academics are not using new and compelling technologies for learning and teaching" (Johnson et al. 2013). Indeed, the pace of technology advancement leaves teacher educators often feeling incompetent and struggling to access their own professional learning to keep abreast of its potential for teaching and learning (Herrington et al. 2014). Therefore, it is not only timely but crucial that we build the capacity of teachers and teacher educators to deliver on societal needs and expectations through effective classroom ICT practices. Development of technology, pedagogy and content knowledge or TPACK (Koehler and Mishra 2009), which is a specific form of pedagogy related to teaching with technology, needs to be considered as an integrated and cross-curriculum priority. Teacher preparation programmes need to carefully consider the potential of ICT for both learning and communicating in and beyond the classroom.

As Jones and Ryan (2014b) note, applications of ICT are wide and varied. The use of mobile devices such as iPods, tablets, smartphones and Flip cameras can support deep, authentic learning, and online learning platforms allow learning to stretch beyond the classroom – in all sectors of education – primary, secondary and tertiary. Technology for communication through the use of email, Skype, Weebly and Google Drive, among many others, also broadens communication with students and parents and is becoming an increasing expectation of teachers in schools.

The principles of *authentic learning*, where the needs and interests of students are the focus of student-centred learning, are paramount in these various uses of technology. Herrington et al. (2014) propose that ICT, and mobile devices in particular, need to be viewed as that reflected by the use of ICT as a "cognitive tool" as well as a "delivery platform". In achieving this more cognitive function, Herrington, Herrington and Mantei (2009) suggest the use of mobile technologies that meet the following guidelines:

   – Real world relevance: Use mobile learning in authentic contexts
   – Mobile contexts: Use mobile learning in contexts where learners are mobile
   – Explore: Provide time for exploration of mobile technologies

- Blended: Blend mobile and non mobile technologies
- Whenever: Use mobile learning spontaneously
- Wherever: Use mobile learning in non traditional learning spaces
- Whomsoever: Use mobile learning both individually and collaboratively
- Affordances: Exploit the affordances of mobile technologies
- Personalise: Employ the learners' own mobile devices
- Mediation: Use mobile learning to mediate knowledge construction
- Prod*use*: Use mobile learning to produce and consume knowledge. (p. 134)

Such an approach requires deep knowledge not just about how to operate various devices, but on their pedagogical integration as a vehicle for the learning itself (Jones and McLean 2012). One strategy that would support teacher education-specific pedagogies such as modelling would be to engage the students themselves in identifying relevant applications and devices and leveraging these, where relevant, for their learning potential more broadly. This engagement of pre-service teachers allows for peer-to-peer learning practices that have been acknowledged for their capacity to promote: learning for those involved, life-long learning, a sense of belonging in a learning community, skill development in managing one's self and others, skills in providing and receiving feedback and evaluating one's own learning (Boud et al. 2001). This also supports a strategy of active participation, which, as discussed earlier in this chapter, is paramount to the personalising learning pedagogies we are purporting as important in this volume.

Traditionally, the standard models of organisational uptake of technology and innovation, such as Davis' technology acceptance model (1993), have been applied to understand the adoption of ICT in learning and teaching in tertiary institutions. However, uptake has been sufficiently slow across most institutions such that some authors have begun to look at the barriers and blockages which prevent more widespread and sophisticated use of technologies in university teaching (Schnekenberg 2009). Parallel to this, others have considered factors such as the role of informal advice, trusted colleagues and local support networks in promoting educational innovation (Roxå et al. 2011; Salmon 2005). We suggest that taking a personalising learning focus on both teaching with ICT and engaging in teacher educator professional learning would assist teacher educators, pre-service teachers and students in school to experience authentic, deep, relevant and meaningful learning where ICT is seamless in its integration and as "obvious" as a means of learning as *Googling* about the Easter Bunny was to the 7-year-old niece of one of the authors.

In the words of Herrington et al. (2014):

Pre-service teachers and their university teachers must be adequately prepared for their new roles, and the means to do this requires imagination and forms of professional development that go beyond the simple provision of information about the devices themselves and how they work. Such endeavours may ensure that teachers will no longer prohibit the use of mobile devices in classrooms, but embrace them as powerful tools for learning. (p. 149)

Taking an approach that personalises learning for pre-service teachers and perhaps even teacher educators helps to address these issues. Personalising learning in ICT use and skill development for teaching promotes the placement of Learners as Central, uses Communities of Collaboration and instils Lifelong Learning practices.

In many ways, ICT could be viewed not just as the enabler of learning, but as its panacea in twenty-first-century education.

7.6.4   Lifelong Learning

As we have shown in Chap. 6, Lifelong Learning is a critical component of any twenty-first-century approach to education. The rapidly changing nature of society and the workforce, largely due to the increasing domination of advanced technologies, requires people to be flexible, adaptable and able to learn across their lifetime if they are to remain active in their participation in society. In many ways, the achievement of companion tenets of personalising learning – that is, Learner as Central, Communities of Collaboration and ICT – automatically allows for the achievement of Lifelong Learning.

Lifelong Learning is characterised by a range of factors that are embedded in these other tenets of personalising learning. For example, the tenet of Learner as Central highlights the importance of learners being active in their participation in learning and for learning to be authentic and contextualised in ways that hold relevance for learners (Keamy et al. 2007; Smit et al. 2014). These features of Learner as Central resound with Saribas' (2015) description of lifelong learners being active in planning and assessing their own learning and the importance of holistic approaches that acknowledge the significance of context (Bronfenbrenner 1994). Another core feature of placing the Learner as Central lies in providing choice in content and approaches to learning (Florian 2009; Keamy et al. 2007) which is representative of the "co-designing" of learning opportunities that Owen (2016) refers to in describing the transferrable skills needed to address issues of Lifelong Learning.

Saribas (2015) also highlights the place of formal and informal learning settings and the need to learn from peers, teachers and mentors when engaging in the skills for Lifelong Learning. These characteristics of Lifelong Learning align with those of Communities of Collaboration where learning from participation in a community of peers and "old-timers" is definitive (Lave and Wenger 1991). The social nature of Lifelong Learning (Aspin and Chapman 2012) is core to Communities of Practice. Wenger (2011), in discussing the nature of participation in social practices underpinning Communities of Practice, states the ways in which this serves "the Lifelong Learning needs of students by organising Communities of Practice focused on topics of continuing interest to students" (p. 5).

The relationship between ICT and Lifelong Learning hardly needs explanation. With Lifelong Learning's primary focus on active participation in society across the lifespan (Halttunen et al. 2014) and the pervasiveness of an increasingly digitalised and technologised society (Manyika 2016), the ability to adapt to growing forms and uses of technology is fundamental to Lifelong Learning. Not only will ICT and technology take over many low-skilled jobs requiring manual labour (Manyika 2016), but it is also infiltrating personal life as much, if not more, than the workforce. The implication of this promotes the importance of Lifelong Learning as all members of society will need to maintain capacity and competency to engage in the ever-increasing technologised world.

Ultimately, what we see here is that the natural alignment (or one might even say, the constructive alignment) of the tenets of personalising learning occurring through the complementary features of Learners as Central, Communities of Practice and ICT engenders Lifelong Learning. Operationalising the first three tenets means that the fourth tenet of Lifelong Learning becomes inherent in how teaching and learning is enacted and experienced. With the importance of Lifelong Learning for meeting personal life goals and participation in society across the lifespan, we see another reason for the adoption of personalising in teacher education.

7.7 Personalising Learning: Meeting Policy and Quality Imperatives

Linking current policy imperatives with research about effective teaching and teacher education leads to some consideration of how personalising learning in the field of teacher education may serve as a helpful vehicle for meeting these policy and quality imperatives. As we have noted earlier, a number of aspects of personalising learning are not necessarily new approaches to education, but rather, draw together a number of known elements of successful teaching and learning in a collective to assist thinking around education.

Personalising learning involves placing the learner at the centre of the learning and ensuring that the learning experiences they undertake elicit active participation and collaboration with their peers. Clinical study of their practice (Grossman et al. 2009) and critical reflection on their teaching practices (Loughran 2006), both supported by expert facilitation and embedded in both universities and schools (Patrick et al.'s (2008) work integrated learning), is essential in achieving the Learner as Central tenet. As discussed above, these approaches encourage constructive alignment and deep learning and provide the basis for meeting the partnerships imperative that is of interest to the whole of the education sector as well as those informing its policy directions.

Collaborations between various stakeholders, pre-service teachers and teacher educators, pre-service teachers and classroom teachers, classroom teachers and teacher educators and pre-service teachers between themselves, are all important in establishing small and large Communities of Collaboration that make up a larger constellation of practice (Wenger 1998) in which clinical analysis and critical reflection on practice can occur. This clinical study of practice and critical reflection are particularly important for teachers to enhance awareness and prevention of the tendency that can otherwise occur for learners with more social capital to dominate the learning resources and space. Again Communities of Collaboration can assist in not only addressing ideas around quality but also supporting the partnership directions in which teacher education is being pushed. Hence again this tenet of personalising learning helps to address both research and policy directions for enhancing teacher education.

Meaningful use of ICT as a key enabler of learning needs to be authentically embedded in teaching, learning and assessment to both leverage learning potential and to equip pre-service teachers with twenty-first-century skills. There is potential here for students' active participation through peer teaching, which has some potential to address what can otherwise be an overwhelming expectation on teachers and teacher educators to remain abreast of the seemingly infinite number of applications and platforms that can support learning.

Finally, as many authors warn (e.g. Biggs and Tang 2011; Loughran 2006), no one framework or theory should be relied on alone or used as a set of prescriptive rules for approaching teaching and learning. Indeed, as Hattie tells us:

> it is not a particular method, nor a particular script, that makes the difference; it is attending to personalising the learning, getting greater precision about how students are progressing in this learning, and ensuring professional learning of the teachers about how and when to provide different or more effective strategies for teaching and learning. (Hattie 2009, p. 245)

Personalising learning is no exception to this warning, although one of its strengths is in its drawing together of other established and convincing approaches to effective teaching and learning and its capacity to align with and support other established pedagogies that are specific to higher education and teacher education in particular. From this, and the preceding discussion in this chapter, we see that the tenets of personalising learning of Learners as Central, Communities of Collaboration, ICT and Lifelong Learning are highly felicitous for meeting the policy, stakeholder and quality imperatives regarding improved teaching and teacher education.

In the remaining chapters of this manuscript, we attempt to illustrate a selection of ways in which the tenets of personalising learning have been applied in our teacher education practice and demonstrate the outcomes from our own critical reflection on these examples, as well as the responses of the pre-service teachers involved. These exemplar chapters illustrate the ways in which personalising learning can be achieved in teacher education and provide some research evidence of its effectiveness in achieving learning for all.

References

Aspin, D., & Chapman, J. (2012). Towards a philosophy of lifelong learning. In D. Aspin, J. Chapman, K. Evans, & R. Bagnall (Eds.), *Second international handbook of lifelong learning* (Vol. 26, pp. 3–35). Dordrecht: Springer.

Aspland, T. (2006). Changing patterns of teacher education in Australia. *Educational Research and Perspectives, 33*(2), 140–163.

Biggs, J. (1996). Enhancing teaching through constructive alignment. *Higher Education, 32*(3), 347–364.

Biggs, J., & Tang, C. (2011). *Teaching for quality learning at university* (4th ed.). New York: Open University Press.

Boud, D., Cohen, R., & Sampson, J. (Eds.). (2001). *Peer learning in higher education: Learning from and with each other*. London: Kogan Page.

Boyd, P. (2014). Using 'modelling' to improve the coherence of initial teacher education. In P. Boyd, A. Szplit, & Z. Zbróg (Eds.), *Teacher educators and teachers as learners: International perspectives* (pp. 51–73). Poland: Wydawnictwo Libron.

Boyle-Baise, M., & McIntyre, D. J. (2010). What kind of experience? Preparing teachers in PDS or community settings. In M. Cochran-Smith, S. Feiman-Nemser, D. McIntyre, & K. Demers (Eds.), *Handbook of research on teacher education: Enduring questions in changing contexts* (3rd ed., pp. 307–330). New York: Routledge.

Brandenburg, R., Glasswell, K., Jones, M., & Ryan, J. (Eds.). (2017). *Reflective theory and practice in teacher education*. Singapore: Springer.

Bronfenbrenner, U. (1994). Ecological models of human development. In T. Postlethwaite & T. Husen (Eds.), *International encyclopedia of education* (Vol. 3, 2nd ed., pp. 37–43). Oxford: Elsevier.

Brookfield, S. (1995). *Becoming a critically reflective teacher*. San Fransisco: Jossey-Bass.

Catelli, L. (1995). Action research and collaborative inquiry in a school-university partnership. *Action in Teacher Education, 16*(4), 25–38.

Chance, S. (2014). Bringing it all together through group learning. In P. Eddy (Ed.), *Connecting learning across the institution. New directions for higher education* (Vol. 165, pp. 107–119). Hoboken: Wiley.

Cochran-Smith, M. (2004). The problem of teacher education. *Journal of Teacher Education, 55*(4), 295–299.

Coia, L., & Taylor, M. (2017). Let's stay in the swamp: Poststructural feminist reflective practice. In R. Brandenburg, K. Glasswell, M. Jones, & J. Ryan (Eds.), *Reflective theory and practice in teacher education, Self-Study of Teaching and Teacher Education Practices* (Vol. 17, pp. 49–62). Singapore: Springer.

Cox, M. (2010). The changing nature of researching IT in education. In A. McDougall, J. Murnane, A. Jones, & N. Reynolds (Eds.), *Researching IT in education: Theory, practice and future directions* (pp. 11–24). London: Routledge.

Darling-Hammond, L. (2006). Constructing 21st century teacher education. *Journal of Teacher Education, 57*(3), 300–314.

Darling-Hammond, L. (2012). *Powerful teacher education: Lessons from exemplary programs*. San Francisco: Wiley.

Darling-Hammond, L. (2014). Strengthening clinical preparation: The Holy Grail of teacher education. *Peabody Journal of Education, 89*(4), 547–561.

Darling-Hammond, L. (2015). *The flat world and education: How America's commitment to equity will determine our future*. New York: Teachers College Press.

Darling-Hammond, L., & Bransford, J. (2005). *Preparing teachers for a changing world: What teachers should learn and be able to do*. San Francisco: Jossey-Bass.

Davis, F. (1993). User acceptance of information technology: System characteristics, user perceptions and behavioral impacts. *International Journal of Man-Machine Studies, 38*(3), 475–487.

Department of Education Victoria [DET Victoria]. (2017). *Teaching academies of professional practice* (TAPP). Retrieved from www.education.vic.gov.au/about/programs/partnerships/.../tapp.aspx

Florian, L. (2009). Towards an inclusive pedagogy. In P. Hick, R. Kershner, & P. Farrell (Eds.), *Psychology for inclusive education* (pp. 38–51). Oxon: Routledge.

Fluck, A. (2010). From integration to transformation. In A. McDougall, J. Murnane, A. Jones, & N. Reynolds (Eds.), *Researching IT in education: Theory, practice and future directions* (pp. 62–71). London: Routledge.

Gewirtz, S. (2013). Developing teachers as scholar-citizens, reasserting the value of university involvement in teacher education. In L. Florian & N. Pantić (Eds.), *Learning to teach. Part 1:*

Exploring the history and role of higher education in teacher education (pp. 10–13). York: The Higher Education Academy.

Grossman, P., Hammerness, K., & McDonald, M. (2009). Redefining teaching, re-imagining teacher education. *Teachers and Teaching, 15*(2), 273–289.

Halttunen, T., Koivisto, M., & Billet, S. (Eds.). (2014). *Promoting, assessing, recognizing and certifying lifelong learning. International perspectives and practices*. Dordrecht: Springer.

Hattie, J. (2009). *Visible learning – A synthesis of over 800 meta-analyses relating to achievement*. New York: Routledge.

Herrington, J., Herrington, A., & Mantei, J. (2009). Design principles for mobile learning. In J. Herrington, A. Herrington, J. Mantei, I. Olney, & B. Ferry (Eds.), *New technologies, new pedagogies: Mobile learning in higher education* (pp. 129–138). Wollongong: UOW. Retrieved from http://ro.uow.edu.au/newtech/

Herrington, J., Ostashewski, N., Reid, D., & Flintoff, K. (2014). Mobile technologies in teacher education: Preparing pre-service teachers and teacher educators for mobile learning. In M. Jones & J. Ryan (Eds.), *Successful teacher education: Partnerships, reflective practice and the place of technology* (pp. 137–151). Rotterdam: Sense Publishers.

Johnson, L., Adams Becker, S., Cummins, M., Freeman, A., Ifenthaler, D., & Vardaxis, N. (2013). *Technology outlook for Australian tertiary education 2013–2018: An NMC horizon project regional analysis*. Austin: The New Media Consortium.

Jones, M., & McLean, K. J. (2012). Personalising learning in teacher education through the use of technology. *Australian Journal of Teacher Education, 37*(1), 75. https://doi.org/10.14221/ajte.2012v37n1.1.

Jones, M., & Ryan, J. (Eds.). (2014a). *Successful teacher education: Partnerships, reflective practice and the place of technology*. Rotterdam: Sense Publishers.

Jones, M., & Ryan, J. (2014b). Successful and 'transferable' practice. In M. Jones & J. Ryan (Eds.), *Successful teacher education: Partnerships, reflective practice and the place of technology* (pp. 177–194). Rotterdam: Sense Publishers.

Jones, M., Hobbs, L., Kenny, J., Campbell, C., Gilbert, A., Herbert, S., & Redman, C. (2016). Successful university-school partnerships: An interpretive framework to inform partnership practice. *Teaching and Teacher Education, 60*, 108–120.

Keamy, K., Nicholas, H., Mahar, S., & Herrick, C. (2007). *Personalising education: From research to policy and practice*. Melbourne: Department of Education and Early Childhood Development.

Kenny, J. (2009). A partnership based approach to professional learning: Preservice and in-service teachers working together to teach primary science. *Australian Journal of Teacher Education, 34*(6), 1–22.

Koehler, M. J., & Mishra, P. (2009). What is technological pedagogical content knowledge? *Contemporary Issues in Technology and Teacher Education, 9*(1), 60–70.

Korthagen, F. (2001). *Teacher education: A problematic enterprise in linking practice and theory: The pedagogy of realistic teacher education*. Mahwah: Lawrence Erlbaum Associates.

Korthagen, F. (2011). Making teacher education relevant for practice: The pedagogy of realistic teacher education. *Orbis Scholae, 5*(2), 31–50.

Korthagen, F. (2016). Pedagogy of teacher education. In J. Loughran & M. Hamilton (Eds.), *International handbook on teacher education* (Vol. 1, pp. 311–346). Singapore: Springer.

Korthagen, F., Loughran, J., & Russell, T. (2006). Developing fundamental principles for teacher education programs and practices. *Teaching and Teacher Education, 22*, 1020–1041.

Kosnik, C., & Beck, C. (2009). *Priorities in teacher education: The 7 key elements of preservice preparation*. London: Routledge.

Kosnik, C., Beck, C., & Goodwin, A. L. (2016). Reform efforts in teacher education. In J. Loughran & M. Hamilton (Eds.), *International handbook of teacher education* (pp. 267–308). Singapore: Springer.

Kruger, T., Davies, A., Eckersley, B., Newell, F., & Cherednichenko, B. (2009). *Effective and sustainable university-school partnerships. Beyond determined efforts of inspired individu-*

als. Canberra: Teaching Australia [Electronic version]. Retrieved from http://hdl.voced.edu. au/10707/144200

Larabee, D. (2010). An uneasy relationship: The history of teacher education in the university. In M. Cochran-Smith, S. Feiman-Nemser, D. McIntyre, & K. Demers (Eds.), *Handbook of research on teacher education: Enduring questions in changing contexts* (3rd ed., pp. 290–306). New York: Routledge.

Lave, J., & Wenger, E. (1991). *Situated learning: Legitimate peripheral participation (learning in doing: Social, cognitive and computational perspectives).* Cambridge: Cambridge University Press.

Lortie, D. C. (1975). *Schoolteacher.* Chicago: Chicago University Press.

Louden, W. (2008). 101 Damnations: The persistence of criticism and the absence of evidence about teacher education in Australia. *Teachers and Teaching: Theory and Practice, 14*(4), 357–368.

Loughran, J. (2006). *Developing a pedagogy of teacher education: Understanding teaching and learning about teaching.* Abingdon: Routledge.

Loughran, J. (2014). Professionally developing as a teacher educator. *Journal of Teacher Education, 65*(4), 271–283.

Loughran, J., & Hamilton, M. (2016). Developing an understanding of teacher education. In J. Loughran & M. Hamilton (Eds.), *International handbook on teacher education* (Vol. 1, pp. 3–22). Singapore: Springer.

Loughran, J., Keast, S., & Cooper, R. (2016). Pedagogical reasoning in teacher education. In J. Loughran & M. Hamilton (Eds.), *International handbook on teacher education* (Vol. 1, pp. 387–481). Singapore: Springer.

MacBeath, J. (2012). Teacher training, education or learning by doing in the UK. In L. Darling-Hammond & A. Liberman (Eds.), *Teacher education around the world: Changing policies and practices* (pp. 66–80). Oxon: Routledge.

Manyika, J. (2016). *Technology, jobs and the future of work.* Briefing Note prepared for the Fortune Vatican Forum December 2016. McKinsey Global Institute.

McNamara, O., & Murray, J. (2013). The School Direct programme and its implications for research informed teacher education and teacher educators. In L. Florian & N. Pantić (Eds.), *Learning to teach. Part 1: Exploring the history and role of higher education in teacher education* (pp. 14–19). York: The Higher Education Academy.

Owen, J. (2016). Foreward. In Foundation for Young Australians (FYA) (Ed.), *The new basics: Big data reveals the skills young people need for the new work order* (p. 3). Melbourne: Foundation for Young Australians.

Patrick, C.-J., Peach, D., Pocknee, C., Webb, F., Fletcher, M., & Pretto, G. (2008). *The WIL [Work Integrated Learning] report: A national scoping study [Australian Learning and Teaching Council (ALTC) final report].* Brisbane: Queensland University of Technology. Retrieved from www.altc.edu.au. www.acen.edu.au

Pegg, J., Reading, C., & Williams, M. (2007). *Partnerships in ICT learning study: Full report.* Canberra: Department of Science, Education & Training. Retrieved from http://www.deewr. gov.au/schooling/DigitalEducationRevolution/Documents/pictl_full_report1.pdf

Reid, J.-A. (2011). A practice turn for teacher education? *Asia-Pacific Journal of Teacher Education, 39*(4), 293–310.

Reid, J.-A. (2014). 'Practice': Foregrounding the study of teaching in initial teacher education. In M. Jones & J. Ryan (Eds.), *Successful teacher education: Partnerships, reflective practice and the place of technology* (pp. 121–135). Rotterdam: Sense Publishers.

Roxå, T., Mårtensson, K., & Alveteg, M. (2011). Understanding and influencing teaching and learning cultures at university: A network approach. *Higher Education, 62*(1), 99–111.

Russell, T., & Martin, A. (2017). Reflective practice: Epistemological perspectives on learning from experience in teacher education. In R. Brandenburg, K. Glasswell, M. Jones, & J. Ryan (Eds.), *Reflective theory in teacher education practice* (pp. 27–47). Singapore: Springer.

Salmon, G. (2005). Flying not flapping: A strategic framework for e-learning and pedagogical innovation in higher education institutions. *ALT-J Research in Learning Technology, 13*(3), 201–218.

Saribas, D. (2015). Investigating the relationship between pre-service teachers' scientific literacy, environmental literacy and life-long learning tendency. *Science Education International, 26*(1), 80–100.

Schneckenberg, D. (2009). Understanding the real barriers to technology-enhanced innovation in higher education. *Educational Research, 51*(4), 411–424.

Schön, D. A. (1983). *The reflective practitioner: How professionals think in action.* New York: Basic Books.

Shulman, L. (1987). Knowledge and teaching: Foundation of the new reform. *Harvard Educational Review, 57*, 1–22.

Smit, K., de Brabander, C., & Martens, R. (2014). Student-centred and teacher-centred learning environment in pre-vocational secondary education: Psychological needs, and motivation. *Scandinavian Journal of Educational Research, 58*(6), 695–712.

Swennen, A., Lunenberg, M., & Korthagen, F. (2008). Preach what you teach! Teacher educators and congruent teaching. *Teachers and Teaching: Theory and Practice, 14*(5–6), 531–542.

Teacher Education Ministerial Advisory Group (TEMAG). (2014). *Action now: Classroom ready teachers.* Retrieved from http://www.studentsfirst.gov.au/teacher-education-ministerial-advisory-group

Ure, C., Gough, A., Newton, R. (2009). *Practicum partnerships: Exploring models of practicum organisation in teacher education for a standards-based profession.* Australian Learning and Teaching Council. Retrieved from http://www.olt.gov.au/project-practicum-partnerships-exploring-melbourne-2007

Vygotsky, L. S. (1978). *Mind in society. The development of higher psychological processes.* Cambridge, MA: Harvard University Press.

Wenger, E. (1998). *Communities of practice: Learning, meaning and identity.* New York: Cambridge University Press.

Wenger, E. (2011). *Communities of practice: A brief introduction.* Retrieved from http://hdl.handle.net/1794/11736

Wood, E., & Geddis, A. (1999). Self-conscious narrative and teacher education: Representing practice in professional course work. *Teaching and Teacher Education, 15*, 107–119.

Zeichner, K. (2002). Beyond traditional structures of student teaching. *Teacher Education Quarterly, 29*(2), 59–64.

Zeichner, K. (2010). Rethinking the connections between campus courses and field experiences in college-and university-based teacher education. *Journal of Teacher Education, 61*(1–2), 89–99.

Zeichner, Z., & Liston, D. (2014). *Reflective teaching: An introduction* (2nd ed.). New York: Routledge.

Zeichner, K., Payne, K., & Brayko, K. (2015). Democratizing teacher education. *Journal of Teacher Education, 66*(2), 122–135.

Part II
Applications of Personalising Learning in Teacher Education

Chapter 8
Tell Tales: Using Community Partnerships

Community-based after-school learning clubs are the focus of this chapter and Chap. 9. This chapter describes how community-based after-school learning clubs can provide innovative, authentic contexts for pre-service teacher literacy education. The tenets of Learner as Central and Communities of Collaboration are discussed in relation to the designing, planning and implementing of the *Tell Tales* storytelling programme for early years' literacy learning in after-school learning clubs. The authentic learning context provided through after-school learning clubs is examined in relation to assessment for learning of pre-service teachers' and children's learning, and issues pertaining to the sustainability of this personalising learning approach in teacher education are discussed.

8.1 Introduction

The community-based after-school learning clubs discussed in this chapter are programmes run in schools during after-school hours by pre-service teachers enrolled in a teacher education course at a local university. These after-school clubs, termed *Tell Tales*, are run in partnership with the university, a local community service agency and local schools. This chapter describes the *Tell Tales* community-based after-school learning club that runs for children in Foundation (first year of formal schooling in Australia) to Year Two at participating schools. It refers to experiences and outcomes associated with participation in *Tell Tales* that relate to Learner as Central and Communities of Collaboration as tenets of personalising learning (Keamy et al. 2007).

Tell Tales is implemented in regional Victoria, Australia. It is embedded in an elective unit delivered through the university's undergraduate Bachelor of Education programme and uses storytelling as the vehicle for young children's literacy learning. What makes *Tell Tales* and *Digi-Tell* (the second of two complementary community-based after-school learning clubs) different to other programmes

© Springer Nature Singapore Pte Ltd. 2018
M. Jones, K. McLean, *Personalising Learning in Teacher Education*,
https://doi.org/10.1007/978-981-10-7930-6_8

embedded in university teacher education courses is a strong emphasis on providing authentic learning contexts for pre-service teachers' development of pedagogical practices for effective literacy teaching. These programmes also offer a rich school-based (work integrated – Patrick et al. 2008) learning experience that occurs outside of the more traditional practicum. This is achieved using the platform for pre-service teacher learning enabled through the after-school context. Using this platform, pre-service teachers deliver an early literacy programme to children from the school without common restrictions associated with the practicum experience such as the expectation to pick up or follow on from a predetermined point in the school's curriculum or to mirror the pedagogical approaches of supervising teachers (McLean 2017). In Australia, recommendations from the Teacher Education Ministerial Advisory Group (TEMAG) for enhancing graduate teacher capabilities include the integration of theory and practice to enhance pre-service teacher capabilities (TEMAG 2014). This recommendation is addressed through the delivery of a key aim of the *Tell Tales* programme in particular, which is to provide pre-service teachers with an authentic learning context for developing effective pedagogy for the teaching of literacy to children in the first 3 years of formal schooling.

This chapter seeks to consider some of the insights from embedding *Tell Tales* in the elective unit. In discussing these insights in relation to the tenets of Learner as Central and Communities of Collaboration, it seeks to highlight the potential of personalising approaches in teacher education in contributing to enhancing the capabilities of graduate teachers to teach in a variety of diverse educational contexts (TEMAG 2014). This chapter draws on findings from research which aimed to identify outcomes of participation in community-based after-school learning clubs for pre-service teachers, children and schools (McLean 2017) to illustrate these tenets in action. Issues in terms of sustainability and wider uptake of the approach used in the delivery of *Tell Tales* are outlined, and the chapter concludes with consideration of the future of *Tell Tales* as an approach to personalising learning in teacher education against the backdrop of current teacher quality agendas in this country.

8.2   The *Tell Tales* Programme

Tell Tales is informed by a sociocultural theoretical perspective. Vygotsky (1978) described development as a transformative process that involves higher mental functions occurring first on a social and second on an individual level. Vygotsky's theory recognises the underlying importance of social interactions in the development of all higher-order functions and situates the process of learning in, but not restricted to, social practice (John-Steiner and Mahn 1996). Vygotsky (1978) theorised that it is through cooperative interactions with others that learners develop independence. In the beginning, an individual's learning is guided by more experienced others which extends to a gradual release of responsibility to the learner for their own learning (John-Steiner and Mahn 1996). Sociocultural theory is enacted in *Tell Tales* through a co-teaching model that involves pre-service teachers working collegially, individually and in collaboration with the supervising university lecturer to plan, implement and evaluate a storytelling literacy programme for children in the first 3 years of schooling. Similar co-teaching models, such as the model described by Murphy et al. (2013), are also underpinned by sociocultural theoretical perspectives. A key difference between the *Tell Tales* model and others is the after-school context which places responsibility for the delivery of the programme to children with the pre-service teachers. Although weekly attendance by participating children is encouraged by their participating schools, children's individual weekly attendance is largely driven by their engagement in the programmes offered by pre-service teachers. This provides a very *real* context for pre-service teachers' engagement with theory and practice and subsequent motivation for the application of new understandings to enhance pedagogical practice.

As *Tell Tales* is embedded within an elective unit, pre-service teachers are typically united by a common interest in young children's early literacy learning. In this unit, pre-service teachers are encouraged to learn through engaging in collaborative and shared practices (Wenger 2011). *Tell Tales* has an emphasis on learning as a process which is typical of student-centred programmes (Smit et al. 2014). This process-orientated emphasis guides pre-service teacher learning and the delivery of the programme in the after-school context.

Pre-service teachers enrolled in the elective unit work together in small groups to plan, implement and evaluate a 5-week literacy programme for children in the first 3 years of schooling. Using a work integrated learning approach (Patrick et al. 2008), each pre-service teacher group is assigned a group of children from the participating school with whom they work for the duration of the programme. A typical *Tell Tales* programme developed by pre-service teachers involves three to four pre-service teachers working with a group of five to seven children from the participating school. This arrangement provides opportunity for the rehearsal of routines and development of core practices attending to both the "conceptual and practical aspects" (Grossman et al. 2009, p. 278) of practice described by Grossman et al. (2009). The *Tell Tales* programme runs for approximately 2 h each week. Pre-service teachers are supported by the university lecturer throughout the process of planning, implementing and evaluation. Congruent teaching practices including *modelling* and *reflection breaks* are integrated into the programme (Swennen et al. 2008). For example, following the implementation of each session in schools, pre-service teachers are guided by the university lecturer to reflect as a group on the implementation of the programme with a view to enhancing delivery and informing individual pedagogical development. In a further example, *linking modelling and theory* (Swennen et al. 2008) is embedded in the workshop sessions to enable explicit connections to be made between literacy theory and the use of storytelling in the classroom. For the purpose of this chapter, *Tell Tales* refers to pre-service teacher participation in the elective unit and pre-service teacher small group storytelling programmes delivered as a community-based after-school learning club, situated in schools.

Figure 8.1 provides an overview of the *Tell Tales* programme as it is embedded in the elective unit. In the weeks leading up to the delivery of the programme,

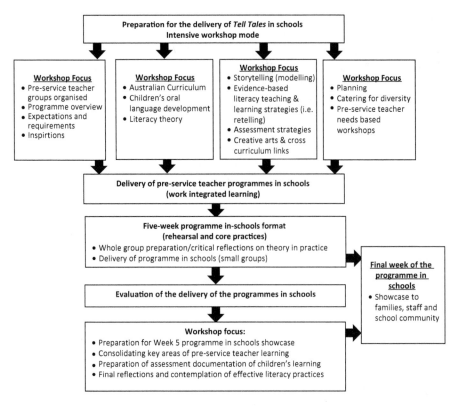

Fig. 8.1 An overview of *Tell Tales* embedded in the elective unit

pre-service teachers engage in workshops aimed at providing important skills, organisational and pedagogical content knowledge for the delivery of the programme in schools. This is achieved through explicit modelling (Loughran 2006) so that pre-service teachers have concrete examples of effective storytelling practice. During implementation, the workshop mode changes to a whole group contemplation and/or reflection session at the university, followed by the delivery of the programme as an after-school learning club in schools. At the end of each session of the programme's delivery in schools, the pre-service teachers engage in whole group and small group round-table (Brandenburg 2008) reflective practices aimed at encouraging problem solving and shaping of their ongoing pedagogical practices. In the final phase of the unit, the workshop mode is revisited to enable pre-service teachers to consolidate key areas of their learning, prepare assessment documentation for the individual children in their programmes, evaluate their programmes and prepare to return to the school for a showcase presentation with the children to families, school staff and the broader school community.

The showcase presentation provides a unique opportunity for pre-service teachers to demonstrate leadership in presenting the showcase to the school community. It also represents the application of sociocultural theory in practice in the pre-service teacher *Tell Tales* programmes where a gradual release of responsibility for story-telling is passed on to the children as part of the delivery of the programme in schools. What began in the first week of the delivery of *Tell Tales* in schools with pre-service teachers' storytelling to the children culminates in the final week of the programme with the children telling the stories they have been learning about in *Tell Tales* to their families and the school community. The workshops in the final part of the unit delivery have a distinct emphasis on pre-service teacher consolidation of learning and contemplation of future practice. The reflective tools and processes used throughout the unit, including round-table reflections (Brandenburg 2008) and critical incident documentation (Kosnik 2001), are orientated towards identifying tacit knowledge and making this knowledge explicit through the examination of praxis (Loughran 2012). As such, a number of pedagogies encouraged for teacher education (work integrated learning, explicit modelling, reflective practice) are evident in the unit.

8.3   Tenets of Personalising Learning in *Tell Tales*

The experience of working with pre-service teachers throughout the elective unit and in the planning and preparation, implementation, assessment and evaluation of *Tell Tales* foregrounds two tenets of personalising learning. The characteristics of the two tenets, (1) Learner as Central and (2) Communities of Collaboration, that are realised in *Tell Tales* are summarised below. These tenets not only provide insight into a personalising learning approach for pre-service teacher education but also how these tenets may be embedded in the future pedagogical practices of these teachers when they graduate and enter the profession.

8.3.1   Learner as Central

As discussed in Chap. 5, Keamy et al. (2007) present an overview of Learner as Central as requiring:

- a highly-structured approach that places the needs, interests and learning styles of students at the centre
- engaged learners who are informed and empowered through student voice and choice
- assessment that is related to meaningful tasks and includes assessment for and from students
- a focus on improving student outcomes for all and a commitment to reducing the achievement gap. (Keamy et al. 2007, p. 2)

An overview of the ways in which these key components of placing the learner at the centre of the learning process were embedded in the *Tell Tales* programme is provided below. This overview includes descriptions of how to support pre-service teachers as learners and how to support the development of pedagogical practices for their future teaching.

Pre-service Teachers as Learners *Tell Tales* employs a *highly structured process*, but within this structured process, pre-service teachers are supported to engage at an individual point of *need* (e.g. knowledge of curriculum), *interest* (e.g. puppetry, art) and *learning style* (e.g. using group and individual reflective tools and processes). This process further involves pre-service teachers in *making decisions* about the *choice* of English content from the Australian Curriculum that will form the basis of their group programme and through taking *responsibility* for how this content will be embedded in the planning, implementation, assessment and evaluation of the storytelling programme. Throughout the unit, university assessment tasks are *meaningful* to the pre-service teachers because these assessment tasks are directly related to the planning of an engaging and effective small group programme, assessment of participating children's learning and evaluation of the programme's implementation as an after-school learning club. An emphasis on the learning *outcomes for all* is fostered through a collegial and co-teaching model where the success of the programme in schools is a cumulative result of the co-teaching effort in an *authentic* teaching and learning context.

Pre-service Teacher Pedagogical Practices The *highly structured Tell Tales process* enables pre-service teachers to explore pedagogical practices aimed at engaging the individual *needs*, *interests* and *learning styles* of the participating children. This includes practices and strategies aimed at (a) finding out what children know about the language, literature and literacy content (e.g. plot, character and setting) through formal and informal assessments, (b) identifying children's interests (e.g. arts, popular culture, hobbies) to make learning connections to these in the programme and (c) catering for different learning needs and styles through presenting new information in a variety of ways (e.g. visual, hands-on, written, oral). Pre-service teachers are supported to explore pedagogical practices that provide children with choice (e.g. choice of props for retellings of the story) and voice (e.g. contributing ideas and sharing feelings). Pre-service teachers actively engage in strength-based assessment of children's learning through ongoing, cumulative and collaborative practices that are *meaningful* to children and their families. The final storytelling presentations to families and the school community provide an *authentic* context for *outcomes for all* to be communicated and celebrated with families and the school community.

8.3.2 Communities of Collaboration

In achieving the tenet of Communities of Collaboration, Keamy et al. (2007) suggest that the setting has characteristics that:

- promote a 'community of learning' approach and cultivate strong relationships between adults and students
- develop and promote the notion of networks rather than existing in isolation
- have strong links with the home, community, local institutions, business and services. (Keamy et al. 2007, p. 3)

The *Tell Tales* programme embedded these characteristics such that pre-service teachers' learning experience and their future teaching practices were shaped as described below.

Pre-service Teachers as Learners Communities of Collaboration are enacted in *Tell Tales* through fostering positive *relationships*. Pre-service teachers are supported to work collaboratively and collegially with peers, university staff and schools to plan, implement and evaluate a storytelling programme. This is achieved through the use of a co-teaching model aimed at fostering supportive learning *networks* for sharing ideas, providing constructive feedback and contemplating future practice. The community partnership model provides pre-service teachers with the opportunity to develop strong *links* between their learning at the university and the teaching profession through connections with schools and families. Moreover, the programme, whilst embedded in pre-service teachers' university course work, is also organised through a local community service agency which provides educational support for children and schools that face some form of social disadvantage. This connection provides pre-service teachers with further *links* to a broader community service.

Pre-service Teacher Pedagogical Practices Pre-service teachers engage in pedagogical practices that strengthen *links* between schools and families. This is achieved through sharing children's learning in the programme in formal [e.g. learning stories documentation (Carr and Lee 2012)] and informal (e.g. weekly conversations with families following *Tell Tales* sessions) ways. Throughout the programme in schools, pre-service teachers are encouraged to explore practices aimed at building *relationships* to support children's learning. These include the use of *networked* strategies for encouraging children to work together in ways that value the unique contributions of classmates and foreground the strengths of contributions to group outcomes (e.g. storytelling presentation). *Links* with the community service agency also increase pre-service teachers' awareness of community services that they could call on depending on the future settings in which they find themselves.

The following section refers to research reported elsewhere (McLean 2017) which considered preparedness of undergraduate teachers involved in community-based after-school learning clubs *Tell Tales* and *Digi-Tell*, to teach literacy in primary schools as graduate teachers. Data from semi-structured interviews (Kvale and Brinkman 2009) with pre-service teachers, school staff and graduate teachers undertaken following completion of the *Tell Tales* elective unit is referred to here to illustrate the tenets of Learner as Central and Communities of Collaboration in this elective unit.

8.4   Pre-service Teacher Learners as Central in *Tell Tales*

As noted earlier, Keamy et al. (2007) describe the tenet of Learner as Central as having the four main characteristics of (1) an enabling structure for attending to students' needs, interests and learning styles; (2) engaged and empowered learners; (3) meaningful assessment; and (4) a focus on learning outcomes for *all* learners. Key elements of personalising learning that have been captured in this tenet in theorisations internationally include the relationship between interests, needs and abilities and motivation (Bransford et al. 2000) and assessment for learning (Black et al. 2003). These four characteristics are each discussed in turn, in relation to pre-service teachers' experiences as learners in *Tell Tales*.

8.4.1   *Enabling Structure for Pre-service Teacher Learning*

Tell Tales has an overarching structured process that utilises reflective practice cycles (Fig. 8.2) for deconstructing and reconstructing pre-service teacher practice (Loughran 2012). These cycles aim to support pre-service teachers to develop in-depth understandings of praxis. Similar approaches are promoted by the Victorian government for effective professional learning for teachers in schools (DETV 2005). In *Tell Tales* the cycles began with pre-service teachers planning a unit of work using the Australian Curriculum (ACARA 2017) and a story of their choosing from a prescribed storytelling text (Winer 2005). During the planning phase, pre-service teachers worked in small groups to plan their programmes with a focus on constructive alignment between planned learning outcomes, teaching and learning strategies and assessment (Biggs 2003). This process involved the embedding of evidence-based assessment and evaluation strategies such as the use of checklists, questioning frameworks and documentation of children's work into each weekly session. During the implementation of *Tell Tales* in schools, these weekly assessments and evaluations were used to guide pre-service teacher reflections and inform planning for the following week. This was followed by a reflective process including documented revisions to planning which were made in response to evidenced children's learning needs, interests and outcomes from each session.

Interviews with pre-service teachers highlighted ways that this structured process enabled pre-service teacher needs, interests and learning styles to be met in the programme as a characteristic of Learner as Central. The process of planning, implementing, reflecting and evaluating meant that pre-service teachers were constantly reflecting on and contemplating their own practices as the basis for building effective practices:

> Planning, and changing plans and actually doing it. It's very authentic and especially because you had to report on it as well, so it went with the full cycle, like it went from planning to implementing to assessment so it was a full cycle. (Pre-service teacher E)

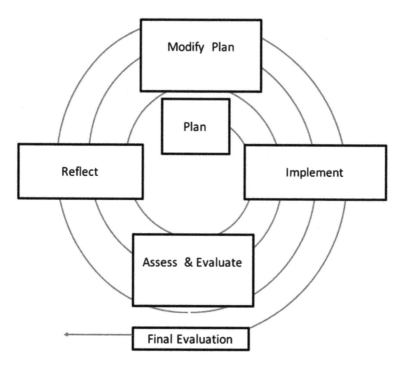

Fig. 8.2   The *Tell Tales* cyclic process

This cyclic process was described in terms of enabling the exploration of creative and innovative ways to deliver the content of the Australian Curriculum English:

> It was enjoyable working with the curriculum and creating [with] it and … presenting it in a way that was creative for those children and interactive for those children. … [and using] strategies for extending, moving forward, where to go next. So just [providing] an understanding of the curriculum so I knew where to jump to next if the children flew through it – and how to back track if it was necessary. (Pre-service teacher H)

In terms of personalising learning, this process was valued by pre-service teachers because exploring and reflecting on their own pedagogy contributed to enhanced individual understanding of the Australian Curriculum through "a better understanding of it and having the knowledge of different ways to present literacy [content]" (Pre-service teacher H).

The opportunity to go through the cyclic process in the small group structure had further benefits for pre-service teachers which extended into other learning contexts:

> I think when you have the smaller group [of children] it's easier to work around with what you are doing, because you're not having to manage [behaviour management] …you're not putting the effort into managing a big group when you could be working on your own approaches. Whereas if you had a bigger group [whole class] you'd be spending a lot more time getting children engaged and behaving, rather than working on things you want to do.

But when you have a smaller group it's easier to manage and engage them ... and you have more time to work on your approaches. (Pre-service teacher R)

After working with a small group ... I'm actually hoping on this placement [practicum] to deliver more focused and individual approaches...It's nothing to have their [children's] ideas and interpretations and modify what you would have done [planning] to suit the group [learning needs] better. ...having the choice and opportunity to do different things, I will be able to transfer that more easily now that we've applied it in smaller groups in *Tell Tales*. (Pre-service teacher Q)

In these examples, the small group context supported personalising learning by scaffolding (Wood et al. 1976) the pre-service teacher experience to support the construction of knowledge needed for application to the whole class context of practicum.

8.4.2   *Engaged and Empowered Pre-service Teacher Learners*

Pre-service teachers described a sense of empowerment to explore theory in their own developing practice from a point of relevance to their learning. For example, pre-service teachers described themselves as engaged learners through learning about themselves as teachers and exploring creative and innovative approaches to using storytelling in the teaching of English in the early years:

A lot of the time you don't take risks in your placement classroom because you're worried that if it flops, it's going to reflect badly on you. ...you've got a role model in your associate teacher, and subconsciously you tailor your teaching to how you've seen them teach ... and it's really hard to stray from that. Whereas in *Tell Tales*, you took your own teaching skills and you took who you wanted to be as a teacher and you didn't have to worry about anyone thinking that you weren't good. (Pre-service teacher H)

We were in classes, we were in tutorials, we were in lectures and we're learning ... and we were starting to have placements but they were minimal and you didn't get a lot of – not control, but the freedom in what you did, and to be able to go into schools and do something that you had created and you had come up with [*Tell Tales*] ... It's good practice. (Pre-service teacher L)

Comments such as these tended to place value on the opportunity for individual learning needs to be met through the freedom to explore content and theory in pre-service teachers' own practice. It seemed to be particularly empowering when the construction of knowledge within praxis involved pre-service teachers bringing their own creative interests to the programme:

... doing this programme [*Tell Tales*] it really does open your eyes to just how much you can do [in the classroom] ... it was quite empowering to see I can actually use that creativity in the lessons ... because before this I probably thought, 'Oh no, I can't do that'. (Pre-service teacher K)

For pre-service teachers, the opportunity to be creative in the design of their *Tell Tales* programme tended to be valued for enabling individual needs, interests and learning styles to be reflected in their learning.

8.4.3 Meaningful Assessment for Pre-service Teachers

Meaningful assessment as a characteristic of the tenet of Learner as Central was noted through pre-service teachers' use of the reflective processes and tools used to evaluate the delivery of *Tell Tales* in schools:

> I think because we're constantly assessing ourselves too … you're reflecting on something [but] you don't necessarily assess yourself, whereas in this [*Tell Tales*] because you knew that you had to be engaging every week or the children wouldn't come back you were assessing yourself to make sure you were better every week. (Pre-service teacher A)

Comments such as this one draw attention to connections between the assessment task for pre-service teacher learning of documentation for the programme and children's participation in the programme in schools. In this way, the process of assessment itself supported learning (Schwartz et al. 2009) by pre-service teachers participating in *Tell Tales*. The personalising learning tenet of Learner as Central was recognised in meaningful assessment where responsibility for the outcomes of the programme was attributed to both individual and social processes for planning, implementation, evaluation and reflection.

8.4.4 Learning Outcomes for All Pre-service Teacher Learners

Pre-service teachers indicated that their experiences in *Tell Tales* supported learning outcomes for all members of the *Tell Tales* pre-service teacher group. As a characteristic of the tenet of Learner as Central, this was represented in pre-service teacher comments that highlighted individual and group learning:

> I think competence with literacy [teaching and learning] too, like we did the planning, we linked it to the curriculum, we saw the outcomes, we implemented it [programme] … I think it's all there [learning] to be able to do something like this in the future as well. I think we would all feel confident to do so. (Pre-service teacher B)

> I feel like Pete [pseudonym] and I worked really well together in the fact that he listened to what I had to say and I listened to what he had to say, and then we talked about and combined our ideas to make a better activity. (Pre-service teacher J)

Comments such as these show a willingness of pre-service teachers to work together to improve their own learning, the learning of other group members and the delivery of the programme. In the words of one pre-service teacher, working together ensured outcomes for all because pre-service teachers "were focussed on the same things … driven to do the same amount … and striving to get to the same place" (Pre-service teacher R).

8.5   Learners as Central in *Tell Tales*: **Pedagogical Practices**

For Learner as Central as a tenet of personalising learning in this teacher education unit to be fully realised, it would seem that there is a need for it to be evident not only in pre-service teacher learning but also in the pre-service teacher pedagogical practices. This appears to be essential if pre-service teachers are to embrace personalising learning approaches as teachers in their own classrooms. The characteristics of (1) an enabling structure for attending to students' needs, interests and learning styles; (2) engaged and empowered learners; (3) meaningful assessment; and (4) a focus on learning outcomes for *all* learners are considered in relation to pre-service teacher experiences of their own pedagogical practices in *Tell Tales* which may serve to inform personalising learning practices in their future classrooms.

8.5.1   Enabling Structure for the Development of Effective Pedagogical Practices

Pre-service teachers described the application of a personalising approach through the tenet of Learner as Central in their teaching. This was noted in relation to providing an enabling structure for children to learn. It included presenting information to children in different ways and the employment of flexible approaches to better cater for children's learning needs, styles and interests:

> … probably the biggest thing would be making sure that I approach it [teaching] in multiple ways for multiple children so I'm not just going in with one focus on how things need to be done … there's multiple ways to achieve that outcome. (Pre-service teacher H)

> I realised how flexible I actually could be with my teaching, with how quickly I could just come up with a different idea or change something slightly to suit the children, to what we had in our original plan. I was really surprised by that. (Pre-service teacher A)

> Look at the children's experience, rather than just delivering them this exact plan of how we wanted it to be, it came out better in the end because we changed it. We looked at what the children actually liked doing and then we worked with that. (Pre-service teacher E)

Comments such as these from pre-service teachers were reflective of their attention to an enabling structure for utilising a repertoire of strategies to meet the individual learning needs of the children participating in their group programme. These comments also indicated a degree of recognition by pre-service teachers of the complex relationship between children's engagement in learning and the learning environment (Land et al. 2012). In terms of an enabling structure for pedagogical practice, this included the identification of children's funds of knowledge (Moll et al. 1992) and utilising these in the delivery of the programme.

8.5.2 *Engaging and Empowering Pedagogical Practices*

Pre-service teachers' engagement in empowering pedagogical practices to support children's learning was recognised in the storytelling and creative arts focus in the programmes. This seemed to present possibilities for engaging children in learning that extended beyond worksheets:

> A lot of what we planned was very similar to what you would generally do when you were focussing on narrative and exploring narrative. But it was a tiny step …to modifying it [planning] so it became more engaging. So, we had stepping stones, we were going to do beaded bracelets of all the different events that took place. We did the character biscuits, we had them dancing and moving and acting like the monkey. They acted out, 'If this happened what would happen, if this happened [pause]' and they just acted … it's a lot more beneficial … it gave them [children] the opportunity to demonstrate their knowledge in a totally different way. (Pre-service teacher R)

> I never thought I could spend a whole unit on the one story; it's one story, you're telling it to the children every week, you think they'd get tired of it but they don't. You can do so much with one story and take so much out of it and it's not writing pen on paper it's actually getting them [children] to be the characters or getting them to really draw out the main ideas in the story through manipulating play dough. It is amazing, that was one of the biggest things, how much you could do with one story and how engaged the students could be. (Pre-service teacher M)

> It was the storytelling aspect, I thought that was effective and engaging for the children and having the props for the children to see while you're telling them the story. It's more engaging, and you develop more of a relationship with the children. (Pre-service teacher Q)

The opportunity to explore the delivery of English content from the Australian Curriculum in less traditional ways than pre-service teachers were generally familiar with seemed to support the development of effective practices. These included connecting to children's lifeworlds (Yelland et al. 2008) because making "connections with the real world outside of what was happening at school was … engaging" (Pre-service teacher H) for the children.

8.5.3 *Meaningful Assessment for the Development of Pedagogical Practices*

The exploration of a range of pedagogical approaches for teaching literacy through storytelling also provoked the need for the use of assessment strategies to gather evidence of children's literacy learning. Pre-service teachers identified ongoing assessment as an important aspect of their pedagogical practice for ensuring that children were engaged learners:

> The learning story [assessment tool] helped me say, 'John [pseudonym] can do this, this and this,' and not say, 'He can't do this, this and this.' And I feel like that will be a better practice for me going forward, to focus on the positive not the negatives. (Pre-service teacher A)

> I'd really like to include the strengths based assessment … it's really effective. Every student has something [strength], there's always something nice to say about students … there's always a strength. (Pre-service teacher F)

> We looked back at our [curriculum] content descriptors, We had them [Australian Curriculum English content descriptors] at the bottom of our notes [individual learning logs]… so we could look back at them [in team meetings] and say, "When they made this statement, they were talking about the characters." So it supported the content descriptor we had [identified]. We tried to bring it [discussion] back to our notes every week … so we didn't get to the end [of the program] and think, "I don't know whether they've achieved it [learning outcome] or not." (Pre-service teacher E)

In their reflections, pre-service teachers described connecting planning and assessment and using observational and strength-based approaches to assess children's literacy learning as important aspects of their developing pedagogy. This awareness by pre-service teachers of meaningful and authentic assessment in *Tell Tales* was further recognised as having relevance or deeper learning beyond the programme (Maeten et al. 2010). This was noted in descriptions which tended to highlight an awareness of the child Learner as Central in their work as teachers where curriculum content, activities and assessment are aligned and meaningfully connected.

8.5.4 Pedagogical Practices to Support Learning Outcomes for All

An enabling structure to support the exploration of a range of pedagogical practices for the delivery and assessment of content from the Australian Curriculum English seemed to also provide a context for the achievement of learning outcomes for all children who participated in the group programme. One pre-service teacher summarised this in the following way:

> You know you need to have activities to match curriculum and … encourage outcomes, but having like a filing cabinet of them [activities] in your brain to know which ones to pull out and when to pull them out, this [*Tell Tales*] has really helped me to do that. Like to know what links with what, and what I can bring out and what's a five-minute activity that will enhance literacy and what's a 20 or 30-minute activity, but with excellent outcomes at the end that all the children can reach and then move forward from. So, sensory fishing, we had everyone using descriptive language, but then let's take it one step further, let's write that, let's draw pictures of that and then keep building on it … making connections with the curriculum – like moving forward in the curriculum, [thinking] how can I expand on that? (Pre-service teacher H)

Comments such as this one were indicative of pre-service teachers being deeply committed to ensuring that all children experienced success in their literacy learning through personalising approaches that situate the child Learner as Central. In a further example, a pre-service teacher described how all children in their *Tell Tales* group demonstrated achievement of one of the learning outcomes (i.e. to sequence the events in the story) for their programme through drawing, speaking and writing:

> When we did the story map … they [children] drew four pictures from the story and … sequenced it – start, middle, end. You'd say, "Tell me the story using your story map" and they would say it and then the next step would be to write it down and then they created a piece of writing that started with them drawing. (Pre-service teacher S)

In a further example, effective practice was described in the repetition of key concepts from the story to ensure that all children were provided with a strong model to engage in new learning:

> Ours [programme] used the words that were in the story from the outset so we [children and pre-service teachers] just talked about the story and talked and talked and talked and they understood the alliteration – that there was a ruby red rose … they were trying to remember the words that went with each item that started with the same letter. And they heard it again and again and again and I think just the reinforcement of hearing the same thing [repeated story] really helped them. (Pre-service teacher M)

Pre-service teachers described a focus in their practice on ensuring all children in the group were able to demonstrate learning, which required attention to each child learner as a central focus of the programme.

8.6   Communities of Collaboration in *Tell Tales*: Pre-service Teachers

The personalising learning tenet of Communities of Collaboration was realised in the *Tell Tales* elective unit through co-teaching as a vehicle for pre-service teacher learning. The co-teaching arrangement sought to provide collaborative and collegial relationships between pre-service teachers, university staff, school staff, families and children. Pre-service teacher co-teaching groups were encouraged to work within and across peer co-teaching group networks to share ideas and learning together:

> We listened to the other groups and they gave us ideas just by what they were discussing … we could try something similar, and we just helped each other. (Pre-service teacher B)

Working together in this way further supported the establishment of links between theory and practice through connections with the teaching profession. This was realised through school staff interactions with pre-service teachers during the delivery of *Tell Tales* and through shared responsibility for the delivery of a successful programme:

> What it's [*Tell Tales*] really brought up for me is the fact that teaching is not an isolated thing. On our placements [practicum] … we go home and we plan whatever it is they've

[teacher] told us to do, we bring it back we show them in the morning, they say, 'Yep good run with it' and it feels like a very individual thing. And this [*Tell Tales*] brought to light the fact that if there are other graduates, if you've got a really good mentor, even if you just build a relationship with one of the other teachers … you can really benefit from each other. We've got different strengths, we've got different ideas, discussing those, exploring them, helps improve us all. (Pre-service teacher V)

This shared responsibility seemed to contribute to the development of learning networks (Bray and McClaskey 2013; Keamy et al. 2007) among pre-service teachers as opposed to a sense of learning in isolation. Although demonstration of individual pre-service teacher learning was an essential component of participation in the unit, pre-service teachers described an interdependence between individual learning and group learning. This interdependence was realised through sustained interactions between peers to support one another (Lee and Smagorinsky 2000), which necessitated a high level of professional conduct for the overall success of the after-school programme for the school community. The individual learning of pre-service teachers seemed to be driven by collaborative social processes, which, in turn, set rise to individual critical reflection and contemplation:

I think it makes you reflect on your own teaching, watching somebody else … you might see something that they do and think, 'I like the way that they do that, maybe I can try and incorporate that'. Or then there might be another way where you see them do something and you think, 'I don't think I would do that'. (Pre-service teacher J)

It makes you look at your own practice as well, and then if you see … your co-teacher was, lacking in something [needing assistance], you might be able to support them and say, 'Well how about you try this' – and give them some support that way too. (Pre-service teacher I)

As a tenet of personalising learning, Communities of Collaboration enacted in the *Tell Tales* unit ensured individual and social processes were entwined to support pre-service teacher learning.

8.7   Communities of Collaboration in *Tell Tales*: Pedagogical Practices

Pre-service teachers described practices for realising personalising learning aligned to the tenet of Communities of Collaboration that were not typically experienced during practicum. These included building positive relationships, establishing links with families and the use of networked strategies.

Although building positive relationships with children is embedded in practicum experience, these relationships are usually developed through the classroom teacher. In contrast, in *Tell Tales* pre-service teachers worked together in the co-teaching group to identify children's funds of knowledge (Moll et al. 1992), including interests and learning needs, as a basis for establishing relationships to support children's learning. This seemed to be significant because it provided pre-service teachers with the direct experience of building relationships from a *grass-roots* level for personalising learning. One pre-service teacher described these relationships as mutually beneficial:

> I had a really good relationship with all of my children and it made a difference for me and it made a difference for them … because they felt comfortable in speaking up and sharing and all those sorts of things. (Pre-service teacher H)

Tell Tales further provided opportunities for pre-service teachers to establish communication links with families. Children's talk at home about *Tell Tales* often prompted parents, carers and extended family members to arrive early to collect children and find out more about the programme. For example:

> Kramer's [pseudonym] mum and dad came in all the time … Marsha's [pseudonym] parents came in once. Martin's [pseudonym] mum came in. And they would just constantly ask questions about what they [children] were doing … (Pre-service teacher H)

Pre-service teachers indicated that knowing parents, carers and teachers were likely to ask questions and show interest in the programme contributed to pedagogy for effective communication with families as part of the extended learning community:

> If you're on placement [practicum] the teacher always deals with parents because they know them. For us, we were in charge of their children and they would talk to us … which helped us. (Pre-service teacher K)

These opportunities to interact with families were also seen as having reciprocal benefits because pre-service teachers gained experience in establishing these links and families benefited from learning more about children's participation in *Tell Tales*:

> It was good to be able to tell the parents what we were doing and they were so much more involved in what their children were doing because we were telling them what they were achieving in *Tell Tales*. (Pre-service teacher H)

In this sense *Tell Tales* offered pre-service teachers the opportunity to experience the tenet of Communities of Collaboration in their role as teachers through interacting and sharing children's learning with families in informal (i.e. at the end of each session) and formal (i.e. *Tell Tales* presentation to the school community) contexts.

8.8 The Future of *Tell Tales*

The delivery of *Tell Tales* as an after-school storytelling club foregrounds two tenets of personalising learning in teacher education. These are (1) Learner as Central and (2) Communities of Collaboration. The extent to which these tenets are embraced in the practice of graduates following participation in *Tell Tales* is yet to be determined. However, from the pre-service teacher experience described here, it would seem that there is potential to explore these tenets further through other similar modes of delivery. *Tell Tales* provided a model for pre-service teacher learning that also enabled pre-service teachers to experience these tenets through the rehearsal and enactment (Grossman et al. 2009) of literacy-centred practice. This demonstrates the power of using a congruent teaching pedagogy (Swennen et al. 2008) that is followed by pre-service teachers' own opportunity to trial the approach being taught. Such a combination of practice would seem to be important for the sustainability of *Tell Tales* moving forward. Aslan and Reigeluth (2016) identify the need for a change in children's or students' mindset about education towards inquiry and responsibility as a key challenge for schools pursuing learner-centred approaches. It may be that *Tell Tales* provides a way to prepare pre-service teachers to be *classroom ready* to attend to this challenge through direct experience of learner-centred pedagogies in their own learning (i.e. their experience of modelling). The sustainability of programmes such as *Tell Tales* requires a willingness of universities, schools and communities to work together. This may be one of the biggest challenges for embracing the tenets of Learner as Central and Communities of Collaboration in teacher education units in the future as it requires a commitment to ensuring that pre-service teachers experience personalising tenets in their own learning. This is not easy to achieve against the prevailing backdrop of prescription and regulation in teacher education, but it is possible. What *Tell Tales* does provide is an example of how the tenets of Learner as Central and Communities of Collaboration can be leveraged as a part of teacher education pedagogy that supports other established practice such as work integrated learning (Patrick et al. 2008) and congruent teaching (Swennen et al.) in pre-service teacher learning and practice. It shows what is possible working within the traditional boundaries of teacher education programmes whilst gently stretching the creative potential of pre-service teachers to embrace these tenets in praxis.

References

Aslan, S., & Reigeluth, C. M. (2016). Examining the challenges of learner-centred education. *Kappan, 97*(4), 63–68.

Australian Curriculum Assessment Reporting Authority [ACARA]. (2017). *Australian curriculum*. Retrieved from http://www.australiancurriculum.edu.au/

Biggs, J. (2003). *Teaching for quality learning at university* (2nd ed.). Maidenhead: Open University Press.

Black, P., Harrison, C., Lee, C., Marshall, B., & William, D. (2003). *Assessment for learning: Putting it into practice*. Berkshire: Open University Press.

Brandenburg, R. (2008). *Powerful pedagogy: Self-study of a teacher educator's practice*. Berlin: Springer.

Bransford, J., Brown, A., & Cocking, R. (Eds.). (2000). *How people learn: Brain, mind experience and school*. Washington, DC: National Academy Press.

Bray, B., & McClaskey, K. (2013). A step-by-step guide to personalize learning. *Learning & Leading with Technology, 40*(7), 12.

Carr, M., & Lee, W. (2012). *Learning stories: Constructing learner identities in early education*. London: Sage.

Department of Education and Training Victoria [DETV]. (2005). *Professional learning in effective schools*. Melbourne: DET.

Grossman, P., Hammerness, K., & McDonald, M. (2009). Redefining teaching, re-imagining teacher education. *Teachers and Teaching, 15*(2), 273–289.

John-Steiner, V., & Mahn, H. (1996). Sociocultural approaches to learning and development: A Vygotskian framework. *Educational Psychologist, 31*(3/4), 191–206.

Keamy, K., Nicholas, H., Mahar, S., & Herrrick, C. (2007). *Personalising education: From research to policy and practice.* Melbourne: Department of Education and Early Childhood Development.

Kosnik, C. (2001). The effects of an inquiry oriented teacher education program on a faculty member: Some critical incidents and my journey. *Reflective Practice: International and Multidisciplinary Perspectives, 2*(1), 65–80. https://doi.org/10.1080/14623940120035532.

Kvale, S., & Brinkman, S. (2009). *InterViews: Learning the craft of qualitative research interviewing* (2nd ed.). Thousand Oaks: Sage.

Land, S., Hannafin, M., & Oliver, K. (2012). Student-centered learning environments: Foundations, assumptions and design. In D. Jonassen & S. Land (Eds.), *Theoretical foundations of learning environments* (2nd ed., pp. 3–25). New York: Routledge.

Lee, C., & Smagorinsky, P. (2000). *Vygotskian perspectives on literacy research: Constructing meaning through collaborative inquiry (Learning in doing).* Cambridge: Cambridge University Press.

Loughran, J. (2006). *Developing a pedagogy of teacher education: Understanding teaching and learning about teaching.* Abingdon: Routledge.

Loughran, J. (2007). Researching teacher education practices: Responding to the challenges, demands and expectations of self study. *Journal of Teacher Education, 58*(1), 12–20.

Loughran, J. (2012). *What expert teachers do: Enhancing professional knowledge for classroom practice.* Florence: Taylor and Francis.

Maeten, M., Kyndt, E., Struyven, K., & Dochy, F. (2010). Using student-centered learning environments to stimulate deep approaches to learning: Factors encouraging or discouraging their effectiveness. *Educational Research Review, 5*(3), 243–260.

McLean, K. (2017). Using reflective practice to foster confidence and competence to teach literacy in primary schools. In R. Brandenburg, K. Glasswell, M. Jones, & J. Ryan (Eds.), *Reflective theory and practice in teacher education* (pp. 119–139). Singapore: Springer.

Moll, L. C., Amanti, C., Neff, D., & Gonzalez, N. (1992). Funds of knowledge for teaching: Using a qualitative approach to connect homes and classrooms. *Theory Into Practice, 31*(2), 132–141.

Murphy, C., Bianchi, L., McCullagh, J., & Kerr, K. (2013). Scaling up higher order thinking skills and personal capabilities in primary science: Theory-into-policy-into-practice. *Thinking Skills and Creativity, 10*, 173–188.

Patrick, C.-j., Peach, D., Pocknee, C., Webb, F., Fletcher, M., & Pretto, G. (2008). *The WIL [Work Integrated Learning] report: A national scoping study [Australian Learning and Teaching Council (ALTC) final report].* Brisbane: Queensland University of Technology. Retrieved from www.altc.edu.au and www.acen.edu.au

Schwartz, D., Lindgren, R., & Lewis, S. (2009). Constructivism in an age of non-constructivist assessments. In S. Tobias & T. Duffy (Eds.), *Constructivist instruction: Success or failure?* (pp. 34–61). New York: Routledge.

Smit, K., de Brabander, C., & Martens, R. (2014). Student-centred and teacher-centred learning environment in pre-vocational secondary education: Psychological needs, and motivation. *Scandinavian Journal of Educational Research, 58*(6), 695–712.

Swennen, A., Lunenberg, M., & Korthagen, F. (2008). Preach what you teach! Teacher educators and congruent teaching. *Teachers and Teaching: Theory and Practice, 14*(5–6), 531–542.

Teacher Education Ministerial Advisory Group [TEMAG]. (2014). *Action now: Classroom ready teachers.* Retrieved from http://www.studentsfirst.gov.au/teacher-education-ministerial-advisory-group

Vygotsky, L. S. (1978). *Mind in society: The development of higher psychological processes.* Cambridge, MA: Harvard University Press.

Wenger, E. (2011). *Communities of practice: A brief introduction.* Retrieved from http://hdl.handle.net/1794/11736

Winer, Y. (2005). *Stories for telling.* Castle Hill: Pademelon Press.

Wood, D., Bruner, J., & Ross, G. (1976). The role of tutoring in problem solving. *Journal of Child Psychology and Psychiatry, 17,* 89–100.

Yelland, N., Lee, L., O'Rourke, M., & Harrison, C. (2008). *Rethinking learning in early childhood education.* Maidenhead: McGraw-Hill Education.

Chapter 9
Digi-Tell: Using Technology for Authentic Learning

This chapter builds on the discussion around the tenets of Learner as Central and Communities of Collaboration for pre-service teacher literacy education through community-based after-school learning clubs. This chapter introduces the tenet of information and communication technology (ICT) for learning to the authentic learning context provided through community-based after-school learning clubs. The discussion in this chapter will explore how the tenets of personalising learning are realised in the teacher education context through the delivery of *Digi-Tell*, a digital storytelling programme for children in the middle and upper years of primary education. In a core unit in their course, pre-service teachers plan, implement and evaluate a literacy programme designed to use ICT in authentic ways as part of an explicit literacy teaching focus. These descriptions provide insight into authentic contexts for effective literacy teaching and learning essential for personalising learning in teacher education.

9.1 Introduction

Digi-Tell is a community-based after-school literacy learning club for children in years three to six in primary [elementary] school. Like *Tell Tales* described in the previous chapter, *Digi-Tell* is enabled through a long-standing partnership between the university, local schools and a community service agency operating in the regional community. It is delivered by pre-service teachers enrolled in a core literacy education unit at a regional campus of the university. *Digi-Tell* uses a similar reflective practice (Loughran 2007, 2012) and co-teaching model (Murphy et al. 2013) to that described for *Tell Tales* in Chap. 8 and hence has the personalising learning tenets (Keamy et al. 2007) of Learner as Central and Communities of Collaboration embedded in the programme. The school-based component also addresses established teacher education pedagogy of work integrated learning (Patrick et al. 2008) and preparatory university-based congruent teaching (Swennen

© Springer Nature Singapore Pte Ltd. 2018
M. Jones, K. McLean, *Personalising Learning in Teacher Education*,
https://doi.org/10.1007/978-981-10-7930-6_9

et al. 2008) to model effective achievement of a *Digi-Tell* approach to literacy learning. In addition, *Digi-Tell* further employs the personalising learning tenet of information and communication technology (ICT) as an enabler of learning. In this chapter, these tenets are discussed in relation to the delivery of *Digi-Tell* with an emphasis on ICT as a key driver for pre-service teacher learning and pedagogical practices. These tenets are explored through descriptions of *Dig-Tell* in action and pre-service teacher reflections on participation in the core literacy education unit for the delivery of *Digi-Tell* as an after-school learning club in schools. In discussing the contribution of *Digi-Tell* to understanding the potential for personalising learning to be realised in teacher education, consideration is given to the applicability of key elements of the programme to other contexts. It is the intention of this chapter not necessarily to provide a model for replication, but rather to act as a catalyst for further thinking to drive innovative personalising learning practice for pre-service teacher learning in teacher education courses.

9.2   The *Digi-Tell* Programme

Extending on the model used in the sister programme of *Tell Tales*, in *Digi-Tell* pre-service teachers deliver a 5-week after-school literacy programme to middle and upper primary school children from participating schools. Pre-service teachers work in groups of three to five to deliver the programme to a group of five to seven children. The focus of *Digi-Tell* is on the teaching of written text types (i.e. narrative, recount, persuasive, discussion, procedure, response, explanation, description) using an inquiry-based model for children's learning. A template for group planning is used that is based on an inquiry model designed for literacy programmes (Wilhelm 2007). Throughout the delivery of the core literacy education unit, pre-service teachers engage with literacy theory to design, implement and evaluate their own group *Digi-Tell* programme, which aims to teach the language features, structure and conventions of a chosen written text type to participating children. The programme culminates in the production of a digital text for each participating child that has been jointly constructed by the group of children with the support of pre-service teachers. To enable this to occur, specific design elements and features of digital texts (e.g. video, images, audio, hyperlinks, headings) are modelled through an integrated, multiliteracies approach (The New London Group 2000) to the delivery of the unit and to the programme in schools.

Figure 9.1 provides an overview of the *Digi-Tell* programme as a dual student- and teacher-centred approach (Elen et al. 2007) embedded in the core literacy education unit at the university. Prior to the commencement of *Digi-Tell*, the lecture mode is used to introduce key literacy theoretical concepts and content required for the successful implementation of *Digi-Tell* in schools. In the tutorial mode, the content and concepts from the lecture are unpacked further through tutorial activities that provide explicit modelling (Loughran 2006) of skills relevant to the *Digi-Tell* programme. Tutorial activities also involve pre-service teachers in applying the

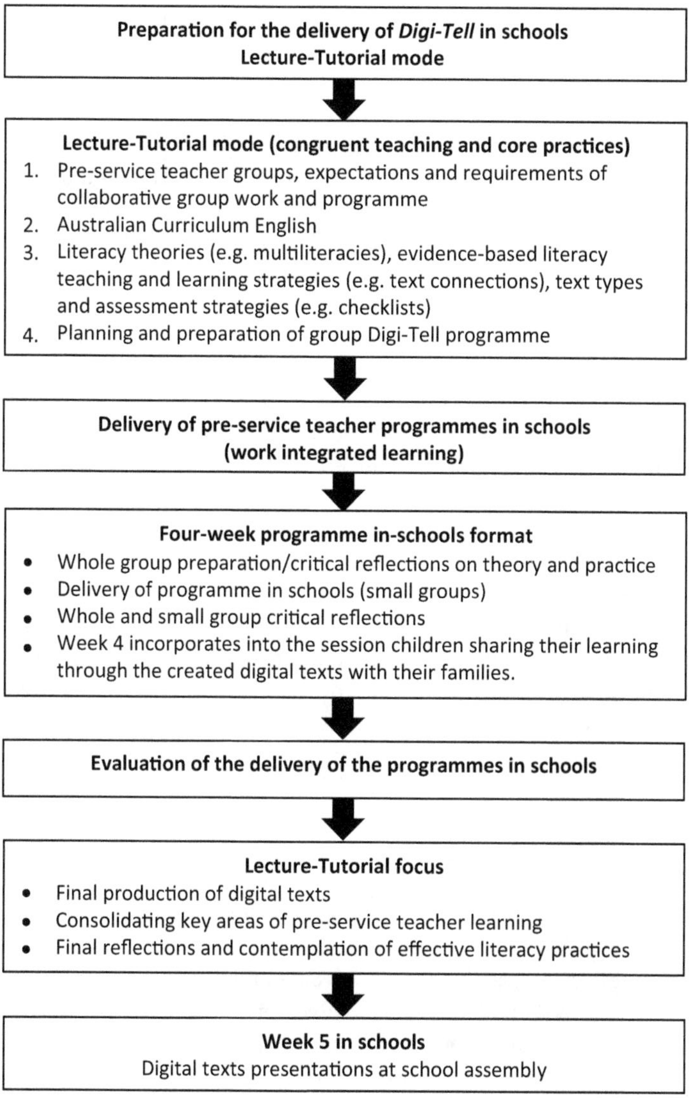

Fig. 9.1 An overview of *Digi-Tell* embedded in the core literacy education unit

theoretical content of the lecture to the planning of group *Digi-Tell* programmes. For example, tutorial activities may include the examination of culturally responsive pedagogy (Seely Flint et al. 2014) to identify child-centred assessment practices for getting to know children's learning interests, styles and needs. Following this tutorial activity, pre-service teachers would be expected to incorporate relevant aspects of culturally responsive pedagogy to cater for diversity through the tenet of Learner as Central in their small group *Digi-Tell* programmes. Tutorial activities such as this are aimed at ensuring that each pre-service teacher group develops in-depth knowledge of the Australian Curriculum English, text type, digital texts and teaching, learning and assessment strategies necessary for the successful delivery and outcomes associated with the *Digi-Tell* programme as an after-school learning club in schools.

Tutorial activities have an additional focus on the preparation of pre-service teachers to work collaboratively and collegially in groups and on the production of a digital text prepared by each pre-service teacher group for use as a model with children participating in the programme. This focus enables attention to both "conceptual and practical aspects" (Grossman et al. 2009, p. 278) of literacy educator practices. For example, a typical tutorial activity may involve pre-service teachers working in their small group to develop a narrative digital text. This process begins with each pre-service teacher completing a team working skills inventory and sharing this inventory with group members prior to delegating tasks for the preparation of the narrative digital text such as writing a script, organising and creating props and managing software. This process aimed to support pre-service teachers to form an identity as a collective group (Fuller 2007), which was critical for their collaboration as a community of practitioners (Lave and Wenger 1991). Practising skills of group organisation and collaboration like these aligns with the embedding of core practices (Grossman et al. 2009), where studying ways of organising effective group work is a high-frequency practice for teachers. The collaborative aspect of this activity addresses Communities of Collaboration as a central tenet and also the tenet of Learners as Central through enabling pre-service teachers to identify and work predominantly within their areas of expertise. The lecture and tutorial mode prior to the commencement of *Digi-Tell* focuses on the four forms of guidance to scaffold learning identified by Land et al. (2012). These are conceptual guidance (e.g. written text types), metacognitive guidance (e.g. planning, assessment and evaluation), procedural guidance (e.g. procedures and protocols for working with children in an after-school learning club in schools) and strategic guidance (e.g. engaging children, managing behaviour using positive behaviour strategies).

During the implementation of *Digi-Tell* in schools, the delivery mode of the unit switches to a reflective practice model for examining practice as both teacher and learner (Loughran 2012). This mode involves pre-service teacher groups using a template for reflecting on theory in practice back at the university in small group and whole group contexts (Brandenburg 2008).

9.3   Conceptual Framework

Edwards (2012) describes a *transfer problem* (p. 586) in teacher education that situates teacher educators as vessels for the transference of theoretical knowledge for uptake by pre-service teachers in practice. This problem is characterised in teacher educators' practice by what Edwards (2012) describes as "the disconnection between the theory and their [teacher educator] practice" (p. 586). Edwards (2012) reports on her own efforts as a teacher educator to address this problem using the sociocultural concept of learning activity to understand teaching of theory/practice in teacher education as embodied within "pedagogical and assessment practices" (p. 587). Edwards' (2012) work challenges teacher educators to seek out authentic learning opportunities for pre-service teacher learning which enable theory and practice to be experienced "as an integrated concept" (p. 587). *Digi-Tell* arises from similar efforts in teacher education to provide authentic learning experiences for pre-service teachers. The provision of authentic learning experiences in *Digi-Tell* aims to support the development of effective praxis to ensure teacher education graduates are not only "classroom ready" (TEMAG, p. xiii) but also engaged in processes for future learning (Wise and O'Neill 2009). Praxis, as it is used in this chapter, refers to theory as embodied in practice through pre-service teacher participation in *Digi-Tell*.

In this chapter, the sociocultural concept of learning activity is used to understand the personalising learning tenets of Learner as Central, Communities of Collaboration and ICT (Keamy et al. 2007) embedded in the delivery of *Digi-Tell* as part of the core literacy education unit. Learning activity has been used previously to examine pre-service teacher learning in online environments in teacher education (Edwards 2012). Understanding how these personalising learning tenets are experienced in pre-service teacher learning and enacted in pre-service teacher practice through participation in *Digi-Tell*, may serve to inform how personalising learning may be more fully embedded in teacher education programmes to support the preparation of teacher education graduates for teaching in contemporary classrooms.

Vygotsky (1978) refers to learning activity as one of five types of leading or *bridging* activity that an individual progresses through to achieve full cognitive development. Learning activity as a bridging activity is important because mastery of learning activity brings about self-change in the learner (Repkin 2003). Vygotsky (1978) describes the social situation of development that an individual is in as giving rise to a new psychological function for development. Through a sociocultural theoretical lens, *Digi-Tell* creates a social situation of development for "collective theorising" about praxis. For example, pre-service teachers collectively theorise when they talk about, share experiences of and enact theory in practice together. Mastery of learning activity in the social situation of development for collective theorising occurs when the learner can verbalise or communicate his/her learning activity (Kravtsova 2006). Mastery of learning activity creates a new social situation of development for theory of practice which gives rise to the psychological function of reflection. Reflection supports "learning with intent" (Edwards 2012, p. 593), which generates self-growth in the learner. This is realised in *Digi-Tell* when pre-service teachers act as agents of their activity (Repkin 2003) and can relate the content (i.e. theory and practice) of their learning to their own development.

Learning activity as a bridging activity is described as having three dimensions relevant to the tenets of personalising learning in teacher education, including the learning task, the learning actions and the structural components. These dimensions are outlined below in relation to *Digi-Tell*.

9.3.1   The Learning Task

The learning task dimension focuses on theoretical knowledge or *what* the learner is learning as an agent of their learning activity. In the authentic learning context provided by *Digi-Tell*, this theoretical knowledge includes theory about children's literacy learning and development and pedagogical approaches for effective literacy teaching and learning in the primary [elementary] school. This involves, but is not restricted to, the three tenets of personalising learning (Learner as Central, Communities of Collaboration and ICT) in the context of literacy education. For example, in *Digi-Tell* theoretical knowledge of ICT as an enabler of literacy learning would include multiliteracies (The New London Group 2000) theory and theory-driven content about the integration of ICT and literacy to create multimodal projects (Seely Flint et al. 2014).

9.3.2   The Learning Actions

The learning actions dimension involves physical and conceptual tools that enable the learner to engage with relevant theoretical knowledge. Learning actions refer to *how* the learner is learning. In *Digi-Tell* these learning actions are facilitated through explicit modelling (Loughran 2006) in tutorials and followed by pre-service teacher planning, implementation and evaluation of the *Digi-Tell* programme. These learning actions also include physical tools such as textbooks (e.g. Seely Flint et al. 2014; Wing Jan 2009) and websites (e.g. Australian Curriculum – ACARA 2017) and the use of reflective tools such as a question framework to guide small group reflections following the delivery of each *Digi-Tell* session in schools.

9.3.3   The Structural Components

The structural components dimension refers to the design elements that enable the learner to engage in learning activity. Mastery of the structural components for supporting the learning tasks and learning actions represents mastery of learning activity. In the core literacy education unit described in this chapter, *Digi-Tell*, as the key structural component, supports mastery of learning task and learning actions by pre-service teachers. Mastery of learning activity as a leading or bridging activity is described by Kravtsova (2006) as occurring when the learner "is capable of verbalising it" (p. 14). In *Digi-Tell* this would include pre-service teachers communicating understanding of content covered in the unit in their practice through the delivery of the *Digi-Tell* programme.

In this chapter learning activity is used to consider *Digi-Tell* as an authentic pre-service teacher learning context for personalising learning in teacher education. The

associated research referred to stems from a broader study that examined preparedness of pre-service teachers to teach literacy in primary schools (McLean 2017).
Ethics approval was granted as part of the broader study, and all data reported in this
chapter is used with permission.

9.4   *Digi-Tell* and the Tenets of Personalising Learning

To understand how personalising learning tenets are experienced by pre-service
teachers through participation in *Digi-Tell*, it is important to consider how these
tenets are embedded in pre-service teacher learning activity associated with this
core unit. Table 9.1 uses the example of written *text types* as a core content area in
the literacy education unit and uses *Digi-Tell* to show how the tenets of Learner as
Central, Communities of Collaboration and ICT are embedded in the learning task,
learning actions and structural components. This is followed by an expanded
description of the tenet of ICT as an enabler of learning in *Digi-Tell*. Davydov et al.
(2003) describe learning activity as the place where "reflection emerges and develops" (p. 71). As mastery of learning activity leads to self-change or growth in the
learner through reflexive development (Repkin 2003), the chapter concludes with
consideration of pre-service teachers' reflections on their experiences in *Digi-Tell* in
relation to the tenets of personalising learning.

9.5   ICT As an Enabler of Learning in *Digi-Tell*

The personalising learning tenet of ICT as an enabler of learning is considered in
relation to pre-service teacher participation in *Digi-Tell*. Repkin (2003) notes that
the goal of learning activity is "change within oneself as the agent of the activity"
(p. 15). This change or development occurs through interactions with others (i.e.
other peers and/or experts) as joint activity. This is similar to Lave and Wenger's
(1991) description of a community of practitioners where individuals learn as part
of a community of peers and is considered here in relation to Communities of
Collaboration. Through participation in *Digi-Tell*, pre-service teachers work collaboratively to plan, implement and evaluate a digital storytelling literacy programme. Following the university lecturer's use of purposeful modelling (Loughran
et al. 2016) for making explicit connections between theory and practice, pre-service
teachers' interpretations of praxis are enacted in a co-teaching model of delivery
with a small group of children. ICT as an enabler of learning embedded in the learning activity of pre-service teachers serves as an important driver for the development of "reflexive control" (Repkin 2003, p. 27) of problem situations in pre-service
teachers' future literacy education praxis.

   ICT as an enabler of pre-service teacher learning is recognised in the presentation of theoretical material required for the successful implementation by pre-service

Table 9.1 Examples of personalising learning tenets embedded in the learning task, learning actions and structural components using written text types as the core content area

Dimension	Learner as central	Communities of collaboration	ICT
Learning task *What* pre-service teachers are learning about written text types	Pre-service teachers use textbooks, lecture, tutorial and online educational resources to access descriptions of the purpose, language features and structure of selected written text types and determine the text type that will be the focus of their small group *Digi-Tell* programme	Pre-service teachers access sociocultural theory relating to effective literacy learning environments for learning language, learning about language and learning through language (Halliday 2004) to teach written text types	Pre-service teachers access the online learning management system (LMS) for recorded lectures, presentation notes and shared resources about written text types. Pre-service teachers also access online resources such as YouTube videos and software applications for the teaching of text types such as *Kids Write Text Types*™
Learning actions	Pre-service teachers experience purposeful modelling (Loughran et al. 2016) by university lecturer of teaching written text types	Pre-service teachers experience "coaching and immediate feedback" (Grossman et al. 2009, p. 285) on practice by university lecturer during programme delivery	Pre-service teachers experience the thinking aloud approach (Swennen et al. 2008) to demonstrate intentions for use of ICT template
How pre-service teachers are learning about written text types	Pre-service teachers access descriptions of the purpose, language features and structure of text types to create a checklist for their chosen text type. This checklist is used by pre-service teachers to determine children's prior knowledge of the text type through oral, written, visual and/or performance modes of communication	Pre-service teachers apply sociocultural theory relating to learning language, learning about language and learning through language (Halliday 2004) to the planning and implementation of their group *Digi-Tell* programme for their chosen text type and to the joint construction of a digital text for use in the programme	Pre-service teachers use a software programme (e.g. iMovie™, Moviemaker) to create a digital text for use in their group *Digi-Tell* programme as a model "for point of need teaching as well as planned teaching focuses" (Wing Jan 2009, p. 41)

(continued)

Table 9.1 (continued)

Dimension	Learner as central	Communities of collaboration	ICT
Structural components Design elements for learner engagement	Pre-service teachers access theoretical materials and draw on their participation in *Digi-Tell* to work through a critical incident relating to the teaching of the text type from their group *Digi-Tell* programme. Pre-service teachers combine theory and practice to interpret the critical incident using a problem analysis framework (Brandenburg 2008)	Pre-service teacher groups use the problem analysis framework (Brandenburg 2008) template to present their critical incident to the tutorial group. Pre-service teachers in the tutorial group, as a wider learning network, respond to each presentation using an established literacy teaching strategy of text connections (Keene and Zimmerman 1997)	Pre-service teachers use a digital template to create a digital, multimodal presentation of a critical incident relating to the teaching of the text type from their group *Digi-Tell* programme. This presentation is shared in the wider learning network of the tutorial group and combines theory and collective participation in *Digi-Tell* to generate understanding of the incident

teachers of the *Digi-Tell* programme in schools. This material was available as online content in the LMS and included presentation notes, recorded lectures and links to educational websites and resources. Mobility associated with this online content provided pre-service teachers with broad access to theoretical materials to support their learning as required. Importantly, ICT contributed to meeting diversity of pre-service teacher learning needs (Keamy et al. 2007) through access to theoretical material outside of the university and during the implementation of *Digi-Tell* in schools. This was enabled through the use of internet-enabled mobile devices such as iPads and mobile laptop and desktop computers. The mobility of ICT used in this way meant that theoretical material for teaching written text types was accessible during the planning, implementation and evaluation processes and at the point of need (Hmelo-Silver et al. 2007) to support the learning task.

During the preparation stage and prior to the implementation of *Digi-Tell* in schools, pre-service teachers used ICT to create digital, multimodal texts. As a learning action, this involved pre-service teachers using a software programme of their choice that was also available in schools, to create a model exemplar of the text type for use with the children during explicit teaching foci in the delivery of *Digi-Tell*. This learning action provided a context for pre-service teacher engagement with multiliteracies theory and content knowledge of the Australian Curriculum, digital texts and written text type conventions in the creation of a digital text for use with children. In the creation of this digital text, pre-service teachers' needs, interests and learning styles were recognised through the collaborative process, including groups having choice and control of the elements that contributed to the final digital text. The element of choice, as noted by Deci and Ryan (1985), makes an important contribution to intrinsic motivation. In the creation of digital texts, these options for pre-service teachers included choice of text type (e.g. persuasive, narrative, information), media (e.g. photographic images, video), creative content (e.g. puppets, play dough, painted scenes, costumes) and programmes (e.g. iMovie™, Moviemaker). The element of choice in *Digi-Tell* enabled pre-service teachers to ensure that the digital texts they created met pre-service teacher learning foci and the delivery of the group programmes in schools.

ICT contributed to the structural components of pre-service teacher learning activity. Pre-service teachers accessed theoretical materials to create a digital text for use with children and then used these materials (theoretical and practical) to teach a small group of children about a selected written text type. The implementation of *Digi-Tell* involved the creation of digital texts with children that, in turn, enabled participating children to demonstrate and share their learning about the text type with their families and the wider school community. This provided an authentic context for pre-service teachers to examine their praxis. A digital template provided a problem analysis framework (Brandenburg 2008) for the examination of praxis. Group pre-service teachers' digital, multimodal presentations provided the catalyst for wider discussion in tutorials. These discussions utilised the collective expertise of all pre-service teachers through engagement with theoretical materials and participation in *Digi-Tell*, in joint problem solving to contribute to the learning of all. When used in this way, ICT enabled theoretical and practical connections and interactivity (Keamy et al. 2007) for enhancing learning within and across the pre-service teacher groups at university and in schools.

9.6 Pre-service Teacher Reflections on the *Digi-Tell* Experience

Edwards (2012) describes the "capacity for reflection" (p. 596) through a sociocultural theoretical lens as important in teacher education because it supports pre-service teachers to act with intention to learn. This can be realised through a change in the relationship between the learner and the object of this learning – theory and practice. Through a sociocultural theoretical lens, reflection is more than problem solving and shared communication as it involves an awareness in the learner "of self-change" (Davydov et al. 2003, p. 72). Recorded focus group interview (Kvale and Brinkman 2009) discussions with pre-service teachers following their participation in *Digi-Tell* highlight pre-service teachers' self-awareness of characteristics aligned with the tenets of personalising learning in praxis. These reflections, as they pertain to the relevant tenets of personalising learning, are described below.

9.6.1   *Communities of Collaboration*

Characteristics aligned to the tenet of Communities of Collaboration were portrayed by pre-service teachers in descriptions of collaborative problem solving, which led to improved knowledge and strengthened practice. This included pre-service teacher comments in relation to supporting each other in their co-teaching groups, as well as through accessing support from the wider tutorial group via observations, interactions and the use of reflective tools such as the problem analysis framework (Brandenburg 2008). A sample of pre-service teachers' comments reflecting these learnings include:

> Working with the other pre-service teachers in the group really helped my knowledge and understanding of actually becoming a professional and having to work alongside other teachers. (Pre-service teacher C)

> I think it's a better way of teaching…because you've got the back up, you've got different ideas, you've got the opportunity to share ideas, to learn from other people. (Pre-service teacher L)

> Just seeing what all the other groups were doing, and not just our own and saying, 'We've used this approach but look at how many other approaches there are to teach it.' Or, 'They're doing this and that's a brilliant idea,' … and seeing a range of ways the multiple different approaches that there are for teaching literacy and how every single one of them could be adapted to work for any text type. (Pre-service teacher T)

The support for pre-service teachers' learning enabled through the tenet of Communities of Collaboration was described in relation to finding a voice within the co-teaching group and in the school community. This was attributed to relationships that enabled pre-service teachers to be more aware of their own individual strengths and weaknesses and to work with the strengths of team members. For example:

> I'm more aware of my own strengths, so I'm able to offer them in a school setting. (Pre-service teacher A)

> It made me very aware of the way I am and the way I work with people, and realising that I sometimes need to stop and think about how others are approaching things … it had its challenges but being able to draw on the strengths of others. So one of us might be very creative … one might be really good with kids. To have all the elements together makes it work really well as a team. (Pre-service teacher O)

> We did procedural text, but being able to watch other groups do narratives or information [texts] gave me ideas as well about how I could implement those in my classroom, so I wasn't just focussed on procedural text. (Pre-service teacher C1)

> I learned that I really liked working with other people on ideas … Nan [pseudonym] was really good on the creative side, Lana [pseudonym] was really good from the practical side … and so you each have a perspective that the other person hasn't thought of." (Pre-service teacher K3)

So it's about finding your own voice, knowing what you know and still contributing to what's going on. Being able to go, "Yes, I agree, let's do this", or "I think this, do you?" – to be able to present your own ideas while accepting their [other group members] ideas and ... having confidence in your own opinion. (Pre-service teacher Q)

It was further described in terms of drawing on networks (including children's contributions) through bringing together collective knowledge and expertise as a means of improving individual knowledge and practice:

You could bounce creative ideas – just anything that came to mind and then get feedback on it [from co-teaching group], rather than just running with it yourself and not knowing where you are going, just ... have their feedback and work on it together, that was really helpful. (Pre-service teacher N)

You don't realise when you are doing the planning [in co-teaching group] how much of the content you are actually learning yourself ... we did procedural texts so you've got to know how it works and what's involved in it to be able to plan different lessons. (Pre-service teacher K4)

Before you go into the lesson [*Digi-Tell*] ... you need to look it [written text type] up and research them [written text types] yourself ... studying them [written text types] in different contexts. One [group] might be reading a sheet of paper [text type], others [groups] may be designing something ... The children were learning and I was learning as well. Sometimes the children can really amaze you ... you can't underestimate how much they know. And with us [co-teaching group] our content knowledge ... sometimes the children helped us with learning and I don't think we should be afraid of that either. (Pre-service teacher M)

Collective expertise also included the knowledge that parents/carers shared with pre-service teachers. The opportunity for pre-service teachers to develop links with families was not typically experienced as part of practicum and was uniquely linked to the work integrated learning (Patrick et al., 2008) of *Digi-Tell*. It provided pre-service teachers with an opportunity to develop further insights into the value of their programme for the children:

We watched the movie [*Digi-Tell*] with the parents and the parents were so thankful and just positive about the whole experience. Also throughout [the programme] when the parents picked the children up I just tried to slip in there and say hello and introduce myself and talk a bit about maybe what the children go home and do because I noticed from some of the children they actually went home and tried to cook what we were cooking that week or they [said they] spoke about it all the way home in the car. (Pre-service teacher R)

When you've got a child that you think might not be all that engaged and then their parent comes and says they talk about it all the time at home ... when the parent tells you that it's a really nice thing to hear. (Pre-service teacher R)

The parents come and give you reinforcement of how much they [children] loved it [*Digi-Tell* programme] the week before and they can't wait to see what happens next week. (Pre-service teacher H)

The tenet of Communities of Collaboration as experienced by pre-service teachers in *Digi-Tell* contributed to pre-service teacher development through building relationships and drawing on networks to support learning. This involved "working together in a professional manner" (Pre-service teacher J) and encompassed working with children, peers, other professionals and families in the rehearsal of routines (Grossman et al., 2009) for establishing effective relationships. The range of comments by pre-service teachers about collaborative and joint practices for learning were further indicative of effective Communities of Practice defined by common interests, collaborative relationships for learning and a repertoire of shared practices to support learning by all members of the community (Wenger 2011).

9.6.2   *Learners As Central*

Pre-service teachers described characteristics aligned with Learner as Central in the delivery of their group *Digi-Tell* programme in relation to strategies for promoting children's literacy learning. This tenet was also described in terms of having choices that enabled pre-service teacher learning needs and styles to be met. Within this tenet of Learner as Central, pre-service teacher comments highlight learner-orientated elements of their own and children's participation.

Digi-Tell provided the opportunity for pre-service teacher co-teaching groups to negotiate the written text type that would be the focus of their programme and the development of the planning for implementation. An inquiry planning template adapted from Wilhelm (2007) was used by each group. This template was intended to provide a clear structure for the delivery of literacy content using the Australian Curriculum, but also provided scope for pre-service teachers to engage creatively with the content through weekly frontloading and scaffolding activities. Frontloading activities (Wilhelm 2007) are designed to activate children's prior knowledge of the content, and scaffolding activities are designed to build or extend on this prior knowledge. Pre-service teachers were given scope within their planning to explore the delivery of content using frontloading and scaffolding activities:

> We got to choose a particular text type and ... the action of actually choosing which text type also involved having to go through how you would teach it ... putting things into practice, for me in particular, is always a better way to learn ... all of the theory we've learnt in literacy, putting it into practice ... was really, really helpful because you got to see it. ... (Pre-service teacher L)

> I could see what we had done and what I had done with the kids actually worked ... so that made me better able to see the directions you can go with literacy and how to make it accessible for kids as well, and more engaging for them. (Pre-service teacher L)

Pre-service teachers further noted that the structure provided a platform that could be used in other learning contexts – a base or "building block to move into other areas" (Pre-service teacher T). This was described in terms of providing a relatable experience (Pre-service teacher A2) that could easily be talked about and applied to other contexts:

> I went for an interview for a nanny position and I put this [*Digi-Tell*] on the resume and the mother was so interested, so I had to talk about it. It gave me a lot of confidence to talk about something that I'd done at University … and I got the job. (Pre-service teacher K4)

The authentic context for pre-service teacher learning in *Digi-Tell* also provided impetus to improve practice:

> The chance to re-evaluate what you are doing, as a teacher you need to be able to step back and rethink what you're going to do. (Pre-service teacher S)

> I liked how you planned your unit, you implemented your unit and then you analysed your unit and you did the learning log [analysed children's literacy learning]. That's something we need to do – we need to plan, implement and then analyse. (Pre-service teacher U)

When used in this way, critical reflection had a meaningful focus for pre-service teacher learning – to improve practice.

Pre-service teachers described characteristics aligned with tenet of Learners as Central in using "approximations of practice" (Grossman et al. 2009, p. 283) in the setting of the after-school learning club. This was noted in pre-service teacher use of assessment strategies to identify prior knowledge (Land et al. 2012) of the written text type and through providing opportunities for children to demonstrate learning in different ways. The delivery of literacy content using a variety of strategies was also considered important for catering for diversity and in empowering children as learners in the *Digi-Tell* programmes:

> I enjoyed that it was child orientated. … So they [children] were doing the filming, they came up with the script. … It made a really good film … because it was all their work. (Pre-service teacher C3)

> We did the storyboard and the graffiti wall, the students were putting all their own words on the board. Then we moved on to writing out the sequence for the movie. So that's where they [children] started putting in the illustrations and add more vocabulary words to actually building a sentence for what they wanted each scene to be about. (Pre-service teacher C3)

> … making the digital movie – by finding their interests and then incorporating that into the movie it provided them [children] with more ownership, they knew it was theirs and had an opportunity to say what they wanted to be included. (Pre-service teacher J2)

> In *Digi-Tell* the children own the text, they own what they were working with. So, I think for me it's taught me that there are different ways to do things and you can make it [learning] much more fun and so much more – I don't remember a lot of what I did in primary school, but I can guarantee that had I done something like that [*Digi-Tell*] … I'd remember a lot more because you've got the personal connections to it. (Pre-service teacher O)

For pre-service teacher learning, Learner as Central was an important tenet in their group programmes with the children because recognising high levels of motivation in the children contributed to motivation for self-growth among the pre-service teacher group:

> It was really positive to know that the children were coming because they wanted to come [to *Digi-Tell*] to the point where we extended the programme ourselves, we kept going back, because the kids really loved it and we loved it. (Pre-service teacher O)

In this reflection, the pre-service teacher describes intrinsic motivation (Deci and Ryan 1985) associated with learning with intent through extending the programme in response to the children's engagement.

9.7   ICT As an Enabler of Learning

Pre-service teachers described the integration of ICT and literacy in their programmes as important for their developing practice as teachers. The approach taken in *Digi-Tell* was one of inquiry for both pre-service teacher learning with ICT and children's engagement in the programmes.

> I've seen in the classroom traditional ways of teaching text types, but I really enjoyed being able to incorporate technology into it. (Pre-service teacher J2)

> *Digi-Tell* was really good for my development of ICT and digital media, because I didn't have a very strong background in that at all when I started the degree. … I learned a lot … about what there is out there and the types of digital technologies and applications … that you can use. And the idea of digital text had never occurred to me. I'd always thought of – when you had children [in the classroom] … you have to sit down with a pen and paper and write, and all of a sudden this whole new world opened up. … Text does not have to be pen on paper with a pen, it can be on a computer, it can be video, it can be filmed, it can be photo, it can be all sorts of things, because it's the same thing – you're still telling an audience something, you're just doing it in a different way, and that was huge. I remember thinking that was massive for me. (Pre-service teacher L)

The inquiry focus meant that pre-service teachers were encouraged to engage with integral practices (Grossman et al. 2009, p. 283) for the use of ICT in creative and flexible ways and to take a multiliteracies approach to the delivery of their programmes. The integration of ICT and literacy throughout *Digi-Tell* was largely achieved through a focus on written text types. ICT in an inquiry-based approach seemed to offer pre-service teachers the opportunity to use ICT to create in the literacy programme:

> Letting them [children] explore it [ICT]… letting them create … instead of just using it [ICT] … actually giving them [children] an iPad or giving them a laptop, showing them how to use Movie Maker or whatever the programme you're going to do, and let them create something. (Pre-service teacher L)

> I learnt a lot of things, but a key thing for me was using ICT as part of the lesson, so working with the kids to develop their own ICT [digital] text. That was a big thing for me, because I always tend to avoid technology. (Pre-service teacher S)

The opportunity to integrate ICT and literacy through the creation of digital texts with children seemed to encourage broader views by pre-service teachers of literacy as communication (Cope and Kalantzis 2000). This was particularly apparent in the group programmes where pre-service teachers recognised that literacy extended beyond print and paper-based texts:

> Today it's just as important to learn how to create different types of texts rather than just reading and writing, now it's more about ICT texts and being able to communicate to different audiences through that. (Pre-service teacher H)

> It [text type] doesn't have to be in their book either. It could be that they create a comic strip about the weekend instead of just – like you know, the different forms it [text type] could take. (Pre-service teacher K)

Learning opportunities with ICT in *Digi-Tell* were summarised in terms of engagement – for pre-service teachers and children. As a primary goal for many graduate teachers, the final pre-service teacher comment in this section of the chapter captures the essence of the tenet of ICT as an enabler of learning through engagement in learning:

> I will be using digital text types and creating digital texts in my classroom because it is almost the most engaging way you could possibly teach text types when you think about it … writing and reading is very important, being able to create something completely different [digital text] makes them [children] feel like they're not really doing the work, but they are actually learning a lot. (Pre-service teacher L)

9.8   Conclusion

Digi-Tell provided an authentic, work integrated learning context for the use of ICT by pre-service teachers to learn about literacy theory and practice as part of a core literacy education unit. The tenets of ICT, Learner as Central and Communities of Collaboration underpinned the approach taken in this unit for pre-service teacher learning and the delivery of *Digi-Tell* as an after-school learning club. The application of this model to other teacher education contexts is possible but would seem to be incumbent on these tenets existing in synergy with reflective processes for examining praxis. In this chapter, the concept of learning activity was used to consider tenets of personalising learning in relation to pre-service teacher experiences in *Digi-Tell*. Pre-service teachers' recognition that their individual actions and interactions with others through participation in *Digi-Tell* contributed to change or self-growth provides impetus for the further exploration of similar models in other teacher education contexts. The relevance of the approach taken in this unit for giving rise to reflection is summarised in the following pre-service teacher comment:

> Reflection was a big one because … We talk about reflection a lot and we go into our placement [practicum] and we do reflection and journal, but not having somebody there [in learning clubs] such as the actual teacher in the room the whole time we had no choice but to reflect on it [the session] and actually *really* reflect on it. Because you actually had to go back the next week and extend upon it [the learning]. (Pre-service teacher T)

In bringing to life the tenets of personalising learning explored in this chapter through *Digi-Tell*, it must be acknowledged that replicating the authentic learning context provided by *Digi-Tell* in other teacher education contexts is not without challenges. *Digi-Tell* provides a unique platform for bringing pre-service teachers, children and families together in schools to enhance learning for all. The *context* provided by *Digi-Tell* is a powerful intrinsic motivator (Deci and Ryan 1985) for pre-service teacher learning and at the same time it pushes the boundaries of traditional lecture and tutorial modes of delivery in teacher education. Although well supported through the three dimensions of learning activity (learning task, learning actions, structural components), the success of *Digi-Tell* ultimately rests on the commitment of all pre-service teachers to the programme. This is where the personalising learning tenets of Learners as Central, Communities of Collaboration and ICT are critical. Embedding these tenets in the programme would seem to contribute to the empowerment of pre-service teachers to act as agents of their learning (Repkin 2003) and self-growth:

> It's about adapting the new content knowledge you get to put it into practice, because the truth is, we're not supposed to know everything [as graduate teachers]. This is like our foundation, we're supposed to continue learning. … we are forever researching new content, new teaching styles so that we've got something [a foundation] that we can work with, then we continue to learn and adapt it and build on it and change our knowledge. (Pre-service teacher T)

Captured in this concluding comment is the essence of empowerment as experienced by pre-service teachers when these tenets come together in *Digi-Tell*. In this comment, the pre-service teacher embraces learning in *Digi-Tell* as a process and leaves the discussion open to further thinking about what needs to happen next through the tenet of Lifelong Learning in teacher education.

References

Australian Curriculum Assessment Reporting Authority [ACARA]. (2017). *Australian curriculum*. Retrieved from http://www.australiancurriculum.edu.au/

Brandenburg, R. (2008). *Powerful pedagogy: Self-study of a teacher educator's practice*. Berlin: Springer.

Cope, B., & Kalantzis, M. (Eds.). (2000). *Multiliteracies: Literacy learning and the design of social futures*. South Yarra: Macmillan.

Davydov, V. V., Slobodchikov, V. I., & Tsukerman, G. A. (2003). The elementary school student as an agent of learning activity. *Journal of Russian & East European Psychology, 41*(5), 63–76.

Deci, E., & Ryan, R. (1985). *Intrinsic motivation and self-determination in human behaviour*. New York: Plenum Press.

Edwards, S. (2012). Teaching through assessment: Reconsidering the transfer problem through a convergence of technology and assessment in early childhood teacher education. *Teachers and Teaching, 18*(5), 585–599. https://doi.org/10.1080/13540602.2012.709733.

Elen, J., Clarebout, G., Lèonard, R., & Lowyck, J. (2007). Student-centred and teacher-centred learning environments: What students think. *Teaching in Higher Education, 12*(1), 105–117.

Fuller, A. (2007). Critiquing theories of learning and communities of practice. In J. Hughes, N. Jewson, & L. Unwin (Eds.), *Communities of practice: Critical perspectives* (pp. 17–29). Oxon: Routledge.

Grossman, P., Hammerness, K., & McDonald, M. (2009). Redefining teaching, re-imagining teacher education. *Teachers and Teaching, 15*(2), 273–289.

Halliday, M. A. K. (2004). Three aspects of children's language development: Learning language, learning through language, learning about language. In M. A. K. Halliday & J. J. Webster (Eds.), *The language of early childhood* (pp. 308–326). New York: Continuum.

Hmelo-Silver, C., Duncan, R. G., & Chinn, C. (2007). Scaffolding and achievement in problem-based and inquiry learning: A response to Kirschner, Sweller, and Clark (2006). *Educational Psychologist, 42*(2), 99–107.

Keamy, K., Nicholas, H., Mahar, S., & Herrrick, C. (2007). *Personalising education: From research to policy and practice*. Melbourne: Department of Education and Early Childhood Development.

Keene, E. K., & Zimmerman, S. (1997). *Mosaic of thought: Teaching comprehension in a reading workshop*. Portsmouth: Heinemann.

Kravtsova, E. E. (2006). The concept of age-specific new psychological formations in contemporary developmental psychology. *Journal of Russian & East European Psychology, 44*(6), 6–18.

Kvale, S., & Brinkman, S. (2009). *InterViews: Learning the craft of qualitative research interviewing* (2nd ed.). Thousand Oaks: Sage.

Land, S., Hannafin, M., & Oliver, K. (2012). Student-centered learning environments: Foundations, assumptions and design. In D. Jonassen & S. Land (Eds.), *Theoretical foundations of learning environments* (2nd ed., pp. 3–25). New York: Routledge.

Lave, J., & Wenger, E. (1991). *Situated learning: Legitimate peripheral participation (learning in doing: Social, cognitive and computational perspectives)*. Cambridge: Cambridge University Press.

Loughran, J. (2006). *Developing a pedagogy of teacher education: Understanding teaching and learning about teaching*. Abingdon: Routledge.

Loughran, J. (2007). Researching teacher education practices: Responding to the challenges, demands and expectations of self-study. *Journal of Teacher Education, 58*(1), 12–20.

Loughran, J. (2012). *What expert teachers do: Enhancing professional knowledge for classroom practice*. Florence: Taylor and Francis.

Loughran, J., Keast, S., & Cooper, R. (2016). Pedagogical reasoning in teacher education. In J. Loughran & M. Hamilton (Eds.), *International handbook on teacher education* (Vol. 1, pp. 387–481). Singapore: Springer.

McLean, K. (2017). Using reflective practice to foster confidence and competence to teach literacy in primary schools. In R. Brandenburg, K. Glasswell, M. Jones, & J. Ryan (Eds.), *Reflective theory and practice in teacher education* (pp. 119–139). Singapore: Springer.

Murphy, C., Bianchi, L., McCullagh, J., & Kerr, K. (2013). Scaling up higher order thinking skills and personal capabilities in primary science: Theory-into-policy-into-practice. *Thinking Skills and Creativity, 10*, 173–188.

Patrick, C.-J., Peach, D., Pocknee, C., Webb, F., Fletcher, M., & Pretto, G. (2008). *The WIL [work integrated learning] report: A national scoping study, Australian Learning and Teaching Council (ALTC) final report*. Brisbane: Queensland University of Technology. Retrieved from www.altc.edu.au and www.acen.edu.au.

Repkin, V. V. (2003). Developmental teaching and learning activity. *Journal of Russian and East European Psychology, 41*(5), 10–33.

Seely Flint, A., Kitson, L., Lowe, K., & Shaw, K. (2014). *Literacy in Australia: Pedagogies for engagement*. Milton: Wiley.

Swennen, A., Lunenberg, M., & Korthagen, F. (2008). Preach what you teach! Teacher educators and congruent teaching. *Teachers and Teaching: Theory and Practice, 14*(5–6), 531–542.

Teacher Education Ministerial Advisory Group [TEMAG]. (2014). *Action now: Classroom ready teachers.* Retrieved from http://www.studentsfirst.gov.au/teacher-education-ministerial-advisory-group

The New London Group. (2000). A pedagogy of multiliteracies. In B. Cope & M. Kalantzis (Eds.), *Multiliteracies: Literacy learning and the design of social futures* (pp. 9–37). Melbourne: Macmillan.

Vygotsky, L. S. (1978). *Mind in society: The development of higher psychological processes.* Cambridge, MA: Harvard University Press.

Wenger, E. (2011). *Communities of practice: A brief introduction.* Retrieved from http://hdl.handle.net/1794/11736

Wilhelm, J. D. (2007). *Engaging readers and writers with inquiry: Promoting deep understandings in language arts and the content areas with guiding questions.* New York: Scholastic.

Wing Jan, L. (2009). *Write ways: Modelling writing forms* (4th ed.). Melbourne: Oxford University Press.

Wise, A., & O'Neill, K. (2009). Beyond more versus less: A reframing of the debate on instructional guidance. In S. Tobias & T. Duffy (Eds.), *Constructivist instruction: Success or failure?* (pp. 82–105). New York: Routledge.

Chapter 10
The Science Teaching in Schools Experience (*STISE*)

This chapter outlines the *Science Teaching in Schools Experience (STISE)*, a school-based approach to science teacher education that profiles, in particular, the application of a Communities of Collaboration and Learner as Central tenets of personalising learning. The context for this example of personalising learning is the teaching of a science education unit within a pre-service teaching Bachelor of Education course for both primary and early childhood and primary teacher candidates at a local university. In these courses, the science teaching self-efficacy levels of the teacher candidates commencing the unit are persistently low. Efforts to address this widespread concern led to an example of situated learning theory forming the basis for the redesign and delivery of the unit. The ways in which Learners as Central and Communities of Collaboration were established and maintained showcase a successful example of personalising learning within science teacher education that addresses traditionally low science teaching self-efficacy beliefs among pre-service teachers.

10.1   Introduction

The school-based approach to the *STISE* teacher education programme described in this chapter arose from the lecturer's concern as a relatively new academic, that the then current unit design was not holding enough relevance for, or making the sort of impact desired, on primary pre-service teachers' ability and confidence to teach science. Anecdotally, the lecturer, who had been teaching secondary school science for 10 years and primary science teacher education for approximately 2 years, reported that pre-service teachers had negative attitudes to science and a lack of confidence in their own science content knowledge, fears about meeting safety requirements and a general lack of confidence to teach science. These consistent reports of negativity served as an impetus for redesigning the science teacher education learning experience

© Springer Nature Singapore Pte Ltd. 2018   155
M. Jones, K. McLean, *Personalising Learning in Teacher Education*,
https://doi.org/10.1007/978-981-10-7930-6_10

to achieve increased opportunities for mastery experience (Bandura 1977) and, thus, increase pre-service teachers' self-efficacy beliefs in their ability to teach science.

The concerns reported by these pre-service teachers are not unique to this one context. In fact, it is widely reported that undergraduate primary pre-service teachers in Australia, and indeed across the world, hold poor attitudes to science and, generally, lack confidence in their ability to teach it (e.g. Freeman 2013; Goodrum et al. 2001; Jones et al. 2016; Nilsson and van Driel 2010; Tschannen-Moran and Woolfolk Hoy 2007; Tytler 2007). Many of these studies indicate that these poor attitudes and low levels of confidence are related to individuals' own negative experiences of science and science teaching in secondary school. It is suggested that these teacher candidates' past experiences of science teaching and learning are didactic in approach, disconnected from "real-world" everyday contexts, and are, generally speaking, considered to be for the elite – the "smart" kids – those looking to study science/engineering beyond the compulsory years of schooling.

Exacerbating this issue is the fact that relatively few people engage in post-compulsory science education and those who do rarely enter initial teacher education programmes. This creates a paucity of teacher education candidates who actually like science, let alone a majority cohort who have studied it in their senior years of schooling. Given evidence that most people hold onto their formed beliefs tenaciously (Loughran 2010), any effort to impact science teaching self-efficacy levels of teacher candidates who hold such a pessimistic outlook is not a task that can be undertaken lightly.

There is a range of efficacy information sources that may serve to address these common self-efficacy issues among primary science teacher education candidates. In his seminal work, Bandura (1977) identified four main sources of efficacy information: mastery experience (first-hand experiences of success), vicarious experience (bearing witness to a "like" other performing a task successfully), social persuasion (positive feedback and encouragement) and physiological response (physiological changes in the body induced by stress, e.g. heart rate). Bandura asserts that, of these, mastery experience is the most influential source of efficacy-building information. Whilst there have been some studies that suggest otherwise (e.g. Mulholland and Wallace 2001; Palmer 2011), most self-efficacy studies conducted support the notion that experiences of personal success, that is, mastery experience, are one of the most critical sources of self-efficacy information (e.g. Tschannen-Moran and Wolfolk Hoy 2007).

Providing mastery experience opportunities can be difficult in teacher education. The university-based setting that serves as the predominant location for teacher education courses cannot provide the authentic, first-hand success of science teaching that is needed to build mastery experience. Indeed, opportunities for mastery experience can only be achieved if the experience is situated within the setting in which it would normally take place – that is, in the classroom, with a class of children. Such a change in the setting where the learning takes place aligns with a work integrated learning approach (Patrick et al. 2008) that is informed by situated learning theory and, subsequently, with the notion of Communities of Practice.

10.2   Situated Learning Theory and Communities of Science Education Practice

In Chap. 3 we outlined the ways in which situated learning theory underpins the Communities of Practice and Collaboration approach that we are endorsing as a key tenet of personalising learning in this book. In essence, situated learning theory attempts to embrace the individual learner as a social being and recognises, at the same time, the context in which the learning takes place. This notion of situated learning recognises that all components of a particular system need to be incorporated into the learning about that system. For learning how to teach, the "system" involves university theoretical ideas and critiques as well as classroom-based practice. Biggs (2003) states that "in a good system, all aspects of teaching and assessment are tuned to support high level learning, so that all students are encouraged to use higher-order learning processes" and that "a poor system is one in which the components are not integrated" (p. 1). This helps to explain why the most effective approaches to theory-practice integration (or "bridging the theory-practice gap") are those which contain a "tight coherence and integration" (Darling-Hammond 2014, p. 549) between theoretical course work and practical classroom teaching experiences. Situated learning that embeds work integrated learning provides a platform for such an approach in teacher education.

The ways in which situated learning theory and Communities of Practice were applied to the *STISE* programme that is the focus of this chapter were threefold. The first Community of Practice was established through the university situated learning experience that provided pre-service teachers with explicit modelling (Loughran 2006) of science teaching and subsequent opportunities to analyse these examples of teaching for learning theories introduced in the course work. The second set of communities was established by placing pre-service teachers in small groups where they applied their understanding of the theories covered to plan their own mini-unit of science. Together, they engaged in the work integrated learning element of *STISE* whereby they implemented their mini-units in a classroom with children where they were engaged in the teaching, assessing and reflecting on their unit of work. Pre-service teachers were provided tutorial time in lieu of the periods of teaching in schools but still attended a university-based lecture in which the small groups came together to discuss and reflect on their experience and where the teacher educator facilitated this reflection within a theory-informed framework. This provided a third type of practice community. The Communities of Practice were adopted in these three main ways, each intended to support the other. The small and larger communities also reflect what Wenger (1998) refers to as "constellations of practice" (p. 127) in which the multi-faceted and permeable boundaries of groups within a larger community work together.

Wenger (1998) describes a "constellation of practice" as a particular way of seeing the interconnectedness of multiple Communities of Practice. One example Wenger (1998) gives of a constellation that is particularly relevant to this context is "the connections that tie communities of practice [which] may take intentional forms, such as the deliberate straddling of boundaries by a supervisor" (p. 128). In this instance, the "supervisor" is the science teacher educator facilitating the learning, and the intentional forms connecting the smaller communities are the critical reflection and sharing of experience, discussed within a theoretical framework that are facilitated by the teacher educator and conducted concurrently with the school-based teaching experience.

The emphasis on the context of the learning in situated learning theory means that the learning needs to take place in the setting that best reflects what it is that is being learnt. Thus, for someone who is learning how to teach, the learning must account for not only the social and cultural experience of the individual but also the school and classroom in which teaching normally takes place. Such a definition aligns with that of work integrated learning where learning takes place in a relevant associated work setting (Patrick et al. 2008). Applying such a concept to science teacher education requires at least some of the course delivery to be undertaken in the school classroom, teaching science. However, this comes with some warning.

When it comes to science education, extra care and attention needs to be given to what is known about situated learning and Communities of Practice that may see graduates adopting the prevailing culture and pedagogies of the school/classroom community they have entered. Research has shown that many primary school and early childhood teachers have low self-efficacy when it comes to science and science teaching (e.g. Kenny 2010; Jones et al. 2016; Nilsson and van Driel 2010). This low efficacy is said to influence teachers' selection of teaching approaches taken to science (Jones and Carter 2007) and, indeed, whether or not it is taught at all. In an Australia-wide study, Goodrum et al. (2001) revealed that primary school teachers tended to avoid the teaching of science, or when it was taught, it was limited to particular topics and/or taught predominantly through literacy- and humanities-based approaches. This does not align with current ideas about the best practice approaches to science teaching, which are focused on hands-on, investigative, inquiry-based learning.

Other studies have shown that teachers also identify issues with the additional time it takes to prepare science activities and to a lack of access to the appropriate resources and facilities for appropriate science teaching and learning to take place (Jones and Carter 2007). As self-efficacy research also demonstrates, however, those with high self-efficacy are far more likely to overcome inhibiting challenges such as the identified issues of time and resources related to science teaching (Jones and Carter 2007; Goddard 2003). Thus, as was discussed earlier, whilst situating science teacher education in the classroom is essential for providing the mastery experience opportunities for building self-efficacy, it does not, on its own, hold any promise of imparting the types of teaching and pedagogies for effective science learning that science teacher educators would be aspiring for their students.

Addressing the need in science teacher education for both a situated, work integrated, classroom learning experience and an appropriately informed knowledge base of science teaching pedagogies can be achieved through a balance between university-based and school-based learning in which other established teacher education pedagogies are employed (e.g. congruent teaching and critical reflective practice). Through a concurrent school and university-based model, theory and practice can be entwined in a more seamless and useful manner (indeed it could be argued that this is needed not just in science teacher education but in teacher education more broadly).

Whilst the traditional practicum component, usually a block of time ranging from 2 to 6 weeks, is often looked to for providing the situated and practice-based learning experience, it is rife with issues, especially for science teacher education. Reasons for this are threefold. Firstly, the block placement is often completed in isolation from university peers and teachers; thus, adopting the practices of the classroom teacher (be they good or bad) will be a likely outcome. Secondly, the block placement often occurs as a unit separate from curriculum and pedagogy units, which makes it difficult for subject-specific assessment to be embedded in practicum tasks. Finally, and for science in particular, the lack of science teaching and the forms of science teaching modelled in schools if it is taught, do not align with the outcomes of science teacher education courses; thus, pre-service teachers are unlikely to gain opportunities for or exposure to the types of science teaching that are desirable in science teacher education during the block practicum.

If the traditional practicum component of teacher education cannot provide the type of exposure to science teaching that is desired, then other form(s) of classroom experience must be sought. This is essential for addressing the ways in which situated learning theory applies to the impact on learning, for building effective Communities of Practice and for providing the mastery experience opportunities that are essential for improving science teacher self-efficacy beliefs. In the example of science teacher education that is the focus of this chapter, situated learning theory was applied by embedding a school-based experience within the science education course work. Furthermore, the school-based component occurred after a period of congruent teaching where science lessons were modelled and analysed for evidence of relevant theories and approaches that served as outcomes of the science education course. The school-based component was also conducted concurrently with ongoing university-based course work to allow for expert-facilitated critical reflection and discussion of pedagogy. This embedded and concurrent approach helped to ensure that the theoretical- and the practical-based components of learning to teach science could be addressed.

10.3   Science Teacher Education Where the Learner Is Central

Situating the Learner as Central to the teaching and learning is another of Keamy et al. (2007) tenets for personalising learning to which we subscribe. We are, however, also cognisant of the need for teacher guidance and support as a "mutually reinforcing feature" (Elen et al. 2007, p. 115) of effective pre-service teacher education. Thus, ways in which learners were made central in *STISE* involved elements of both student- and teacher-centred learning. Following the five categories identified by Smit et al. (2014) – tasks, student activities, teacher activities, sources of information and assessment which are summarised in this volume (Fig. 4.1, Chap. 4) – the learning environment provided a rich authentic context for the learning and assessment, opportunities for collaboration and negotiation and active and self-regulated learning. In addition, there were core aspects of learning that were theoretical and identical for the cohort and that were, at times, more passive and teacher-paced. Moreover, there was substantial scaffolding and guidance provided throughout. The more detailed description of these facets of the learning environment, based on Smit et al.'s five categories, is outlined below, demonstrating the compatibility of the student- and teacher-centred aspects that collectively place the Learner as Central.

The unit was established with integrated learning and assessment tasks. With a focus on developing ideas and skills about effective science teaching, a number of theoretical models and approaches supporting them were introduced. This was achieved through experiential-based learning: completing a hands-on activity and, then, after introduction to the theory/approach through explicit teaching, analysing the activity in relation to the theory or approach being targeted for that lesson (e.g. 5Es, discovery learning, interactive teaching, etc.). Such an approach aligns with Swennen et al.'s (2008) congruent teaching, a pedagogical approach specific to teacher education that has been recognised for its effectiveness. An example of how this was achieved in one particular lesson is outlined below.

10.3.1 Application of Student-Centred Learning: An Example

In the second session for the unit, the 5Es (Bybee 1997) inquiry learning framework is introduced to pre-service teachers. The way in which this occurs is outlined through the series of steps that were applied with annotations to highlight the mutually supported student- and teacher-guided aspects of the lesson.

10.3.1.1 Pre-lesson Requirement

Pre-service teachers are provided access to some literature around the 5Es inquiry model through the online learning platform and asked to read these prior to coming to class.

Lesson Step 1
Pre-service teachers are asked to draw a diagram of a battery, a single wire and a globe connected in such a way that the globe would light up. Once they have drawn their own diagrams, pre-service teachers are encouraged to compare it with others of those around them, to discuss any differences and to adjust anything they want to in their own diagram accordingly.

Student-centred accessing prior knowledge – opportunities for social interaction, explaining to others and learning as a community

Teacher-guided explicit instructions on what to draw – providing a problem for consideration

Lesson Step 2

Equipment is distributed, and pre-service teachers work in pairs to test their diagrams using the provided equipment. If their globe does not glow, they are asked to keep "playing" with it until they can get it to light up. Pre-service teachers are asked to redraw their diagrams to correctly represent the configuration required to make the globe glow and explain how/why it works.

Student-centred activity allows for the affirming of ideas or creation of cognitive dissonance; it is self-regulated and self-paced; students are active and the context is personal (related to their own prior knowledge by testing their own diagrams).

Teacher-guided appropriate equipment is provided to allow everyone to have a hands-on experience; teacher educator roams the room to check progress. Questioning/direction is used to provide appropriate scaffolds at appropriate levels for different pre-service teachers; e.g. pre-service teachers who are close to achieving are encouraged with "you're on the right track, keep playing with that arrangement". Those with a completely incorrect approach are (after an appropriate amount of time) encouraged to try placing the globe on one end of the battery and just moving the wire around. Those who succeed early are encouraged to try the activity with the globe in different positions (standing upright, lying flat).

Lesson Step 3

The teacher educator draws three images on the board that show three common initial diagrams in this activity. Two are incorrect, one is correct. Pre-service teachers are asked which one is correct. They are then asked to discuss in pairs and report back to the class why the other two diagrams, although common, are incorrect. Pre-service teachers are encouraged to draw their ideas on the board, showing the path of the electricity to assist their explanations. Terminology is gradually introduced (circuit, closed circuit, open circuit, short circuit).

Student-centred involves pre-service teachers' explanations to one another and to the whole class.

Teacher-guided teacher educator provides the prompts to direct thinking (three diagrams) and encourages sharing between small groups and whole class to confirm ideas and language.

Lesson Step 4

Teacher educator introduces the 5Es framework and an overarching definition of each component to the whole class. A worksheet containing a blank table is distributed, and students are asked to identify which components of the 5Es were represented by which parts of the completed activity. They are encouraged to think back on the pre-class reading that also discusses the 5Es.

Student-centred pre-service teachers reflect on their personal experiences of the lesson and discuss the definition of the 5Es components and how they were represented in the activity in order to complete the worksheet table.

Teacher-guided explicit instruction introducing the 5Es framework; the table provided as a graphic organiser to assist the organisation and recording of ideas.

A number of activities following this sort of process to introduce and to consolidate key content were conducted in the first half of the unit. Pre-service teachers then had to utilise the ideas and approaches in the two assessment tasks set in the unit: (1) a folio of selected lectures/tutorials to analyse against the main theoretical frameworks covered in the unit and (2) to design a mini-unit of science for implementation in schools (see Assessment section below for more on this). Both of these tasks saw the assessment embedded into the learning process, as required to achieve a student-centred approach. In addition, they both provided opportunities for pre-service teachers to learn throughout the assessment process, another key feature of student-centred assessment according to Schwartz et al. (2009). Further detail of this is provided in the section on Personalising Assessment below.

10.4   Personalising the Assessment

Nearly all commentaries and studies of teacher education contain a strong focus on teaching and learning pedagogies, often without an accompanying strong consideration of the relationship between these and assessment. The work of scholars, such as Ramsden (2003) and Biggs and Tang (2011), tells us that the profile of assessment in higher education is core to the teaching and learning process. "There is nothing more important than assessment" states Race (2014, p. 28), a view that has permeated thinking about effective higher education for at least two decades. Ramsden (2003) indicates that, for students, "assessment is the curriculum" as it is the assessment that determines what students will put effort into learning. Biggs (2003) echoes this notion, indicating that "Faulty assumptions about and practices of assessment do more damage by misaligning teaching than any other single factor" (p. 3). This highlights the importance of the alignment that assessment has with what it is we want pre-service teachers to know and do. Designing constructively aligned assessment has a number of key features. These features include (but are not limited to):

- Assessing for structure rather than independent facts;
- Teaching and assessing to encourage a positive working atmosphere, so students can make mistakes and learn from them;
- Emphasising depth of learning, rather than breadth of coverage;
- Using teaching and assessment methods that support explicit aims and objectives of the course. (Biggs and Tang 2011, p. 27)

Coupled with the argument to closely integrate theoretical university-based components of teacher education with practical school-based ones (Darling-Hammond 2014; Zeichner 2010), personalising assessment becomes a challenge of how theory and practice can be reflected in performance-based assessment tasks that embed the features noted above. The design of the assessment reported in this chapter aimed to achieve such a goal. It is explained below with reference to the various elements purported for effective, constructively aligned practice.

10.4.1 The Assessment Task

The major assessment task required pre-service teachers to plan, implement, assess and reflect on a mini-unit of science. They had to apply the theoretical ideas covered in the first few weeks of the course, where a number of contemporary, research-informed approaches to effective teaching and learning in science were modelled, analysed and discussed. Pre-service teachers applied this learning to their mini-unit design for five lessons that ran for approximately 2 h per week for 5 weeks. They worked in small groups of between two and four pre-service teachers to complete their unit plan. Group sizes were determined by the allocation of each group to a local school to try to ensure that the ratio of pre-service teachers to children was approximately equal across all groups. The application of their learning in the design and implementation of their unit plans enabled pre-service teachers to "turn analysis into action" which Darling-Hammond (2014, p. 553) indicates is a characteristic of a powerful teacher education programme:

> Powerful teacher education programs have a clinical curriculum as well as a didactic curriculum. They teach candidates to turn analysis into action by *applying* what they are learning in *curriculum plans, teaching applications*, and *other performance assessments* that are organized around professional teaching standards. These attempts are especially educative when they are *followed by systematic reflection on student learning* in relation to teaching and *accompanied by feedback*, with opportunities to retry and continue to improve. (Darling-Hammond 2014, p. 553, emphasis added)

The elements of powerful learning outlined here by Darling-Hammond were embedded in the assessment task in the ways outlined in the following sections.

10.4.2 The Unit Planning: "Applying What They Learn in Curriculum Plans"

Pre-service teachers were provided with a range of contextual information about their class of children to assist them in their planning. For example, they were told how many children would be in the class, what sort of technology access/software the school had, whether there were any special learning needs for which they needed to cater and whether there was an inquiry topic that classes were working on that pre-service teachers could support in the focus of their own mini-units. In this way, the needs of the children and schools could be incorporated into the planning, which helped to maximise the benefits for all partners.

Once pre-service teachers had prepared a draft of their mini-unit, they submitted their plans for feedback. This feedback was qualitative in nature and focused on strengthening the science inquiry and investigative aspects of the teaching and learning. No grades were given at this stage – it was purely a formative assessment, so pre-service teachers could enhance their plans before they implemented them in schools. Providing formative feedback in this way is essential for achieving deep learning (Ramsden 2003). It also supports what Rust et al. (2005) describe as critical engagement with assessment criteria and feedback for assessment supporting a student-centred approach.

10.4.3   The Unit Implementation: "Teaching Applications"

The time pre-service teachers spent teaching their mini-units in schools was counted towards the teaching and learning time associated with their course. In other words, they were given this time in lieu of the tutorial time they would otherwise be attending at university. This allowed for the science-dedicated teaching time in schools (instead of trying to rely on the unpredictable block teaching period to incorporate science teaching experience). It also helped to ensure strong alignment between the pre-service teacher learning experience and the assessment they were completing, especially given that their teaching was not being assessed per se. Assessment targeted their planning, assessment of children's learning and their reflection on the experience. This ensured Schwartz et al.'s (2009) directive for providing students with opportunities to learn throughout the assessment process was achieved.

10.4.4   The Assessment and Reporting: "Other Performance Assessments"

To assess children's learning, pre-service teachers were each required to monitor a small number of children over the 5-week period of the mini-unit's implementation. Pre-service teachers implemented their mini-unit in their groups. This involved them taking turns to lead any whole-class components of a given lesson and taking charge of small group learning activities, which were by far the more significant time-based part of every lesson. As such, each pre-service teacher was able to observe the learning of a small group of children each week. Ensuring they worked with the same small group of children each week enabled pre-service teachers to monitor learning both within individual lessons as well as across the mini-unit. At the end of the unit, pre-service teachers wrote a one-page report for each child that provided an overview of the unit's learning intentions and a comment about the child's learning and achievement. Work samples collected throughout the teaching period were also annotated and attached to the one-page report to form a learning journal type of artefact. Pre-service teachers submitted these reports along with their finalised unit plans for assessment. After being assessed, children's reports were returned to pre-service teachers who then submitted them to the classroom teacher at the schools they had been involved with. Teachers sent these science reports home to parents as a part of the school's larger reporting cycle. This added a layer of rich and authentic task complexity (Smit et al. 2014) that cannot be contrived in the university setting and increased the impetus and motivation for pre-service teachers to perform.

10.4.5 The Reflection: "Reflection on Student Learning in Relation to Teaching"

The requirements to assess and report on children's learning, as well as complete an evidence-based reflection on their own learning, helped to enhance the "powerful teacher education" experience that Darling-Hammond (2014) describes. To increase the meaningfulness of the reflective component of the task, pre-service teachers were asked to think about the different approaches and ideas we had covered in the early weeks of the course and, individually, select an area of science-specific pedagogy that they thought they most needed to improve in their own practice. The Australian Professional Standards for Graduate Teachers (AITSL 2014) were also used to assist pre-service teachers in framing their reflection around professional practice and expectations for graduate teachers. Early identification of a specific, targeted area meant that pre-service teachers could actively trial approaches to improve this self-identified aspect of their teaching and plan for the collection of evidence of its level of success. Pre-service teachers were encouraged to collect a range of data to assist their reflection, including feedback from the children they were teaching, feedback from their peers who were in the classroom with them and their own personal thoughts and feelings. They were also required to align their synthesis of this data with relevant literature when they wrote their reflective pieces for submission. These guidelines for evidencing levels of success not only helped to make the reflection critical in its nature by incorporating a range of lenses (Brookfield 1995) but also meant that over the 5-week period, they had opportunities to trial, evaluate and improve in a key area of their own practice that was important and meaningful to them. This self-regulated, student-elected focus for the task made this aspect of the learning and assessment student-centred and significant on a personal level. It also meets Darling-Hammond's (2014) final component of the description of powerful teaching whereby students had experiences that were "followed by systematic reflection on student learning in relation to teaching and accompanied by feedback, with opportunities to retry and continue to improve" (Darling-Hammond 2014, p. 553).

The final assessment for pre-service teachers incorporated both the group component (the mini-unit plan) and the individual component (reporting on children's learning and reflecting on their own learning). Tied to the embedded nature of the actual teaching experience in schools that was informed by the early course work, the teaching, learning and assessment had the coherence and alignment that Biggs (2003) and others (Biggs and Tang 2011; Ramsden 2003) call for to ensure higher education is deep, purposeful and constructively aligned.

10.5 Designing Mechanisms for Feedback

The influence of *STISE* in meeting its goals of improving pre-service teachers' attitudes towards and confidence to teach science was measured in two key ways. The first measure was through a "consensogram" and the second through an open-ended questionnaire targeting their responses to the teaching experience in schools. Both data collection tools were administered annually for the different pre-service teacher cohorts studying the unit across a 5-year period (2010–2015). A total of 208 pre-service teachers were included in this data collection across the 5 years.

10.5.1 The Consensogram

The consensogram (Fig. 10.1) is a set of axes on which pre-service teachers indicate their confidence to teach science and their attitude towards how important they believe science to be in the primary school curriculum. A position is selected and marked with a sticker such that the vertical height represents level of confidence to teach science and the horizontal length represents how important science is perceived to be in the primary curriculum.

The consensogram was administered at the commencement (pre) and at the end (post) of the science education unit. Once pre-service teachers marked their selected positions (see Fig. 10.2 for an example of pre- and post-consensograms), the horizontal and vertical distances from each axis to the centre of the sticker were measured to provide a numerical score for each item. These numerical data were analysed through a t-test for unequal variance, providing a statistical measure for significant difference between before and after means. These tests were applied to pre- and post-data. All 5 years of data were analysed as a single pre- and post-data set, providing a large sample size ($N = 208$), which is more than sufficient to achieve reliability through the use of statistical tests (Cohen et al. 2013). Data could be treated in this manner because the unit was taught by the same lecturer, covered the same content, included the same assessment task and were conducted in the same schools each year. The analysis provided evidence of the impact of the programme

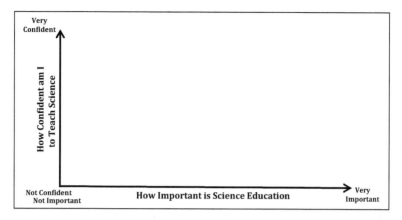

Fig. 10.1 Attitude and confidence consensogram

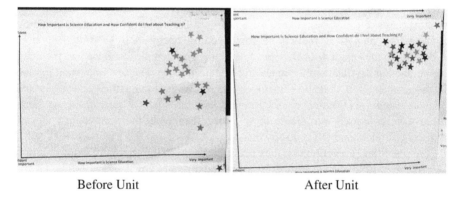

Before Unit   After Unit

Fig. 10.2 Pre- and post-consensograms (2015 cohort)

on pre-service teachers' attitude towards the importance of science and showed changes in their confidence to teach science.

The sample before and after consensograms shown in Fig. 10.2 is typical of the results obtained using this tool across the 5-year period. They consistently demonstrate that pre-service teachers enter this final year unit of their course believing science to be of medium to high importance in primary school curricula. They also consistently reveal a quite varied level of initial confidence to teach science – ranging from very low to reasonably high. After their experience in the unit, which, as outlined earlier, involves exposure to modelling, analysis and discussion of various science-specific pedagogies and work integrated learning with the features of planning, implementing, reporting and reflecting on a mini-unit of science for which the teaching component occurs in schools, both attitudes towards and confidence to teach science improved significantly. This improvement can be seen visually in Fig. 10.2 and is also evident through the statistical analyses conducted showing $p < 0.01$ for t-tests (unequal variance) conducted for both confidence and attitude scales. The significantly reduced variance in responses is also a strength of the findings, demonstrating that as a cohort, pre-service teachers' ideas, beliefs and confidence to teach science were far more similar in their positivity after their experience in the unit. These findings are consistent with those from a study of the early years of the programme (see Jones 2017).

10.5.2   The Questionnaire

Upon the unit's conclusion, pre-service teachers completed an open-ended questionnaire which provided insight into the aspects of the programme that were particularly beneficial or less so. The questionnaire targeted the in-schools teaching component of the course in particular. Bloom's revised taxonomy (Anderson and Krathwohl 2001) was used to provide a framework for structuring the questionnaire. The six resulting questions are shown in Fig. 10.3.

Responses to the questionnaire were analysed through a process of topic coding followed by analytical induction. Topic coding occurred by coding responses according to the category of Bloom's taxonomy in which the response was recorded (remember, understand, apply, analyse, evaluate, create). The first important finding in the analysis was that the remember and understand categories and apply and analyse categories contained exceptionally similar types of responses. As such, these were collapsed into single topic codes, leading to the final topic codes of remember/understand (RU), apply/analyse (AA), evaluate (EV) and create (CR).

The analytical induction that then occurred involved the sorting of responses into key themes within each category. This enabled not only key responses to be identified and summarised but also the strength of response types to be considered based on the proportion of pre-service teachers commenting within each identified theme.

---

1. **Remember -** What will be the main thing you will remember from this teaching experience?

2. **Understand -** What aspect(s) of teaching Science do you understand more clearly out of your involvement?

3. **Apply –** What have you learnt from this experience that you will apply in your future teaching?

4. **Analyse -** What aspect(s) of your teaching might be different as a result of this experience?

5. **Evaluate -** Was the teaching in schools a valuable way for you to learn about how to teach and assess Science? Why/Why not? What would have made it a better learning experience?

6. **Create -** To prepare you to be the best Science teacher possible, what would you suggest this unit needs: More of...   Done differently...   Getting rid of...

Fig. 10.3 Final questionnaire items

The results both support and extend on the findings from the consensogram data by demonstrating substantial improvement in pre-service teachers' general ideas and understanding of how to teach science effectively and increases in their confidence as teachers of primary school science. A summary of each topic code is provided to show representative data on how pre-service teachers' ideas, understanding, beliefs and confidence were affected by their science learning experience in this programme. For most topics, the number of comments exceeds the number of pre-service teacher participants because they often provided more than one response to each item.

Remember/Understand   Themes identified in the remember/understand responses covered a range of aspects including learning about content-based ideas such as the 5Es, the importance of hands-on learning activities and increases in science content knowledge. Some comments referred to more personal, affective notions such as remembering/understanding: the children's enthusiasm for science, growth in their own confidence to teach science and realisations that science was enjoyable to teach – indeed, it could be "fun" and "not scary". A sample of representative comments demonstrating each of the identified themes is provided in Table 10.1. Frequency of response types is also given to demonstrate the prevalence of each theme within the responses.

Six of the top seven most prevalent themes identified align with those identified in an earlier study of this programme that focused on 2009–2010 student data (see Jones, 2017). This demonstrates the consistency of the programme to produce outcomes around:

- Approaches to teaching science (53% of responses in this study; 52% of responses in the previous study)
- Content knowledge (10% of responses in this study; 9% of responses in the previous study)
- Student engagement (9% of responses in this study; 11% of responses in the previous study)
- Authentic classroom experience (8% of responses in this study; 15% of responses in the previous study)
- Being prepared (8% of responses in this study; 4% of responses in the previous study)
- Science can be fun and easy to teach (5% of responses in this study; 2% of responses in the previous study)

Apply/Analyse   When considering the aspects of their experience that pre-service teachers thought they would apply in their own teaching, and ways in which their ideas about teaching science might be different as a result of their experience in this programme, pre-service teachers noted again that their ideas about approaches to teaching science were considerably affected. Most of these responses were concerned with their intention to utilise the 5Es framework and inquiry-based learning in general when teaching science, which is commensurate with the most prevalent response in the remember/understand category reported above. The themes

Table 10.1 What pre-service teachers remember/understand from the science education unit

Theme	Frequency	Sample comment
Approaches to teaching science	165 (53%)	The 5Es model and putting it into practice (RU16-2012)
		The benefits of using hands-on interactive approach to teaching science (RU19-2010)
		Best teaching practice from the lectures (RU3-2015)
Content knowledge	35 (10%)	The content – I have more understanding about what I have to know to be able to teach it (RU9-2015)
		Forces, simple machines, how toys work (RU2-2010)
Student engagement	32 (9%)	How excited the children were to learn science and how much they enjoyed the hands-on activities (RU33-2015)
		How excited all the students were regarding the unit and how engaged they were (RU32-2010)
Authentic experience	26 (8%)	Actually teaching the unit (RU26-2011)
		Going into a school and getting to put into practice what we had learnt in the unit (RU6-2012)
Being prepared	26 (8%)	Be prepared and have your resources readily available (RU9-2011)
		Be prepared – do the science experiment at home (RU25-2015)
How to plan a unit of science	21 (6%)	Being able to see the student learning about science through a sequence rather than a single lesson (RU38-2012)
		I understand what it takes to plan a science unit (RU21-2011)
Science can be fun/easy to teach	18 (5%)	Science is a fun thing to teach and that students can learn it easily (RU41-2015)
		Science isn't scary – it's fun. The kids enjoy exploring and investigating which makes teaching experiences easier (RU51-2010)
Increased confidence	13 (4%)	I have gained confidence in using these [5Es/SIS] in my science teaching and learning (RU7-2012)
		I feel I am better prepared and more comfortable with teaching science in a classroom and choosing appropriate activities and resources (RU46-2010)
Importance of questioning	11 (3%)	I understand the importance of good questioning (RU13-2015)
		The importance of using open questioning and allowing students to make their own connections (RU9-2012)
	347 (100%)	

identified in this category are listed in Table 10.2 along with their associated frequency and representative comments.

Four of the themes identified in Table 10.2 align with themes also identified in the earlier study. These included:

- Approaches to teaching science (59% of responses in this study; 50% of responses in the previous study)

Table 10.2 What pre-service teachers will apply/change about their science teaching

Theme	Frequency	Sample comment
Approach to teaching science	200 (59%)	Students need to explore before explain to make sense of their learning (AA8-2015)
		I understand the importance of inquiry learning instead of direct teaching (AA30-2015)
Planning a unit	44 (13%)	Planning skills and linking lessons together to have a successful learning sequence (AA47-2011)
		My approach to planning – the 5Es framework and PoLT and how to implement them (AA27-2010)
Questioning	23 (7%)	Question styles – open-ended questions (AA3-2011)
		Focus on questioning to encourage higher-order thinking – preparing them before teaching (AA6-2015)
Being flexible	17 (5%)	Planning is important but so is being flexible and adaptable (AA50-2011)
		Allowing flexibility and versatility. Ability to move off the expected lesson steps (AA11-2010)
Reporting and assessment strategies	14 (4%)	Use assessment as a starting point to build on knowledge (AA32-2015)
		I will incorporate more assessment opportunities (AA29-2010)
Team teaching	18 (5%)	I guess I learnt about teaching collaboratively. I didn't enjoy all aspects of this but will be better placed to do so in future (AA54-2010)
		Team teaching techniques (AA43-2012)
Time management	9 (3%)	Timing – making sure the activities planned run on time and smoothly (AA5-2011)
		Time management – don't put so much work in such a small timeframe (AA31-2015)
Behaviour/classroom management	7 (2%)	Class management as well as managing a group of teachers teaching the same content. Very beneficial (AA1-2011)
		Behavioural management (AA13-2012)
Student reflection	4 (1%)	I would always make sure that students have time to reflect on their learning (AA30-2011)
Attitude to the importance of science	4 (1%)	The importance of science teaching/investigating/exploring (AA37-2015)
		Learnt that science isn't easy to teach but it is critical to the curriculum (AA8-2010)
		My entire outlook on science is different due to this experience (AA22-2010)
	340 (100%)	

- Reporting and assessment strategies (4% of responses in this study; 10% of responses in the previous study)
- Team teaching (5% of responses in this study; 1% of responses in the previous study)

- Behaviour/classroom management (2% of responses in this study; 5% of responses in the previous study)

A fifth theme which was very similar to that of the previous study was also identified:

- Time management (3% of responses in this study) and allowing time (1% of responses in the previous study)

The themes of relatively high prevalence in this study that were not as prevalent in the earlier study include Planning a unit (13% of responses), Questioning (7% of responses) and Being flexible (5% of responses).

Evaluate In evaluating the experience, pre-service teachers were asked to consider the value of the programme for assisting their learning about teaching science and ways that it could be improved. In noting what was of value, the clear majority of the responses identified the benefit of the authentic teaching experience. Some suggestions for improvement were also provided, although the majority of the participants left this section of the questionnaire blank or wrote "nothing". The suggestions that were provided centred on increasing the amount of time in the schools. Other less prevalent but, nonetheless, useful suggestions included wanting to know more about the children before the unit began, changing the size of the groups that they worked in/with and a desire for increased involvement from the classroom teacher. These and other suggestions provided in this category are noted in Tables 10.3 and 10.4.

Pre-service teachers' evaluation comments were predominantly demonstrative of the value of the authentic classroom experience. Every single response given in answer to the question about the value of the programme was positive. This was represented through general responses like "Yes it was valuable" or specific responses "It was really beneficial to do a 'real' report" (EV17-2015). None of the respondents left this section of the questionnaire blank, and no one responded with a negative view of the experience. There were, however, a number of suggestions provided to the query about how to improve the programme. These suggestions generally targeted some of the finer details concerned with the administration of the programme rather than macro changes that would alter the overall concept of what the programme looks like and how it works. For example, pre-service teachers wanted more contact with schools, more modelling of teaching ideas at university, more preparation time, etc. Many of the improvement ideas would be difficult to achieve given the relatively short (12-week semester) period in which theory, modelling and practice all need to be incorporated. Elements that could be improved initially include investigating opportunities to collect more prior knowledge of children before the teaching commences and investigating ways to increase the involvement of classroom teachers.

Create The responses to the create section of the questionnaire came in three subcategories aligned with the three questions pre-service teachers were asked to respond to in this section of the questionnaire. These three questions asked (1) what

Table 10.3 How pre-service teachers evaluated the science education unit in terms of its value

Theme	Frequency	Sample comment
Authentic experience	121 (81%)	Yes it was [valuable] because we were working with real children (EV4-2012)
		Yes – it was hands-on and took us through the whole planning and evaluating process (EV19-2012)
		Yes. Teaching science is something I have rarely come across on my teaching rounds (EV4-2010)
General response of its value	16 (8%)	Yes [it was valuable] (EV12-2012)
		Definitely – do not change it (EV20-2010)
Opportunity to write reports	10 (5%)	It was really beneficial to do a "real" report (EV17-2015)
		The journals made you reflect on students' learning and ours (EV53-2011)
Increased confidence	7 (3%)	Being able to plan, conduct and then assess was invaluable. Seeing the full process has made me confident not only in science but other areas too (EV1-2011)
Teaching science for the first time	6 (3%)	Yes – this was my first experience teaching science (EV27-2012)
Total	**210 (100%)**	

Table 10.4 How pre-service teachers evaluated the science education unit in terms of improvements needed

Theme	Frequency	Sample comment
More time in schools	65 (31%)	More time with students in schools (EV9-2010)
Nothing/blank	60 (28%)	I think it all worked well! (EV2-2011)
Content at uni	26 (13%)	I loved the activities we did in discovery learning, electrical currents, etc. I really did get *so much* out of this unit! (EV4-2015)
		More class time/lectures (EV41-2012)
Knowing the students before teaching	20 (9%)	Get to know the students before teaching (EV12-2012)
		Meeting the children before planning for them and teaching them (EV7-2010)
Time for assessment	20 (9%)	Having more time in class to prepare and plan for our assessment (EV43-2011)
Involvement of classroom teacher	7 (3%)	Feedback from your classroom teacher on lessons (EV28-2010)
Smaller PST group size	6 (3%)	I think it would be better to work in smaller groups to be a more realistic experience (EV1-2012)
Co-ordination between the university and school	5 (2%)	More planning at the start with schools (EV37-2012)
Smaller groups of children	2 (1%)	Smaller groups would make assessment and reporting easier, allowing us to gain a better understanding of each child's learning (EV9-2015)
	212 (100%)	

would they like *more of* in the unit, (2) what they would like to see *done differently* and (3) what should be *removed* from the experience. A number of the responses for these subcategories contained themes aligned with the "suggestions for improvement" reported in the evaluate section above. Table 10.5 details the themes identified within each subcategory. There were also 20 out of the 208 questionnaires returned where there was a single, positive comment about the unit. These 20 responses are recorded in the table to ensure other responses are reported proportionately.

10.6   Shifting Mindsets and Forming Science Teacher Identities

One of the key concerns reported in relation to science education is the low self-efficacy levels and poor background content knowledge that primary school and early childhood educators report as a reason for avoiding the teaching of science. Shifting such mindsets of inability to perform is difficult to achieve. This chapter reports on an example of personalising the science learning in a teacher education course to attempt to shift such mindsets and help to develop pre-service teacher participants' identities as teachers of science. This was achieved by utilising established pedagogies for teacher education that were supported by the Communities of Collaboration situated learning and Learner as Central tenets of personalising learning.

The feedback from pre-service teachers provides compelling evidence that personalising the approach was powerful in shifting their ideas and attitudes towards science teaching and learning. The impact of using the 5Es inquiry learning framework to both model science teaching and learning, and as a framework for the pre-service teachers' own planning and teaching of a mini-unit of science, had a strong influence on what pre-service teachers said they remembered, understood and would apply in their own teaching. This aligns with many of the elements of Learners as Central which are outlined in detail in Chap. 5. Ways in which this was achieved were varied. For example, pre-service teachers had an opportunity to negotiate topics of interest – Keamy et al.'s (2007) "choice and voice" – within the scope of the science curriculum. The curriculum and the learning frameworks and theories, along with the modelling and other lecturer support strategies, provided a scaffold and structure for pre-service teachers to guide their planning – Keamy et al.'s (2007) "highly structured approach".

Learning was highly active throughout the unit. This was evident in the modelling, analysis and application of learning approaches that were covered in the early part of the unit and then utilised in open-ended ways when pre-service teachers had to plan and implement their own science unit in schools. In this way Land et al.'s (2012) productive engagement in complex, authentic and open-ended learning

Table 10.5 How pre-service teachers would create the science education unit differently

Theme	Frequency	Sample comment
Do more of:		
Nothing/blank	61 (29%)	n/a really enjoyed the unit (CR34-2015)
Modelling of teaching ideas	46 (22%)	Modelling teaching of science. We did a lot of this but the more the better (CR4-2011)
Science content knowledge	31 (15%)	Content – but that's probably up to the other science units as well (CR8-2012)
Preparation time	21 (10%)	Preparation before heading into schools (CR22-2012)
Positive comment	20 (9%)	I think the unit was great. Very good balance between theory and practice (CR57-2010)
Time in schools	19 (9%)	More weeks in the classroom (CR8-2010)
Lecturer contact time	13 (6%)	Preparation time with the lecturer (CR27-2012)
	211 (100%)	
Do differently:		
Nothing/blank	116 (55%)	I can't think of any changes to make, I liked the unit as it is (CR50-2011)
Assessment	31 (15%)	Not so many assessment tasks (CR1-2010); break the last assignment into two parts (CR7-2012)
Positive comment	20 (10%)	Everything was helpful for my science learning. There were heaps of resources and representations during the lectures and tutorials (CR4-2010)
Folio assignment	15 (7%)	AT1 was too big (CR44-2010)
Explanation of assessments	14 (7%)	More feedback and guidance with assignments (CR10-2010)
Group work	7 (3%)	Smaller group sizes (CR40-2015)
Due dates	6 (3%)	Such full on assessments with large workload – could have been more spaced out (CR14-2011)
	209 (100%)	
Remove:		
Nothing/blank	135 (65%)	Nothing. An excellent unit (CR15-2015)
Specific content	24 (11%)	Ollie's DVD (CR26-2010); Waterwatch excursion (CR3-2011)
Folio assignment	23 (11%)	SIS/PoLT assessment task (CR9-2011)
Positive comment	20 (10%)	I thought it was a brilliant experience and cannot see how to make it a better learning experience. Keep it the same for next year (CR29-2010)
Mode of submission	6 (3%)	The online component – make it a hardcopy assignment (CR6-2012)
Total	**208 (100%)**	

occurred. This also assisted the achievement of Keamy et al.'s (2007) "engaged learners".

Assessment procedures were closely linked to the teaching and learning processes, bringing about strong constructive alignment (Biggs and Tang 2011) between the teaching, learning and assessment employed. The authenticity of the school experience also helped to ensure that the assessment was related to "meaningful tasks" and included "assessment for and from students" (Keamy et al. 2007, p. 2). This experience also meant individual pre-service teachers had opportunities for mastery experience, helping to meet Keamy et al.'s (2007) final criterion for Learners as Central, which requires a focus on improving the learning outcomes for all involved.

The fact that pre-service teachers had to apply their learning in the authentic context of the classroom, teaching their own unit of science and assessing and reporting on students' learning, also ensured that the situated learning associated with the Communities of Practice aspect of personalising learning was achieved. Moreover, aspects of Grossman et al. (2009) rehearsal of complex practices in settings of reduced complexity were enabled by having pre-service teachers work together in groups and with a small group of children each within the classroom. This placement in the classroom was also powerful in pre-service teachers' identity formation as teachers of science. This was evidenced through the many comments provided regarding increases in confidence, knowledge of science and science teaching approaches and attitudes and intention to teach science. It was also captured through one participant's comment about the value of the school experience and being viewed as *the* teacher:

> Yes! It was great. Children refer to us as the "science teachers". (EV10-2015)

Overall, the STISE provided pre-service teachers with a highly authentic experience of learning to be a science teacher through the attention given to key teacher education pedagogies such as congruent teaching, explicit modelling, work integrated learning, rehearsal opportunities in settings of reduced complexity and critical reflective practice. It achieved these through the focus on placing the Learner as Central, engaging pre-service teachers in Communities of Collaboration and promoting Lifelong Learning mindsets. It was an effective and successful example of personalising learning in science teacher education.

References

AITSL. (2014). *Australian professional standards for teachers.* Australian Institute for Teaching and School Leadership. Retrieved from https://www.aitsl.edu.au/australian-professional-standards-for-teachers/standards/list

Anderson, L. W., & Krathwohl, D. R. (Eds.). (2001). *A taxonomy for learning, teaching, and assessing: A revision of Bloom's taxonomy of educational objectives.* New York: Longman.

Bandura, A. (1977). Self-efficacy: Toward a unifying theory of behavioural change. *Psychological Review, 84*(2), 191–215.

Biggs, J. (2003). *Aligning teaching for constructing learning.* The Higher Education Academy. Retrieved from https://www.heacademy.ac.uk/aligning-teaching-constructing-learning.

Biggs, J., & Tang, C. (2011). *Teaching for quality learning at university: What the student does* (4th ed.). Berkshire: McGraw-Hill Education.

Brookfield, S. D. (1995). *Becoming a critically reflective teacher.* San Francisco: Jossey-Bass.

Bybee, R. (1997). *Achieving scientific literacy: From purposes to practices.* Portsmouth: Heinemann.

Cohen, L., Bell, R., Manion, L., Martin, S., McCulloch, G., Morrison, K., & O'Sullivan, C. (2013). *Research methods in education* (7th ed.). Abingdon: Routledge.

Darling-Hammond, L. (2014). Strengthening clinical preparation: The holy grail of teacher education. *Peabody Journal of Education, 89*(4), 547–561.

Elen, J., Clarebout, G., Léonard, R., & Lowyck, J. (2007). Student-centred and teacher-centred learning environments: What students think. *Teaching in Higher Education, 12*(1), 105–117.

Freeman, B. (2013). *Science, mathematics, engineering and technology (STEM) in Australia: Practice, policy and programs.* Melbourne: Centre for the Study of Higher Education.

Goddard, R. (2003). The impact of schools on teacher beliefs, influence and student achievement: The role of collective efficacy beliefs. In J. Raths & A. McAninch (Eds.), *Teacher beliefs and classroom performance: The impact of teacher education* (pp. 183–202). Greenwich: Information Age Publishing.

Goodrum, D., Hackling, M., & Rennie, L. (2001). *The status and quality of teaching and learning of science in Australian schools: A research report.* Canberra: Department of Education, Training and Youth Affairs.

Grossman, P., Hammerness, K., & McDonald, M. (2009). Redefining teaching, re-imagining teacher education. *Teachers and Teaching, 15*(2), 273–289.

Jones, M. (2017). Improving a school-based science education task using critical reflective practice. In R. Brandenburg, K. Glasswell, M. Jones, & J. Ryan (Eds.), *Reflective theory and teacher education practice* (pp. 179–204). Singapore: Springer.

Jones, M. G., & Carter, G. (2007). Science teacher attitudes and beliefs. In S. Abell & N. Lederman (Eds.), *Handbook of research on science education* (pp. 1067–1104). Mahwah: Lawrence Erlbaum Associates.

Jones, M., Hobbs, L., Kenny, J., Campbell, C., Gilbert, A., Herbert, S., & Redman, C. (2016). Successful university-school partnerships: An interpretive framework to inform partnership practice. *Teaching and Teacher Education, 60*, 108–120.

Keamy, R. K., Nicholas, H., Mahar, S., & Herrick, C. (2007). *Personalising education: From research to policy and practice, Paper No. 11. Office of Education Policy and Innovation.* Melbourne: Department of Education and Early Childhood Development.

Kenny, J. (2010). Preparing pre-service primary teachers to teach primary science: A partnership approach. *International Journal of Science Education, 32*(10), 1267–1288.

Land, S., Hannafin, M., & Oliver, K. (2012). Student-centred learning environments: Foundations, assumptions and design. In D. Jonassen & S. Land (Eds.), *Theoretical foundations of learning environments* (2nd ed., pp. 3–25). New York: Routledge.

Loughran, J. (2010). *What expert teachers do. Enhancing professional knowledge for classroom practice.* Abingdon: Routledge.

Mulholland, J., & Wallace, J. (2001). Teacher induction and elementary science teaching: Enhancing self-efficacy. *Teaching and Teacher Education, 17*, 243–261.

Nilsson, P., & van Driel, J. (2010). Teaching together and learning together: Primary science student teachers' and their mentors' joint teaching and learning in the primary classroom. *Teaching and Teacher Education, 26*(6), 1309–1318.

Palmer, D. (2011). Sources of efficacy information in an inservice program for elementary teachers. *Science Education, 95*, 577–600.

Patrick, C.-J., Peach, D., Pocknee, C., Webb, F., Fletcher, M., & Pretto, G. (2008). *The WIL [Work Integrated Learning] report: A national scoping study* (Australian Learning and Teaching

Council (ALTC) Final Report). Brisbane: Queensland University of Technology. Retrieved from www.altc.edu.au and www.acen.edu.au

Race, P. (2014). *The lecturer's toolkit: A practical guide to assessment, learning and teaching.* New York: Routledge.

Ramsden, P. (2003). *Learning to teach in higher education* (2nd ed.). London: Routledge Falmer.

Rust, C., O'Donovan, B., & Price, M. (2005). A social constructivist assessment process model: How the research literature shows us this could be best practice. *Assessment and Evaluation in Higher Education, 30*(3), 231–240.

Schwartz, D., Lindgren, R., & Lewis, S. (2009). Constructivism in an age of non-constructivist assessments. In S. Tobias & T. Duffy (Eds.), *Constructivist instruction: Success or failure?* (pp. 34–61). New York: Routledge.

Smit, K., de Brabander, C., & Martens, R. (2014). Student-centred and teacher-centred learning environment in pre-vocational secondary education: Psychological needs, and motivation. *Scandinavian Journal of Educational Research, 58*(6), 695–712.

Swennen, A., Lunenberg, M., & Korthagen, F. (2008). Preach what you teach! Teacher educators and congruent teaching. *Teachers and Teaching: Theory and Practice, 14*(5–6), 531–542.

Tschannen-Moran, M., & Woolfolk Hoy, A. (2007). The differential antecedents of self-efficacy beliefs of vice and experienced teachers. *Teaching and Teacher Education, 23*, 944–956.

Tytler, R. (2007). Re-imagining science education: Engaging students in science for Australia's future. *Australian Education Review 51*, Australian Council for Educational Research. Retrieved from http://research.acer.edu.au/cgi/viewcontent.cgi?article=1002&context=aer

Wenger, E. (1998). *Communities of practice: Learning, meaning and identity.* New York: Cambridge University Press.

Zeichner, K. (2010). Rethinking the connections between campus courses and field experiences in college- and university-based teacher education. *Journal of Teacher Education, 61*(1/2), 89–99.

Chapter 11
Transitioning to University: A Personal Learning Experience

In this chapter, all four tenets of personalising learning were targeted in a programme that was written to assist pre-service teachers' transition to university in a first year, first semester, core unit in a Bachelor of Education (primary) degree. The chapter describes how student diversity in ICT ability and learning needs were used to frame an approach to teaching and learning the content of the unit, which was focussed on human development and different contexts for learning. The approach is described and demonstrates how ICT can become a vehicle for learning that caters for student diversity and how a seemingly rigid university timetable structure can be used creatively and with flexibility. The notion of value-added assessment is also highlighted.

11.1 Contexts for Learning and Development: A Foundation Education Unit

The unit of focus in this chapter was a first year, first semester unit in a 4-year, undergraduate Bachelor of Education (primary) degree at the regional campus of a national university. The unit, entitled Contexts for Learning and Development, was the first in sequence of six Foundation Education units that were core to the Bachelor of Education programme. Unit content focused on concepts and theories relating to human development with a key goal to instil understanding of the various contexts and developmental issues that might affect school-aged young people as individuals and as members of social groups. In particular, theories of physical, cognitive and psychosocial development were targeted, as was the influence of family, school, peers, culture and other social contexts (local, religious and ethnic communities) on elements of background knowledge, cultural knowledge, inclusiveness and connectedness. This unit was also targeted in the broader Bachelor of Education programme as one that had to have explicit embedding of Information and

© Springer Nature Singapore Pte Ltd. 2018
M. Jones, K. McLean, *Personalising Learning in Teacher Education*,
https://doi.org/10.1007/978-981-10-7930-6_11

Communications Technologies (ICTs) for learning. This content was explicated in the unit's five learning outcomes:

1. Explore and critique basic concepts, theories and research about physical, cognitive and psychosocial aspects of child and adolescent development.
2. Discuss and apply these concepts and theories to an understanding of child and adolescent development.
3. Describe the influences on human development of family, school and peers in relation to cultural and societal context.
4. Consider theoretical frameworks in the observation and explanation of child and adolescent development and behaviour in diverse contexts.
5. Develop and use a range of ICT skills for learning.

11.2 Structure of the Unit

The university ran a 12-week semester in the Bachelor of Education programme with three contact hours per week expected in most units of study. Generally, this expectation translated into weekly 1-h lectures and weekly 2-h tutorials. In order to enhance the personalising of learning in the unit, we trialled a new approach to the traditional structure by designing the unit in two distinct phases. Phase 1 involved the timetabled classes within the university's usual timetable structure of 1-h lectures and 2-h tutorials that ran weekly. This phase ran for the first 6 weeks of the semester. During this phase, pre-service teachers were introduced to a range of theories and models and explored their application to contexts for learning and development. In tutorials, pre-service teachers were placed in one of five "expert" groups and assigned a particular context in which they developed their expertise. These contexts reflected the risk, protective and intervention factors associated with (1) family, (2) gender, (3) culture, (4) health and (5) community. Group members were required to complete the set readings and contribute to discussions and activities both in general and through the particular lens specific to their assigned context. Activities to explore the learning were sometimes run in expert groups and sometimes run in groups of mixed experts, allowing for depth of learning in the assigned context and breadth of learning across contexts.

In Phase 2, pre-service teachers consolidated their learning by applying the content of Weeks 1–6 to an in-depth analysis and reflection on their own transition to university. This analysis and reflection required pre-service teachers to consider the range of contexts and influences in their lives that acted as support structures, risk factors and sources of intervention during their transition to university. The analysis and reflection were linked to a 60% weighted assessment task in which pre-service teachers completed an individual written paper and a group multimedia presentation that utilised selected forms of ICT. To determine the contact time during this second phase of the unit, we conducted an ICT inventory in which pre-service teachers identified ICTs that they were familiar with, confident with and interested in. This enabled us to make an approximation of pre-service teachers' existing exposure, skills and confidence in using different ICTs and to determine the ICTs in which they were most interested in developing their skills. The outcomes of this inventory enabled us to form groups of pre-service teachers who had similar interest areas and, generally, reduced variation in current skill level.

In the first 3 weeks of Phase 2, ICT workshops and group appointments replaced the traditional structure of timetabled classes. These workshops were based on the areas of ICT that pre-service teachers had identified in the inventory as areas they would be interested in. They included PowerPoint design, Web page design, interactive whiteboard, digital photography and video and movie making. Pre-service teachers opted into one, two or more of these workshops depending on their areas of interest and on their group decisions on which forms of multimedia they would present their learning through for assessment. Groups were required to select ICTs to utilise for their multimedia presentations that would enhance their skills and abilities.

Groups with medium-to-low exposure and/or confidence to ICT tended to limit their selection of workshops to two or three, and most group members attended all workshops. Groups with higher levels of exposure and confidence tended to incorporate a wider range of ICTs into their work and often had only one or two group members in attendance at a particular workshop. These group members subsequently became the "expert" for the relevant ICT within their group. Overall, each pre-service teacher was required to attend a minimum of two workshops in a 3-week period. As there were three separate tutorials running in this particular year, we offered three different workshops per week. Some workshops ran more than once (based on demand), and not all workshops were offered each week.

The final few weeks of the unit provided pre-service teachers with time to collate their presentations (Week 10), present them (Week 11) and, finally, reflect on their learning (Week 12). In the presentation week, tutorials were open to other members of the unit (staff and students) as well as invitees from different areas of the university (e.g. student experience office). A summary of the unit's structure and content over the 12-week semester is provided in Table 11.1.

11.3   Unit Assessment

Two assessment tasks contributed to the measurement of pre-service teachers' learning in the unit. The first required pre-service teachers to complete an analysis of a particular context from a period of their own lives in relation to Bronfenbrenner's ecological systems theory (social ecology model). The second task was an individual analysis of transition to university using the theories and models discussed in the unit as a framework for analysis and a group multimedia presentation that highlighted the collective insights of the group in regard to risk, protective and intervention factors that can impact on the transitioning to university. Each task is detailed further below.

Table 11.1 Overview of the unit's content and structure

Week	Content focus	Mode of delivery
1	Structure of unit – modes of delivery and ICT inventory; establish learning group "experts" for different contexts	1-h lecture
		2-h tutorial
2	Contexts – family, gender, health, culture, community	1-h lecture
	Risk and protective factors	2-h tutorial
3	Bronfenbrenner's ecological systems theory	1-h lecture
	Case studies – applying to Bronfenbrenner model	2-h tutorial
4	Stages of development – early stages of development "experts" to contribute perspectives from different contexts	1-h lecture;
		2-h tutorial
5	Middle stages of development "experts" to contribute perspectives from different contexts	1-h lecture
		2-h tutorial
6	Adulthood stages of development	1-h lecture
	Share ICT needs and interests to decide group ICT focus and sign up for Weeks 7–9 workshops	2-h tutorial
7	Group appointment times and voluntary ICT workshops	Workshops
8	Voluntary ICT workshops	Workshops
9	Voluntary ICT workshops	Workshops
10	Presentation preparation/research time	Group work time
11	Multimedia presentations	Presentations in tutorials
12	Reflection and evaluation	1-h lecture
		2-h tutorial

11.3.1 Task 1 Written Analysis

In completing the analysis of a personal life experience in relation to Bronfenbrenner's (1977) ecological systems theory of development (or social ecology model), pre-service teachers needed to provide an overview of the situation/experience and identify and discuss their stage of development and the different influential factors present in their life at this time. Links to theoretical ideas covered through unit content and readings as well as extant literature in the field were also required.

11.3.2 Task 2: Transition to University: Written Paper and Multimedia Presentation

The second task required pre-service teachers to reflect on their transition to university by producing a written paper and a multimedia presentation of their learning over the first 10 weeks of the Bachelor of Education course, which showed an analysis of their experience with respect to the particular ideas covered in the Foundation Education unit.

The Written Paper   To assist the writing of the individual written paper component of the task, pre-service teachers were provided with four initial questions: *Where have I come from? Where am I at in my transition? Where am I going? What factors influence my future direction?* They were asked to consider the theories and models studied in the first 5 weeks of the unit to inform their responses and to submit an interim paper in Week 7. Feedback on areas of strength and those in need of development or refinement was provided on the interim paper, which pre-service teachers then developed into a full and final paper that they submitted for assessment at the end of the unit in Week 12.

The final 1500-word paper was structured in three sections:

1. Application of Theories and Models: where pre-service teachers provided an overview of their transition experience and related it to the theories and models introduced in the unit.
2. ICT Learning: where pre-service teachers reported and reflected on the use of ICT for their group multimedia presentation, showing evidence of growth in their ICT learning.
3. Reflection on Group Work: where pre-service teachers provided a short reflection on the contribution each person made to the group, including themselves. This reflection was based on feedback from their fellow group members and noted what they would do next time to improve their personal contribution and the group's overall productivity.

The Multimedia Presentation   Pre-service teachers were placed in groups to complete the multimedia presentation component of the task. These groupings were based on the results of the ICT inventory described earlier, such that each pre-service teacher worked with others wanting to develop ICT skills in similar areas. Group members also tended to be at approximately similar levels of confidence and/ or prior experience with ICT. The multimedia presentation had to portray the collective insights of the group regarding different aspects of university life and the analysis of these with respect to both the individual and group factors that contributed to an effective transition to university. Attention was required to be given to the identification of risks, protective factors and possible interventions for university students moving through such a transition process. The content for this analysis was to be drawn from each group member's individual written component of the task.

In determining the form(s) of ICT utilised to prepare the multimedia presentation, groups were encouraged to select the ICT medium(s) such that each group member could demonstrate growth in the development of their ICT skills, knowledge and understanding. Selection also needed to be made with consideration to available resources.

11.4   Constructive Alignment of Outcomes Activities and Assessment

The first key reflection in looking at the structure of the Foundation Education unit is on its constructive alignment. As noted earlier in this volume, constructive alignment is critical for achieving deep learning and promotes the placement of the learner at the centre of learning through their active participation (Biggs and Tang 2011). The overview of the unit, reported earlier in this chapter, demonstrates the active participation of students in teaching and learning activities through the use of the "experts" appointed to different contexts for Phase 1 of the unit and through the use of personal experiences of transition to university to develop and present a multimedia presentation that formed the basis of Phase 2 of the unit.

As Biggs and Tang (2011) note, constructive alignment is achieved when learning outcomes, teaching and learning activities and assessment are aligned. They note the common linking of learning outcomes and assessment and the less common linking of teaching and learning activities, particularly with assessment. The importance of constructive alignment between these elements, particularly with assessment, which, in universities, tends to predominantly rely on more surface-type approaches (Ramsden 2003), is that each element of the teaching, learning and assessment mutually supports the other. If, for example, assessment is going to be based on short-answer or, worse, multiple choice-type examinations and tests, then students are unlikely to feel compelled to engage in unit learning activities on a deeper level than that which is required to pass the test. The assessment sets the curriculum as far as students are concerned and also determines the value that students place on different activities (Ramsden 2003). Authentic, meaningful assessment that is closely linked to the teaching and learning activities and learning outcomes will far better motivate and assist students to learn in deep and meaningful ways. Here we illustrate how alignment occurred across all three factors in the way we designed and implemented the Foundation Education unit.

11.4.1   Alignment of Learning Outcomes with Assessment

The 1500-word written piece of work that formed the first assessment piece enabled pre-service teachers to engage with unit concepts, theories and research about physical, cognitive and psychosocial aspects of child and adolescent development (Learning Outcome 1) and apply these concepts and theories (Learning Outcome 2) to explore and understand a situation in their own lives. In doing this, they also engaged with unit content regarding influences of family, school, cultural and societal factors (Learning Outcome 3) on their response to the selected situation whilst drawing on theoretical frameworks in the observation and explanation of child and adolescent development and behaviour in diverse contexts (Learning Outcome 4).

The second task is aligned with the first four learning outcomes in a similar manner to the first task. The first section of Task 2 required pre-service teachers to relate the theories and models introduced in the unit to their personal experience of transition into various aspects of university life. The purpose of this section was to provide pre-service teachers with an opportunity to demonstrate their understanding of the theories and models discussed in the unit (Learning Outcome 1) and how they apply to real life experiences (Learning Outcome 2). In analysing the risks and support structures in their own lives, pre-service teachers were able to identify and understand the influence of various personal, cultural and social contextual factors such as family, school, gender, health, sporting clubs and religious communities, etc. (Learning Outcome 3). Overall, this part of the task focused strongly on the theoretical frameworks in the observation and explanation of their own development and behaviour (Learning Outcome 4).

The group multimedia component of Task 2 consolidated pre-service teachers' engagement with and achievement of learning outcomes. The content of these presentations required pre-service teachers to consider their collective experiences and thus form a more generalised discussion of risk and supportive structures that incorporated the various contexts of individual group members and thus enabled the consideration and application of theories and models across more diverse contexts. As such, Learning Outcomes 1–4 were deepened in the learning that took place through this synthesis work; and the diversity element of Learning Outcome 4 could be more fully addressed.

To achieve the development and use of ICT skills for learning (Learning Outcome 5), we provided a structured and informed process for pre-service teachers to identify their strengths, weaknesses and interest areas in the use of ICT. Through this identification process, pre-service teachers were able to select and demonstrate relevant ICTs through which to complete their multimedia presentation. This ensured their ability to, in particular, demonstrate development of their skills and knowledge of ICT use for learning (Learning Outcome 5).

11.4.2 Alignment of Teaching and Learning Activities with Assessment

With the nature of assessment playing an integral part in how students are said to respond to teaching and learning activities (Ramsden 2003), we were resolute in our intention to provide a deep, meaningful, student-centred approach to the teaching and learning experiences in the unit and to have these closely aligned to the assessment. The first challenge in achieving this was designing the first 6 weeks of the unit (Phase 1), which were heavily content-focused as the various theoretical ideas underpinning human development and social and cultural contexts that influence development and learning were introduced. These theoretical, content-driven aspects of the unit were also incorporated into Phase 2 of the unit in a meaningful way by requiring pre-service teachers to represent their understandings of the content as they applied to their own transition experiences. Furthermore, the highly student-centred ICT-focused workshops made available on the basis of pre-service teachers' selection allowed for additional relevance and meaning to be layered into the learning experience. Each phase of learning and its alignment to assessment is outlined further below.

Phase 1 Teaching and Learning Activities In devising a strategy that would engage pre-service teachers with a sense of responsibility in and importance of both their own and others' learning, we decided to establish "expert" groups around the five key contexts that relate to human development and which were targeted in the unit. These contexts included:

1. Family: age, structure, relationships, etc.
2. Gender: identity
3. Health: physical, mental, emotional, activity and disability
4. Culture: ethnicity and cultural practices
5. Community: church, school, neighbourhood, workplace and clubs

Pre-service teachers as an "expert" in their assigned context were responsible for representing the key ideas, issues and implications of the various discussion topics throughout Phase 1 learning. They met in expert groups to discuss the set readings, using their context as a particular lens for these discussions. At times, one "expert" from each group joined others to form a group of mixed "experts" where topics could be discussed and considered from multiple perspectives. In this way learning had depth for individuals in their particular context area and breadth as they shared insights and issues with their peers from other expert groups.

As noted earlier, topics throughout Phase 1 were focused on human development and ecological systems theory, where pre-service teachers considered risk and protective factors from the different contexts of their expert groups and within different layers of Bronfenbrenner's Social Ecology Model. A number of case study situations were provided to ensure pre-service teachers could engage with the material in an analytical and creative way, thus engaging higher-order thinking approaches to the teaching and learning. These case studies also allowed for a number of opportunities to "rehearse" the application of theory to practical examples, thus utilising an aspect of Grossman et al. (2009) core practices approach as a pedagogy specific to effective teacher education in the current literature.

This Phase 1 learning aligned closely with both assessment tasks and the first one in particular, where pre-service teachers applied the range of learning and ideas in an analysis of an experience from their own past. The types of experiences selected by students included the birth of a sibling, the death of a family member, parents' separation/divorce, a significant sporting achievement, etc.

Phase 2 Teaching and Learning Activities Phase 2 learning was highly student-centred as it focused on pre-service teachers' own stories regarding their transition to university and was presented through forms of ICT they selected as both areas of interest and areas of ICT in which they could demonstrate personal skill development. These selected ICTs were then used to create a multimedia presentation through which they communicated their transition stories. The learning activities were selected by pre-service teachers from a suite of ICT workshops, of which availability was based on preferences identified by pre-service teachers in an ICT inventory. This ensured that selection of workshops were relevant to pre-service teachers' skills and interests and met them at their level of need.

Working in groups assigned on the basis of ICT interests and past experiences, pre-service teachers were challenged to select ICTs that would enable them to demonstrate growth in their ICT abilities. Evidencing this growth was supported by the pre- and post-ICT inventory as well as through a reflective discussion that was incorporated into the individual written paper that formed one component of the second assessment task, the individual written paper.

As noted earlier, the individual written paper also required pre-service teachers to present their university transition story in light of the Phase 1 theoretical ideas covered in the unit. The third component of this task targeted the pre-service teachers' contribution to their group. Each group member had to write a short review of the strengths that each other person brought to the group. They were asked to share these insights with one another, so when they came to write the reflection on their own contribution, they could draw on their own insights as well as those of their fellow group members. This informed assessment by helping to identify appropriate contributions to group work, as it became quickly evident if someone had not made suitable contributions to the group's productivity without engaging pre-service teachers in a blaming and accusatory form of reflection that can sometimes inhibit personal reflection when group work is employed. Grades associated with group components of the task were adjusted if particular individuals appeared to have made insufficient *collaborative* efforts in their group.

The alignment between the workshop focus of Phase 2 learning and the group multimedia presentation is self-evident. The approach used was also highly student-centred, ICT-focused and collaborative and encouraged a focus on Lifelong Learning. As such, this and other aspects of the unit were delivered in a manner that aligned with tenets of personalising learning. These connections are outlined further in the remaining sections of this chapter.

11.5   Personalising Learning in the Foundation Education Unit

The first five chapters of this book unpack the various theoretical and practical ideas that inform the tenets of personalising learning. These tenets (Learner as Central, Communities of Collaboration, ICT and Lifelong Learning (Keamy et al. 2007)) are considered below in relation to how they were achieved in the Foundation Education unit. Pre-service teachers' feedback from unit evaluations is embedded in these descriptions to illustrate the ways in which the approach was received and how it impacted the learning process and perceptions of the outcomes.

11.5.1 Learner As Central

Placing the Learner as Central in teacher education is essential for a host of reasons. These have been discussed both in this chapter and earlier in this book and are generally related to active participation, deep learning and student motivation and engagement. Learner as Central also addresses issues of student diversity and better enables for inclusivity. It is an important focus given concerns around teachers' lack of preparation for managing diverse learning needs (Rouse 2017). Placing pre-service teachers at the centre of the learning was a particular challenge in the planning of the unit as it contained a highly theoretical content focus. We were loathe to deliver this heavy content focus in the traditional transmission-type approaches associated with what Ramsden (2003) describes as the usual passive-type instruction of university teaching, which had certainly been the primary mode of delivery in the past years that this unit had been taught.

Whilst direct instruction modes of delivery can have a place in teaching and learning, we share the views of many researchers in the field of social constructivism, that more participatory modes of learning should be employed in university teaching if student engagement is to be achieved. As Schwartz et al. (2009) describe:

> Direct instruction can be very effective, assuming that people have sufficient prior knowledge to construct new knowledge from what they are being told or shown. In many cases, they do not. For example, a challenge in pre-service teacher education courses is that the students do not have sufficient prior knowledge of teaching in the classroom. In their teacher preparation courses, it is hard for the students to see the significance of the theories and map them into their future pupils' behaviours. Moreover, they lack a repository of personal instances that round out the specific examples used during instruction. (p. 39)

Outside of non-compulsory senior secondary school psychology, it is highly unlikely that pre-service teachers in their first semester of teacher education study would have encountered much in the way of human development theory or ecological systems theory; and even if they had prior exposure to these fields of study, it is unlikely they had been considered through the lens of being/becoming a teacher. This context made Schwartz et al.'s (2009) warning of particular relevance to us as we decided how to best assist pre-service teachers' meaningful engagement with the unit content. It was with consideration of this issue that we decided to contextualise the teaching and learning around pre-service teachers' own lives and learning experiences. This was the first key manner in which learners were placed at the centre of learning and something that pre-service teachers indicated in their unit evaluations as being valuable to their knowledge development and their overall experience of learning in the unit.

The lectures have been very informative and the tutorials enabled me to feel valued and empowered me with a feeling that I can make a difference to my students. (Pre-service teacher – 13)

A second key strategy used to ensure learners were central to the teaching and learning approach was through the use of "expert" groups in Phase 1 of the unit and through self-identified and selected ICT focus areas for completing the multimedia presentation. As described earlier, ICT workshops and group appointments were scheduled in Weeks 7–9 of the unit in lieu of timetabled lectures and tutorials. This allowed us to cater for differing needs of individuals within groups. Each group was expected to attend at least two workshops relevant to their identified ICT and one group appointment with teaching staff. The final multimedia product and individual written paper had to clearly demonstrate skills attained by each person in their targeted ICT.

It (the unit) encouraged individual learning. (Pre-service teacher – 4)

The way we were able to follow what we were interested during our ICT component was helpful as it made me responsible for my research into the topics. I found it helpful instead of being told what I should learn. (Pre-service teacher – 27)

To strengthen the sense of personalisation, once we had collated the results of the ICT inventory and grouped pre-service teachers accordingly, we provided them with a personal letter of invitation outlining their allocation to a group and offering suggestions for the group to commence their planning. A sample of this letter can be found in the Appendix. As can be seen, this letter provided a personal touch to the group allocation process and formalised the learning and collaboration that was expected. Pre-service teachers found the personalised approach empowering and indicated that they felt that their particular learning needs had been carefully considered and planned for.

It (the unit) not only encouraged individual learning but also enabled the development of the ICT of my own choice. (Pre-service teacher – 4)

I personally found the [multimedia] presentation very helpful for my learning. The work done on our own presentation was helpful but I found watching others' presentations were a great learning tool. (Pre-service teacher – 22)

These learning activities, contextualised in the unique individual experiences of each pre-service teacher, meant they were able to engage with learning outcomes in authentic and meaningful ways and in ways that made the learning experience enjoyable. The element of choice in these learning activities was essential in providing this meaning, authenticity and overall experience of enjoyment throughout the learning and assessment. As Froese (2017) notes, providing choice "can enhance both satisfaction and academic performance" (p. 121). Choice also creates a sense of responsibility and ownership, and this is reflected by one pre-service teacher in particular, who commented that:

Through not having structured lectures and tutorial, the onus was put on us to take responsibility for our own learning. (Pre-service teacher – 25)

11.5.2 Communities of Collaboration

Promoting Communities of Collaboration is another critical component of personalising learning and was instrumental in the design and delivery of the Foundation Education unit. The "expert" groups in Phase 1 of the unit provided the initial experience of learning both individually and through collaboration, a twofold experience Keamy et al. (2007) claim to be important in achieving their Communities of Collaboration tenet. Individual learning merged with collaboration was promoted throughout lectures and tutorials and in instances of student-centred and direct instruction. Individuals were charged with the responsibility to become "expert" (at least relative to others in their tutorial grouping) in a particular context related to learning. Led by teacher educators in lecture and tutorial settings, "experts" were called upon to comment on the given content through the lens of their assigned context. This enabled individual experts to contribute to the collaboration that became the primary method of learning. This involvement and responsibility also helped to ensure the sense of "expertise" and the sense of belonging and contributing were shared equitably throughout the group members. It also engaged pre-service teachers in what Lave and Wenger (1991) described as "legitimate peripheral participation" as they established themselves in the wider community of their peers (other newcomers) and teacher educators (old-timers) and established their identity within the community as a knowledgeable practitioner, as encouraged by Fuller (2007).

In Phase 2 of the unit, the Communities of Collaboration relied even more heavily on one another's and their own participation in the group. Being challenged to incorporate multiple examples of ICT in their multimedia presentations, groups had to nominate members to attend particular ICT workshops and lead the integration of the relevant ICT in the group's presentation. They also had to work collaboratively to share their experiences of transition to university and to analyse and synthesise these experiences into a coherent framework for inclusion in their presentations. Only through active participation and authentic collaboration could this be achieved.

> I enjoyed the independent and flexible learning coupled with the opportunity to be involved with different group work. (Pre-service teacher – 23)

> The group activity on the ICT learning was a good way to not only develop ICT skills, but organisation and cooperation skills. (Pre-service teacher – 34)

Removing the traditional timetable structure from this second phase of the unit was important in promoting an authentic Community of Collaboration in this component of the learning. Had we attempted to deliver Phase 2 learning through the traditional lecture-tutorial approach, learning would be contrived, and the timetable would serve as an artificial structure to deliver content that was meaningful to some but not others throughout the ICT-focused learning. Moving to an elective-based programme in which pre-service teachers discussed within their groups who should attend and take responsibility for what better ensured authentic collaboration before, during and after the workshops, pre-service teachers decided as a group what their individual and collective ICT goals were in relation to creating a multimedia presentation. Individuals then attended selected workshops, making the learning meaningful and relevant, and subsequently became the group expert in ensuring this area of ICT was utilised effectively and efficiently in the creation of the multimedia presentation. In this way, Phase 2 saw the Communities of Collaboration become the vehicle for the learning, something that Hughes et al. (2007) purport as a defining factor in establishing learning through a Communities of Practice approach.

11.5.3   ICT As a Key Enabler

The inclusion of ICT as a key enabler of learning was self-evident in the unit as it dominated the whole of Phase 2 learning. The ICT was used as the topic, content and medium of learning and assessment throughout this component of the unit.

In planning for the incorporation of ICT in the unit, our primary concern was in ensuring that an authentic and seamless integration of ICT was taking place, where the ICT was more than just a "tool" for learning. We were interested in the more powerful application of ICT as a "vehicle for learning" (Jones and McLean 2012). As noted in Chap. 4, making ICT the vehicle for learning relies on the relationship between pedagogical considerations and the characteristics of ICT applied to the learning episode or activity. This relationship is evident in the design of the Foundation Education unit in the way in which pre-service teachers were given ownership of the ICTs they were to learn about and the instructional design supported this choice in a meaningful way. This approach to choice of learning and associated workshop attendance also validates Keamy et al.'s (2007) assertion of the capacity of ICT to cater for diversity in both skills and interests and enhances interactivity between peers. This was achieved in the Foundation Education unit through the culmination of pre-service teachers' individual learning in the jointly prepared multimedia presentation. The process and product of creating the multimedia presentation was also demonstrative of the way in which ICT can be "a personal cognitive and social tool" that the Organisation for Economic Co-operation and Development [OECD] (2006, p. 11) encourages.

The assessment of the ICT component of the unit received significant attention and extremely careful consideration as we designed the multimedia task and associated marking criteria. The unit's learning outcome concerned with ICT states that pre-service teachers were expected to *develop* and *use* a *range* of *ICT skills* for learning (Learning Outcome 5). We read the intention of this learning outcome as targeting the extent to which pre-service teachers were able to *develop* their use and skills of ICT and to incorporate a *range* of ICTs when considering this development. This focus on *development* led us to query how we could demonstrate *equity* in the measurement of ICT use and skill development in the task.

In the mid-2000s, the level of ICT exposure and capability among our commencing teacher candidates was quite varied. This may have been exacerbated by the fact that we worked at a regionally based university campus, which attracted candidates from surrounding regional and rural settings where ICT access is historically known to be behind that of larger, more metropolitan settings (Lyons et al. 2006). Even though rural and regional students did make up the majority of the student population, being situated reasonably close to a large regional centre and an even larger metropolitan city, the student population profile did attract some of its candidates from these larger regional and metropolitan settings, leading to something of a mixed pre-service teacher demographic. To ensure background privilege in regard to previous ICT exposure and access was not weighted too heavily in how pre-service teachers were assessed on their ICT skill development, we decided to use a "value-added" form of assessment of ICT-related criteria. After all, if a person is already highly skilled in the use of ICT, it can be difficult for them to show further development compared to someone who begins at a lower level of ability. Furthermore, the ICT product of someone who is already highly skilled is likely to be superior to that of another who enters the task with a relatively lower skill base. We wanted to ensure that all pre-service teachers had an opportunity to demonstrate and be acknowledged for meaningful growth and development in their ICT skills and usage, regardless of their ability entry point.

This was another significant way in which the assessment was designed with a focus on personalising the learning.

Measurement of ICT Skill Development It is well known that learners respond to learning challenges based on a range of factors, including their interest in and perceived relevance of the topic, their sense of what they will gain from their engagement and effort and their perception of the task's difficulty and achievability (Barber 1999; Eccles and Wigfield 2015). Barber suggests that expecting more from students whilst building their self-esteem is more likely to result in feelings of competency, motivation and, overall, more successful learning outcomes. Meanwhile, Eccles and Wigfield (2015) indicate that both internal (self) and external (others') expectations have an effect on establishing a sense of competency in learners. Hence, when designing assessment, the level of challenge needs to be carefully set to allow for individual differences. Only when these individual differences are catered for will the task be successful in eliciting maximum effort and motivation from all learners. Given the known diversity in individual differences when it comes to ICT, the notion of personalising learning to set an appropriate challenge for all pre-service teachers is paramount. This also helps to address the more general concern in education at all levels that meaningful participation in learning be available to and accessible by all learners (Rouse 2017). A value-added approach to assessment is one way of achieving such a state for maximising meaningful engagement and learning potential for all.

In light of this need for differentiation to motivate and engage all pre-service teachers, we designed the ICT components of the multimedia task around how much growth pre-service teachers were able to evidence in their final submission. They were able to demonstrate this growth through the pre- and post-ICT inventory results as well as through their personal reflection on their ICT experience, which was a section of the individual written paper that formed a part of this task. In their unit evaluations, pre-service teachers acknowledged the success we achieved in meeting this goal, as they commented on the relevance and sense of being catered for as an individual within the group. For example:

> I enjoyed the way the ICT skills part of this unit was structured. It allowed me and other students to engage in the ICT skill where we had never engaged in before. Thus my opportunities were great and increase my level of knowledge and skill. (Pre-service teacher – 18)

> I thought that the structure of choosing our own ICT area with our skills in mind was really good as each person could expand on their own learning and no one was bored or way over their own skill level. (Pre-service teacher – 33)

11.5.4 Lifelong Learning

As noted in Chap. 6, it can be difficult to provide a set of steps for operationalising the concept of Lifelong Learning, as it is more of a mindset than a particular action or approach. In spite of this abstract nature of the idea of Lifelong Learning, there are authors who indicate that particular approaches to teaching, learning and assessment are more likely than others to engender the necessary mindset to promote learning across the lifespan. In particular, Saribas (2015), drawing on the work of Knapper and Cropley (2000), suggests that dispositions towards Lifelong Learning are engendered through learning that involves students as active participants; that engage students in both planning and assessment of their learning and when there are opportunities to learn from others, including teachers, mentors and peers. She also encourages learning experiences that take place in a range of settings – formal (e.g. the classroom) and informal (e.g. in the wider environment) – in order to facilitate attitudes that promote Lifelong Learning outcomes.

The ability to cope in a rapidly changing world, particularly in regard to technology (Manyika 2016), provides a strong impetus for promoting approaches to Lifelong Learning in education. In discussing the impact of technology and ICT on such a need, we recall Manyika's recommendation that education emphasises creativity and critical and systems thinking. Along similar lines, the Foundation for Young Australians [FYA] (2016) calls for the incorporation of transferrable skills and practices that promote higher-order thinking. A number of these elements, as well as those from Saribas (2015), were incorporated into the teaching, learning and assessment approaches in the Foundation Education unit, suggesting that the way the unit was delivered is likely to promote a Lifelong Learning outlook among pre-service teachers. We have breifly outlined these elements and the ways we addressed them in the unit below.

Active Participation Pre-service teachers were active participants in the roles they played as "experts" to develop their own and others' learning about the potential impact of an assigned context (family, gender, health, culture, community) on the development of a person. Pre-service teachers were also actively involved in the selection and learning of relevant ICTs and their use in presenting their learning through a group multimedia presentation.

Engaged in Planning Pre-service teachers were active in planning the ICT learning they wished to pursue, relating it to their own, individual learning needs. They were also then able to plan the ways in which the ICTs they were learning about could be used in a group multimedia presentation.

Learning from Others The expert roles assigned to pre-service teachers in Phase 1 of the unit placed responsibility for their own and others' learning on everyone in the class. Sharing insights about human development from the lens they were to be expert in meant there was substantial learning from one another within the structure and stimuli provided by the teacher educators. In Phase 2 of the unit, groups nominated particular members to be responsible for the learning and skill development in different ICTs they wanted to incorporate into their multimedia presentation. These individuals attended workshops specific to the selected ICT, which were focused on skill development and run by the teacher educators. Individuals then returned to and became the expert on the given ICT within their group. Here, learning from others – teachers and peers – was paramount to success. Finally, in presenting their work to one another in the culminating presentation week, pre-service teachers were able to strengthen their knowledge and understanding of the wide range of factors that can impact human development, particularly around the context of transitioning to university.

Formal and Informal Settings Whilst the learning undertaken in the unit was predominantly formal, there were a number of less formal strategies also adopted, including some use of informal settings. In particular, whilst learning about selected ICTs through attendance at the nominated workshop, the fact that there was independence in the selection of which workshop(s) to attend reduced the formality of this part of the unit. There were also weeks in the schedule in which groups attended group meetings with one another and group appointments with the teacher educators, which allowed for less formal settings in which the learning took place.

Creativity and Critical and Systems Thinking Throughout the process of preparing a multimedia presentation, pre-service teachers were engaged in creative thinking, critical thinking and systems thinking. Creativity was utilised in the use of the various ICTs pre-service teachers selected, for example, the way in which they filmed their video or the photographs they took and how these were embedded in the presentation, etc. The content focus being on the synthesis of group members' transition experiences in regard to the theoretical content of the unit (risk, protective and intervention factors associated with their different contexts) meant critical thinking was required to conduct the necessary analysis and subsequent synthesis. Finally, connecting their own and one another's stories to Bronfenbrenner's (1977) ecological model also meant that systems thinking was achieved in regard to how the various systems of the model were at play in their lives.

Transferrable Skills Promoting Higher-Order Thinking Similar to the critical thinking, systems thinking and overall synthesis that were required to complete the multimedia task described above, higher-order thinking was engendered through the nature of the task. According to Bloom (1956), higher forms of thinking, which are represented in his "taxonomy of thinking domains", involve applying, analysing, synthesising and evaluating. Pre-service teachers were engaged in these higher forms of thinking by analysing their own and others' transition experiences, applying Bronfenbrenner's (1977) ecological systems theory to their personal development, synthesising their experiences into a single coherent presentation and creating a multimedia presentation of this synthesis using new or expanded ICT skills. In Phase 1 learning, higher-order thinking was also embedded in the learning experience as pre-service teachers were called upon to analyse case studies in relation to Bronfenbrenner's (1977) ecological systems theory and the "expert" lens defined by their assigned context.

Fostering learning that places the learning responsibility on the pre-service teachers, and having them practice ways in which to enact their learning in this way, hopefully instils the sorts of habits and motivation for learning that hold these learners in good stead beyond their years of schooling and tertiary education. Certainly the work of people such as Deci and Ryan (1985) suggests that the provision of the types of flexible learning with multiple pathways that cater for all students should yield such motivation for learning. Utilising the various approaches to teaching and learning that we have outlined in this section, approaches that are actually embedded in other tenets of personalising learning, should precipitate the mindsets and propensities for Lifelong Learning. Evidencing this, however, requires a longitudinal study that we are yet to undertake.

11.6 Conclusion

As mentioned in the introduction to this book, it was the experience as teacher educators in designing, facilitating and reflecting on this particular unit of work that served as the impetus for us to examine our practice for other ways in which personalising learning could be embedded into teacher education. This example, addressing all four tenets of personalising learning, did not disappoint in its outcomes for pre-service teachers' sense of feeling catered for, in terms of their learning needs, motivational needs and more general emotional needs as they worked through what can be a very difficult transition into tertiary learning. We believe it sets an example for teacher education that looks at the holistic needs of the beginning pre-service teacher and illustrates the creative potential for doing things differently in an otherwise unchanged structure of timetabling. We were successful in leveraging the students' and our own availability to provide learning that allowed for meaningful choice, relevance, appropriate challenge, independence, collaboration and reflection. As it turned out, personalising the learning in this way led to an enjoyable and effective learning experience for our pre-service teachers, as well as an enriching and life-giving teaching experience for ourselves.

Appendix: Sample Letter for Pre-service Teachers' Group Allocation

Name: *Stewart Dent*   **Group Number:**   *3*

Dear *Stewart*

You have been assigned to Group Number *3*. Other members of your group are *Mirander Dobe, John Lemon, and Emily Mose*.

Groups were determined using the information you provided in the ICT inventory, completed online in the first week of the course. This has enabled us to identify how you see your skill level for various ICT applications and the particular areas of ICT you are interested in developing. We have tried to group you with students of a similar skill level who have similar areas of interest.

Your group's self-assessed abilities range from *Medium to Medium-High*. The main areas of interest for development identified by members in your group were: Web Pages and Movie Maker.

You will have some time today to meet your group members and discuss and finalise the ICT media you would like to use for your multimedia presentation assessment task. Please keep in mind the suggestions made in the lecture (and noted below) of applications that might be better suited to the current abilities of the group. We want you to be able to assist you in extending your ICT skills in a manageable and achievable way.

In your group meeting today you will also need to determine the areas you would like to have ICT workshops focus on. Please let your tutor know which areas you identify, and how many members of your group will likely attend each workshop. This will help us finalise the number and types of workshops we run in Weeks 8–9.

All the best with your planning.

Karen and Mellita.

Workshop Suggestions

Generally speaking, groups should consider developing their skills according to their current skill level where we would suggest:

Low to Medium Low skill levels

- PowerPoint
- Digital Photography: – photo download; photo editing and inserting in documents

Medium skill levels

- Interactive Whiteboard/Advanced PowerPoint
- Web Page Development
- Basic Movie-Maker – downloading video; basic editing; inserting movie files in documents.

Medium-high to High skill levels

- Advanced Movie-maker – advanced editing techniques
- Marrying a number of ICTs together for presentation (e.g., Web with Movie/ Photography/Sound file links)

Nb: Names have been changed to protect pre-service teachers' identity.

References

Barber, M. (1999). Taking the tide at the flood: Transforming the middle years of schooling. In *National middle years of schooling conference redesigning the middle years*. Melbourne: Zbar & Schapper Consulting.

Biggs, J., & Tang, C. (2011). *Teaching for quality learning at university* (4th ed.). New York: Open University Press.

Bloom, B. (Ed.). (1956). *Taxonomy of educational objectives. Book I: The cognitive domain*. New York: Longman.

Bronfenbrenner, U. (1977). Toward an experimental ecology of human development. *American Psychologist, 32*(7), 513–531.

Deci, E., & Ryan, R. (1985). *Intrinsic motivation and self-determination in human behaviour*. New York: Plenum Press.

Eccles, J., & Wigfield, A. (2015). Academic achievement motivation, development of. In D. Wright (Ed.), *International encyclopedia of social and behavioral sciences* (2nd ed., pp. 20–25). Elsevier.

Foundation for Young Australians (FYA). (2016). *The new basics: Big data reveals the skills young people need for the new work order*. Report prepared for FYA by AlphaBeta. Retrieved from https://www.fya.org.au/wp-content/uploads/2016/04/The-New-Basics_Update_Web.pdf

Froese, P. (2017). The benefits of choice in education: A Canadian perspective. In M. Etherington (Ed.), *What teachers need to know: Topics in diversity and inclusion* (pp. 121–140). Eugene: Wipf & Stock.

Fuller, A. (2007). Critiquing theories of learning and communities of practice. In J. Hughes, N. Jewson, & L. Unwin (Eds.), *Communities of practice: Critical perspectives* (pp. 17–29). Oxon: Routledge.

Grossman, P., Hammerness, K., & McDonald, M. (2009). Redefining teaching, re-imagining teacher education. *Teachers and Teaching, 15*(2), 273–289.

Hughes, J., Jewson, N., & Unwin, L. (Eds.). (2007). *Communities of practice: Critical perspectives*. Oxon: Routledge.

Jones, M., & McLean, K. J. (2012). Personalising learning in teacher education through the use of technology. *Australian Journal of Teacher Education, 37*(1). https://doi.org/10.14221/ajte.2012v37n1.1.

Keamy, K., Nicholas, H., Mahar, S., & Herrrick, C. (2007). *Personalising education: From research to policy and practice*. Melbourne: Department of Education and Early Childhood Development.

Knapper, C., & Cropley, A. J. (2000). *Lifelong learning in higher education*. London: Kogan Page.

Lave, J., & Wenger, E. (1991). *Situated learning: Legitimate peripheral participation (learning in doing: Social, cognitive and computational perspectives)*. Cambridge: Cambridge University Press.

Lyons, T., Cooksey, R., Panizzon, D., Parnell, A., & Pegg, J. (2006). *Science, ICT and mathematics education in rural and regional Australia the SiMERR national survey: A research report* prepared for the Department of Education, Science and Training, National Centre of Science, ICT and Mathematics Education for Rural and Regional Australia, University of New England.

Manyika, J. (2016). *Technology, jobs and the future of work.* Briefing Note prepared for the Fortune Vatican Forum December 2016. McKinsey Global Institute.

Organisation for Economic Co-operation and Development [OECD]. (2006). *Schooling for tomorrow: Personalising education*. Paris: Centre for Educational Research and Innovation, OECD.

Ramsden, P. (2003). *Learning to teach in higher education* (2nd ed.). London: Routledge Falmer.

Rouse, M. (2017). A role for teachers and teacher education in developing inclusive practice. In M. Etherington (Ed.), *What teachers need to know: Topics in diversity and inclusion* (pp. 19–35). Eugene: Wipf & Stock.

Saribas, D. (2015). Investigating the relationship between pre-service teachers' scientific literacy, environmental literacy and life-long learning tendency. *Science Education International, 26*(1), 80–100.

Schwartz, D., Lindgren, R., & Lewis, S. (2009). Constructivism in an age of non-constructivist assessments. In S. Tobias & T. Duffy (Eds.), *Constructivist instruction: Success or failure?* (pp. 34–61). New York: Routledge.

Chapter 12
A Synthesis of Practice Applications in Teacher Education

This chapter examines the cogent features of the practice examples of personalising learning in teacher education that have been depicted in the second part of this book. The key practices that appear to provide successful achievement of each of the four tenets for personalising learning: Learner as Central, Communities of Collaboration, ICT and Lifelong Learning are synthesised and presented. Taken together, the sections comprising this chapter provide a synthesis of practice that informs the emergence of a guide for visualising personalising learning in teacher education.

12.1 Introduction

In the second part of this book, we have provided a number of examples in which the four tenets of personalising learning have been applied to our teacher education practice. Applications of Learner as Central and Communities of Collaboration have been particularly visible in these examples, inevitability a consequence of our personal philosophies ingrained in sociocultural theory (Vygotsky 1978). Situated learning, through the use of partnerships with schools, and sometimes other community organisations, has also been prolific in the practices we have presented. These situated elements of our work, manifested through school-based practices, are associated with the authenticity and relevance of learning that we constantly aspire to embed in the design of our teaching. The relationship between these predominant elements of our practice, alongside those that are perhaps less prevailing, but selectively placed (such as the use of ICT), and the tenets of personalising learning identified by Keamy et al. (2007) are described in the individual sections dedicated to each tenet below. Together they provide a synthesis of practice for personalising learning in teacher education that supports other established pedagogies of teacher education such as work integrated learning (Patrick et al. 2008), core practices (Grossman et al. 2009), congruent teaching (Swennen et al. 2008) and critical reflective practice (Loughran 2014) that we hope can inform and refine

© Springer Nature Singapore Pte Ltd. 2018
M. Jones, K. McLean, *Personalising Learning in Teacher Education*,
https://doi.org/10.1007/978-981-10-7930-6_12

practice to help ensure that meaningful, relevant, challenging and effective teacher education prevails into the future of Australian teacher education.

12.2   Learner as Central

Making the learner central in teacher education essentially requires less lecture-style approaches to teaching and more collaborative group work that is focused on conducting, analysing, applying and evaluatingconcepts and ideas in meaningful contexts. These elements of Learner as Central can be seen throughout the examples presented in this book. We summarise these elements below in relation to the teaching, learning and assessment that are conducted within meaningful contexts and are constructively aligned.

12.2.1   Meaningful Contexts

Meaningful contexts can have different implications for different learners, due to the very personal nature of something actually being "meaningful". In teacher education, the shared goal of entering the teaching profession helps to narrow the scope of the personal nature of what a meaningful context might be. Hence, for us, the school-based setting presents as significant for providing the personal, meaningful context for the achievement of personalising learning. This focus on school-based settings aligns with the premise of work integrated learning (Patrick et al. 2008), which is established as an approach that provides relevance and was of particular importance for providing the meaningful context in the *Tell Tales,Digi-Tell* and the *Science Teaching in Schools Experience (STISE)* programmes described in Chaps. 8, 9 and 10, respectively. Also important in these school-based elements of curriculum and pedagogy units is the concurrent university-based learning that was featured alongside the schools component, which allowed for effective critical reflection on practice to inform learning (Loughran 2014).

It is already known, although often forgotten, how important both the school and the university settings are in providing the most effective learning about teaching (see, e.g., Darling-Hammond 2012; Korthagen 2011, 2016; Loughran and Hamilton 2016). The reasons for this stem from the importance of learning through mastery experience that builds self-efficacy belief in one's competence (Bandura 1986), as well as expert-facilitated reflective practice, whereby teacher educators can assist pre-service teachers to examine and understand their experiences in light of established theories about teaching and learning.

Some might argue that learning about theory-informed approaches to teaching can occur without the school-based mastery experience opportunities. However, without meaningful school-based mastery experience, connections between theory and practice are more difficult, if not impossible, to achieve. This has been shown historically through the "apprenticeship of observation" approaches to teacher education that have been consistently revealed to be lacking (Aspland 2006; Lortie 1975). The teacher educator's domain is to inform the ways in which theory speaks to practice and, reciprocally, how practice speaks to the evolution of theory. In this space, practice and theory are constantly challenged, refined, reformed and developed. Without the facilitation of this probing of theory and practice, that falls in the realm of teacher education research, teaching and learning risks remaining unchallenged and unchanged.

Some (and often politicians in particular) have implied that there may not necessarily be anything wrong with a return to the traditional curriculum and hence maintenance of the status quo. However, without challenge and change that have accompanied deepening understanding of how different people learn, and how people learn differently, we would still have the old Victorian-era sized classes of 70–100 children, the use of corporal punishment to "encourage" learning and rote learning and transmission of content that, in its time, created a society in which only the privileged few found education accessible. Indeed, through the challenge and evolution of theory and practice, education is more widespread and more accessible today than it has ever been.

Another way in which meaningful context was demonstrated in the examples reported in this book include the assessment links between the teaching and learning process and the culminating products of these experiences; or in other words, the constructive alignment that Biggs and Tang (2011) contend is so important in higher education pedagogy. For example, the presenting to families and the wider school community that was a part of *Tell Tales* and *Digi-Tell*, and the written reports with children's work samples attached that the science pre-service teachers prepared and submitted to their schools, made the assessment products of the pre-service teachers' learning highly authentic. This authenticity added a layer of meaning and relevance to the work that pre-service teachers were undertaking. They saw the requirements not only as the assessment contributing to their university results but something significant for the children, the parents and the schools. The responsibility fell outside of how their effort affected only themselves. The extent of their effort in these examples had implications for others, and this "raised the bar" in their own minds as to the standards of performance and expectations that they set for themselves.

The focus on meaningful context in the transition to universitylearning experience of the Foundation Education unit reported in Chap. 11 was created in two key ways. Firstly, meaningful context was promoted by having pre-service teachers apply and analyse the unit's heavy theoretical basis in the context of their own lives and, in particular, their transition to university experience. Secondly, it was embedded in the multimedia presentations that pre-service teachers created to showcase their synthesised learning about risk, protective and intervention factors in transition to university experiences, using a highly personalised and targeted approach to pre-service teachers' development in skills and use of ICT. This tailored and supported approach to developing pre-service teachers' ICT skills was paramount in making their learning experience meaningful, relevant, challenging, achievable and constructively aligned.

12.2.2   Constructive Alignment

The examples of practice reported through *Tell Tales*, *Digi-Tell*, *STISE* and the design and delivery of the Foundation Education unit focusing on pre-service teachers' transition to university all exemplified the deep learning that is associated with constructive alignment (Biggs and Tang 2011). To consider the parameters to achieve constructive alignment, we recall Biggs and Tang's (2011) requirement for the teaching, learning and assessment processes to be mutually supportive and aligned. This occurs, they say, when what is being assessed is representative of what is required for the learning to be achieved. In other words, it is where processes of learning are consistent with the ways in which the outcomes are measured. Thus, set a test if you want students to learn by rote and memorise facts to recall; engage them in application and analysis if you want them to demonstrate problem solving, knowledge and skills in action. Given the highly active nature of teaching, surely it is the latter of these examples that needs to be pursued in teacher education.

The ways in which the processes and products of learning were achieved in the examples presented in this manuscript are almost self-evident. In *Tell Tales*, *Digi-Tell* and *STISE*, the intended outcomes of the learning were associated with pre-service teachers' development of knowledge and skills to teach the associated discipline areas (literacy and science) and, subsequently, to assess their own and children's learning in effective, theory-informed ways. Aligned with these outcomes, the teaching and learning processes presented relevant theory, engaged pre-service teachers in analysis and application of this theory to plan a learning sequence and then required them to teach the learning sequence to children in a school setting. This process meant that Swennen et al.'s (2008) congruent teaching was embedded and Patrick et al.'s (2008) work integrated learning supported both the constructive alignment and the critical reflective practice touted by many (e.g. Brandenburg et al. 2017; Jones and Ryan 2014; Korthagen 2011; Loughran 2006; Loughran and Hamilton 2016; Zeichner and Liston 2014) as essential for learning and teaching about teaching. Pre-service teachers were also required to monitor and assess children's learning and to reflect on their own learning and development. The link between the activities that pre-service teachers were engaged in here was reflected in the very elements described by the learning intentions. Moreover, the assessment was not conducted on pre-service teachers' responses in a test of questions about theories and actions but rather on the planning, implementation and evidence of assessment conducted. Alignment is strong throughout these examples.

Constructive alignment was also a significant element of the more university-based example of the Foundation Education unit presented in Chap. 11. In this unit, the learning intention was around building pre-service teachers' understanding of the influence human development and particular contexts a person's life (the ecology) has on their learning and development. Development of ICT skills and use was also built into the intended outcomes of this unit. In achieving an understanding of the highly theoretical focus of the unit, the analysis and application of the various theories were aligned with pre-service teachers' own life experiences and the transition to university that they were experiencing as they studied the unit. This alignment between content and personal experience made the otherwise abstract notions of human development and ecological systems theory tangible, because pre-service teachers could link the ideas to their own lives and personal experiences. To complete the alignment in this unit, assessment was also based on the experiences pre-service teachers had, whereby they presented their understandings of the theories and how they translated through a synthesis of experiences in a group multimedia presentation. This aligned both the learning of theory and how it applies in real-life situations and the development and use of ICT skills; a complete sweep, personalising the constructively aligned teaching, learning and assessment.

12.2.3   Active Participation

Tell Tales, *Digi-Tell*, *STISE* and the Foundation Education unit all necessitated the active participation of pre-service teachers. Participation in the former three of these four programmes involved pre-service teachers in planning a learning sequence, teaching this sequence to children in schools and then assessing children and evaluating their own learning. As such, pre-service teachers were active in generating learning and engaged in higher-order tasks of applying, creating, analysing and evaluating (Bloom 1956) and thus experiencing the work integrated learning (Patrick et al. 2008) and critical reflective practice (Loughran and Hamilton 2016) pedagogies of teacher education. In Phase 1 of the Foundation Education unit, the learning through expert roles and groups also ensured that learning was generated with and through one another rather than just through the teacher educator. In Phase 2, pre-service teachers had full control of how they utilised their class time to develop their ICT skills and work collaboratively and cooperatively to create their multimedia presentations. In being given voice and choice, pre-service teachers had control of the focus and number of workshops required in this phase.

The design of each of these programmes ensured that if pre-service teachers were in attendance, they had to be active in the learning process. There was no opportunity to adopt a passive role; there was no way, other than through active participation, for content to be obtained. So much of the learning occurred through *use* of information and knowledge rather than through its delivery. Elements of choice within, and ownership of, these programmes also engendered the intrinsic motivation that Deci and Ryan (1985) refer to when choice is made a meaningful part of the learning experience. This choice and its subsequent motivational effects also engendered active participation of pre-service teachers. The learning experience could not be replicated through a set of "take-home" notes or listening to a recorded lecture. This further instilled a sense of responsibility and motivation for pre-service teachers to attend class and become actively involved in the teaching, learning and assessment processes.

Together, the constructive alignment, provision of highly meaningful contexts both through university-based and work integrated learning and design that demanded significant active participation ensured that the learner was at the centre of the teaching, learning and assessment and also helped them feel like they were central in the concern of the teacher educators involved. Tasks were open-ended, providing flexibility in both the pace at which pre-service teachers could progress and enabling them some control over the types of learning styles they adopted. In this, the teacher educator was still instrumental in assisting the selection of possible tasks and in providing learning experiences to challenge and develop pre-service teachers. Teacher educators also provided essential support to monitor and guide pre-service teachers through their experiences in the units and facilitated the reflective practice that helped them identify in what ways and why their learning was successful. Overall, learners were central because the entire learning experience was tailored to pre-service teachers' differing needs, abilities and interests and provided rich experiences for their individual meaning making, all elements that are consistently called for in a deep, student-centred approach to teaching, learning and assessment (Biggs and Tang 2011; Land et al. 2012; Smit et al. 2014) that align with other established pedagogies of teacher education.

12.3   Communities of Collaboration

The formation of Communities of Collaboration is a practical and natural by-product of the active participation element of the Learner as Central tenet, although these can be promoted and supported in more or less effective ways. All four of the programmes we have exemplified in this second section of the book utilised collaboration as a foundational feature of the teaching, learning and assessment processes. All involved significant group work in dealing with theoretical ideas (e.g. planning learning sequences to align with relevant theories of literacy and science learning and synthesising the risk, protective and intervention factors to create a group presentation on transitioning to university). Collaboration and cooperation were also fostered by requiring pre-service teachers to present their learning through either the delivery of their learning sequences through the work integrated learning (Patrick et al. 2008) in schools or in their multimedia presentations. Activities providing access to and use of theory and content were also collaborative in nature. The expert roles and groups were a particularly strong example of this in the Foundation Education unit described in Chap. 11.

Lave and Wenger (1991) first presented the phrase "Communities of Practice" to describe the sorts of collaborative group work that each of our examples of collaboration exhibit. Lave and Wenger's Community of Practice is based on situated learning theory, that is, participation in the environment (or community) in which the targeted knowledge is used/applied. For higher education (and subsequently for teacher education), this equates to work integrated learning approaches. Situated and work integrated learning in Communities of Practice helps to ensure that pre-service teachers are engaged in "authentic tasks" where the *use* of theories and or skills is able to occur (Barab and Duffy 2012). This *use* of knowledge and skills to plan and teach, particularly in discipline-based subjects such as the literacy and science that formed the basis of three of our examples, requires this to occur with children and in schools. As noted in the chapters specific to these examples (Chaps. 8, 9 and 10), these programmes incorporated a school-based component into their coursework rather than relying on the practicum component the course. This was important in enabling a specific focus on learning through Communities of Collaboration within these units. Practicum tends to involve pre-service teachers in schools such that each pre-service teacher is assigned to a particular classroom where, although supported by the supervising classroom teacher, their planning, teaching and reflective practice is mostly undertaken as an independent activity. The embedded nature of the school component in our examples allowed a shift away from the more isolated experience associated with the practicum, and instead, provided the opportunity for Communities of Practice and collaboration to be formed, both in the schools, and back at the university where the school experiences were discussed and analysed. This provides an added dimension to the notion of work integrated learning in that it could be made specific to the discipline areas of interest and not left at the discretion of the particular schools/teachers involved.

Having pre-service teachers work in Communities of Collaboration in schools provided a different type of support structure than that which could be achieved through more traditional approaches to school-based learning. The collaboration was able to permeate through all aspects of the learning experience. Pre-service teachers analysed and applied theory to their planning together instead of on their own. Feedback on planning ideas and teaching moments were continuous as pre-service teachers worked together, rather than being restricted to moments of consultation with the teacher educator and/or supervising classroom teacher. Pre-service teachers were also involved in team teaching experiences with shared responsibility and accountability, rather than teaching on their own with the knowledge that their supervising teacher was observing them, predominantly for assessment purposes. Finally, they were able to discuss their experiences and reflect together, both in their immediate group, as well as in the larger community of peers when they shared the critical moments (Kosnik 2001) of their learning experiences in the concurrent university sessions, with the facilitation of the teacher educator. Traditional practica are generally too isolated (Le Cornu and Ewing 2008) for this level of collaboration and support to be achieved and are not usually run concurrently with university-based work, which limits the amount of theory-informed, guided reflection on practice that can occur.

The benefits of such a strong collaboration in small and large Communities of Practice link to the pervasive literature regarding the integration of theory and practice. It also addresses Barab and Duffy's (2012) recommendation to ensure that pre-service teachers are engaged in "authentic tasks" where the *use* of theories and or skills is able to occur. The application of situated learning theory, through Communities of Collaboration, enabled this use of theories and skills.

12.4   ICT as a Key Enabler

The "technolution" of education (and indeed, the western world society as a whole) has been subject to various examples of implementation and rigorous debate about the appropriateness of ICT in formal education settings. These considerations have included, firstly, whether or not ICT should be utilised in education and, secondly, if it is used, in what forms, for what reasons and at what points and levels of schooling it should feature. These are not easy questions to answer, and those answers that have been suggested have varied over time and in light of the growing body of evidence provided through this much-researched field of education.

Certainly the question of whether or not ICT should be used in formal education has become obsolete. Despite early concerns about detrimental effects of ICT for learning, particularly in relation to early years education (Romeo et al. 2003), it is now widely accepted that ICT is an important component of the curriculum at all levels of learning (Zaranis 2016). The importance of ICT at all levels of education stems, if for no other reason, from the technolisation of the world, which quite simply requires a citizenship that has capacity to operate through increasingly technological approaches to both work and life (Manyika 2016). However, the questions of what ICT, how, how much and why remain debated. Questions around what ICT range from provided tablet, laptop and PC devices (e.g. Herrington et al. 2014) to "Bring Your Own Device" (BYOD) models of incorporation. Questions around touchscreen versus mouse forms of technology have also been raised (e.g. Romeo, et al. 2003). Alongside these debates are questions about equity and access (Gunter et al. 2014), as well as flexibility and choice (Herrington et al. 2014).

The question around how ICT should be incorporated in education has also traversed the terrain of learning *about* ICT or *with* ICT. It is possibly this aspect of ICT in education that is of most interest and importance to the consideration of personalising learning. Personalising learning *assumes* ICT incorporation in education – it is a key tenet, after all. In personalising learning, the *how* is also strongly advocated towards a particular form. ICT as a key enabler of learning (Keamy et al. 2007) is concerned with an approach that utilises ICT as a vehicle for learning.

As a vehicle for learning, ICT needs to be utilised in the ways that are described by Papert (1993), that is, ways that provide opportunities for creativity and deep thinking. In addition, as explored in more detail in Chap. 4, the importance of student-centred (Newhouse 2015), lifelong (Selwyn 2012) and collaborative (Kruse 2013) approaches to learning with ICT must also be privileged if ICT is to be used as a vehicle for learning. It is through these approaches that the issues of authentic, contextualised and meaningful learning, that are all so paramount to personalising learning, are addressed. These methods require less focus on the skills associated with ICT use, although these obviously emerge as a natural consequence of embedding ICT, and a far stronger focus on embracing ICT for the ways in which it can enhance the learning experience. The examples of ICT used in this way, as a vehicle for enhanced, authentic, contextualised and meaningful learning, are particularly evident in the *Digi-Tell* and Foundation Education unit design examples presented in this volume.

Learning in the *Digi-Tell* and Foundation Education unit programmes privileged ICT as the *vehicle* through which the learning occurred. This meant that ICT was incorporated in a seamless manner and allowed for the personalising learning approaches identified by Keamy et al. (2007), such as allowing students' greater diversity for learning, and enhancing interactivity between individual students and individual teachers. Such diversity and interactivity were clearly evident in these programmes. In *Digi-Tell*, interactivity was addressed through the pre-service teachers' work with one another and with a small group of children in schools, to create a digital text of a story using programmes like iMovie or MovieMaker. Diversity was addressed in both levels of access (mobile or fixed devices; within and beyond the classroom) and in the selection and use of theory to plan the teaching and learning experience associated with a chosen text type, a chosen medium and group-selected software.

Similar levels of catering for diversity and supporting interaction were evident in the Foundation Education unit's design. Diversity in ICT skills, needs and interests were all a feature of the learning design. Skills and interests were revealed through pre-service teachers' completion of an ICT inventory that helped both us as the teacher educators and the pre-service teachers themselves to identify types of contemporary ICTs to which they had been exposed and felt confident in using. In addition, this inventory sought to identify the areas of interest that pre-service teachers had to develop their ICT skills and knowledge. By ascertaining pre-service teachers' ICT learning interests, we were then able to design and offer ICT workshops that were tailored to the number and level of pre-service teachers. For example, many pre-service teachers identified wanting to make a movie as an area of ICT learning interest. Some of these pre-service teachers had limited prior experience with digital devices for learning, and others had been exposed to things like *MovieMaker* in previous schooling. In order to cater to the different learning needs within this same interest area, we designed and delivered a *MovieMaker Basics* workshop for beginners and a *MovieMaker Advanced* for those looking to extend the basic skills that they had previously established. Interactivity was also supported throughout this process as pre-service teachers were placed in groups where they had to negotiate the types of ICT that would be incorporated into the group's work, and who would be the "lead" for a given ICT learning experience, and thus teach it to other members of the group.

As the unit evaluation data collected from pre-service teachers show for both of these programmes (see Chaps. 9 and 11), the learning experience and embedding of ICT within it were motivating, affirming, useful and appropriate. It was the inextricable link between the learning and presenting of the programme's content with the various ICT media that places ICT as a vehicle for and, thus, key enabler of personalisation in the learning undertaken.

12.5   Lifelong Learning

In many ways, Lifelong Learning is a natural consequence of the student-centred, collaborative, contextualised and ICT-enabled learning that has been described in this book. The *process* of learning how to teach was paramount in all of the examples we have provided of personalising learning. This emphasis on process meant that value was given to the skills of learning how to learn, and not just the product of the learning how to teach experience. It is through this participation in learning and the emphasis on how the learning occurred that assurance can be given that proclivities for Lifelong Learning are fostered.

For *Tell Tales* and *Digi-Tell*, it was the very different perspectives and experiences of teaching with children's literature that promoted Lifelong Learning for the pre-service teachers involved in these programmes. Each programme, in its own way, demonstrated a very different medium for children's learning with literature that challenged pre-service teachers' previous conceptions about children's literature as pertaining only to the reading of books. The creative potential that these experiences enabled helped pre-service teachers to view children's literature and storytelling from a new perspective and one that broadened access through the wider incorporation of different learning styles and resources.

In the *STISE* programme, pre-service teachers were involved firstly, in the congruent teaching (Swennen et al. 2008) experience, and secondly, in the work integrated learning (Patrick et al. 2008) and associated reflective practice (Loughran and Hamilton 2016). This culminated in the analysing, planning, teaching, assessing and reflecting on a discipline area that is traditionally avoided in primary school teaching and promoted cultivation of Lifelong Learning tendencies. Pre-service teachers themselves reported their own misgivings about their ability to teach science and how important it was in the repertoire of primary school curriculum. The requisite participation in explicitly modelled (Loughran 2006) science teaching and the authentic experience of teaching science themselves in schools, placed pre-service teachers for a full semester of study, in a position they may well not have elected to be in had they been given a choice. Such withdrawal from science teaching associated with low confidence has been evident in the literature for many years (e.g. Appleton 1995; Goodrum et al. 2001; Kazempour 2014). Engagement in this "forced" participation, however, altered pre-service teachers' attitudes towards and confidence to teach science in significant ways. Thus, the experience of confronting their fear of science teaching and engaging in mastery science teaching experience helped challenge their tendency to otherwise avoid that which may not turn out well. Pre-service teachers were unanimous in the positive influence this supported, work integrated learning experience had on their confidence and intention to teach science in the future and demonstrated the value of facing those areas of perceived weakness in order to develop skills, knowledge, confidence and ability. It is this "let's give it a try" type of attitude that is important for instilling and enacting the behaviours of a lifelong learner.

These same perceived fears and lack of confidence were prevalent among the pre-service teachers experiencing the challenge of learning with and presenting their learning through technology that was the focus of the Foundation Education unit of work. Again, pre-service teachers were supported through a process of identifying their own strengths, weaknesses and interests and encouraged to challenge themselves in areas of ICT in which they could demonstrate learning and improvement. The fact that the pre-service teachers involved in this programme were able to achieve this identification of gaps and improvement further instils the "can do" attitude associated with a Lifelong Learning mindset.

Lifelong Learning mindsets are fostered through flexibility and provision of a range of pathways that meet students at their particular points of learning need (Keamy et al. 2007). It was the choice, tailoring of learning and flexible incorporation of different means of learning (schools, workshops, etc.) that helped provide this flexibility and meeting of learning needs. Pre-service teachers had a voice throughout each of the programme examples, and their voice was used to shape the learning experiences that followed for them. Such practice assists in helping pre-service teachers learn the skills of thinking about what they want and need and examining possibilities and pathways to actively achieve them. This planning and assessing of their own learning and learning needs is what Saribas (2015) highlights as important in the disposition of a lifelong learner.

12.6 Conclusion

This chapter provides a synthesis of the examples of personalising learning in teacher education with respect to Keamy et al.'s (2007) four tenets, Learner as Central, Communities of Collaboration, ICT and Lifelong Learning, and their alignment with other established pedagogies of teacher education. Whilst not every tenet is emphasised in every example, what we demonstrate is that, across a course, personalising learning in teacher education can be achieved and does make the teaching, learning and assessment experience far more meaningful and relevant for pre-service teachers. It can be difficult to otherwise achieve this sense of relevance among pre-service teachers given the theoretical emphasis teacher education tends to have. We are by no means suggesting that this theoretical emphasis is not important. However, making theory-informed practice more accessible to pre-service teachers is paramount for achieving effective teacher education that attends to both the theoretical and the practical elements of this complex and sophisticated craft. It is for this reason that personalising learning is such a significant and useful way of envisaging teacher education of the future. As we have shown, the integration of key theoretical components of coursework with practical experience can be effectively achieved through an approach that pays attention to the tenets of personalising learning.

Personalising learning is informed by long-established theories of sociocultural learning, situated learning, collaboration, active participation, reflection, meaningful and authentic integration of ICT and skills for learning across the lifetime. There is no doubt that some of the cautions associated with these different elements of a personalising learning approach are important, particularly in regard to the learning capital that some students bring to the learning environment that may overshadow and hence disadvantage other learners. An awareness of both the cautionary measures and the processes of operationalising the different components that contribute to personalising learning help to ensure that teacher educators provide an effective teacher education experience that truly prepares graduate teachers, not only to teach in diverse education contexts but also to seek out and engage in ongoing professional learning and development throughout their teaching careers.

Based on this position of the need to move teacher education into a realm of far greater personalisation, we present in the next, concluding chapter, a guide for visualising the personalising of learning in teacher education. This guide is theory and practice informed, and we hope it helps address the current policy imperative of making our graduate teachers more "classroom ready" (TEMAG 2014), than they have possibly been considered up until now.

References

Appleton, K. (1995). Student teachers' confidence to teach science: Is more science knowledge necessary to improve self-confidence? *International Journal of Science Education, 17*(3), 357–369.

Aspland, T. (2006). Changing patterns of teacher education in Australia. *Educational Research and Perspectives, 33*(2), 140–163.

Bandura, A. (1986). *Social foundations of thought and action: A social cognitive theory.* Englewood Cliffs: Prentice-Hall.

Barab, S., & Duffy, T. (2012). From practice fields to communities of practice. In D. Jonassen & S. Land (Eds.), *Theoretical foundations of learning environments* (2nd ed., pp. 29–65). New York: Routledge.

Biggs, J., & Tang, C. (2011). *Teaching for quality learning at university* (4th ed.). New York: Open University Press.

Bloom, B. (Ed.). (1956). *Taxonomy of educational objectives. Book I: The cognitive domain.* New York: Longman.

Brandenburg, R., Glasswell, K., Jones, M., & Ryan, J. (Eds.). (2017). *Reflective theory and practice in teacher education.* Singapore: Springer.

Darling-Hammond, L. (2012). *Powerful teacher education: Lessons from exemplary programs.* San Francisco: Wiley.

Deci, E., & Ryan, R. (1985). *Intrinsic motivation and self-determination in human behaviour.* New York: Plenum Press.

Goodrum, D., Hackling, M., & Rennie, L. (2001). *The status and quality of teaching and learning of science in Australian schools: A research report.* Canberra: Department of Education, Training and Youth Affairs.

Grossman, P., Hammerness, K., & McDonald, M. (2009). Redefining teaching, re-imagining teacher education. *Teachers and Teaching, 15*(2), 273–289.

Gunter, H., Hall, D., & Mills, C. (Eds.). (2014). *Education policy research: Design and practice at a time of rapid reform.* London: Bloomsbury Publishing.

Herrington, J., Ostashewski, N., Reid, D., & Flintoff, K. (2014). Mobile technologies in teacher education: Preparing pre-service teachers and teacher educators for mobile learning. In M. Jones & J. Ryan (Eds.), *Successful teacher education: Partnerships, reflective practice and the place of technology* (pp. 137–151). Rotterdam: Sense Publishers.

Jones, M., & Ryan, J. (2014). Successful and 'transferable' practice. In M. Jones & J. Ryan (Eds.), *Successful teacher education: Partnerships, reflective practice and the place of technology* (pp. 177–194). Rotterdam: Sense Publishers.

Kazempour, M. (2014). I can't teach science! A case study of an elementary pre-service teacher's intersection of science experiences, beliefs, attitude, and self-efficacy. *International Journal of Environmental and Science Education, 9*(1), 77–96.

Keamy, R. K., Nicholas, H., Mahar, S., & Herrick, C. (2007). *Personalising education: From research to policy and practice*. (Paper No. 11. Office of Education Policy and Innovation). Melbourne: Department of Education and Early Childhood Development.

Korthagen, F. (2011). Making teacher education relevant for practice: The pedagogy of realistic teacher education. *Orbis Scholae, 5*(2), 31–50.

Korthagen, F. (2016). Pedagogy of teacher education. In J. Loughran & M. Hamilton (Eds.), *International handbook on teacher education* (Vol. 1, pp. 311–346). Singapore: Springer.

Kosnik, C. (2001). The effects of an inquiry oriented teacher education program on a faculty member: Some critical incidents and my journey. *Reflective Practice: International and Multidisciplinary Perspectives, 2*(1), 65–80. https://doi.org/10.1080/14623940120035532.

Kruse, J. W. (2013). Implications of the nature of technology for teaching and teacher education. In M. P. Clough, J. K. Olson, & S. Niederhauser (Eds.), *The nature of technology: Implications for learning and teaching* (pp. 345–370). Rotterdam: Sense Publishers.

Land, S., Hannafin, M., & Oliver, K. (2012). Student-centered learning environments: Foundations, assumptions and design. In D. Jonassen & S. Land (Eds.), *Theoretical foundations of learning environments* (2nd ed., pp. 3–25). New York: Routledge.

Lave, J., & Wenger, E. (1991). *Situated learning: Legitimate peripheral participation (learning in doing: Social, cognitive and computational perspectives)*. Cambridge: Cambridge University Press.

Le Cornu, R., & Ewing, R. (2008). Reconceptualising professional experiences in pre-service teacher education… reconstructing the past to embrace the future. *Teaching and Teacher Education, 24*(7), 1799–1812.

Lortie, D. C. (1975). *Schoolteacher*. Chicago: Chicago University Press.

Loughran, J. (2006). *Developing a pedagogy of teacher education: Understanding teaching and learning about teaching*. Abingdon: Routledge.

Loughran, J. (2014). Professionally developing as a teacher educator. *Journal of Teacher Education, 65*(4), 271–283.

Loughran, J., & Hamilton, M. (2016). Developing an understanding of teacher education. In J. Loughran & M. Hamilton (Eds.), *International handbook on teacher education* (Vol. 1, pp. 3–22). Singapore: Springer.

Manyika, J. (2016). Technology, jobs and the future of work. *Briefing note prepared for the fortune Vatican forum December 2016*. McKinsey Global Institute.

Newhouse, C. P. (2015). When does technology improve learning? In M. Henderson & G. Romeo (Eds.), *Teaching and digital technologies: Big issues and critical questions* (pp. 197–213). Melbourne: Cambridge University Press.

Papert, S. (1993). *The children's machine: Rethinking school in the age of the computer*. New York: Basic Books.

Patrick, C.-J., Peach, D., Pocknee, C., Webb, F., Fletcher, M., & Pretto, G. (2008). *The WIL [Work Integrated Learning] report: A national scoping study [Australian Learning and Teaching Council (ALTC) final report]*. Brisbane: Queensland University of Technology. Retrieved from www.altc.edu.au and www.acen.edu.au

Romeo, G., Edwards, S., McNamara, S., Walker, I., & Ziguras, C. (2003). Touching the screen: Issues related to the use of touchscreen technology in early childhood. *British Journal of Educational Technology, 34*(3), 329–339.

Saribas, D. (2015). Investigating the relationship between pre-service teachers' scientific literacy, environmental literacy and life-long learning tendency. *Science Education International, 26*(1), 80–100.

Selwyn, N. (2012). *Education in a digital world.* London: Routledge.

Smit, K., de Brabander, C., & Martens, R. (2014). Student-centred and teacher-centred learning environment in pre-vocational secondary education: Psychological needs, and motivation. *Scandinavian Journal of Educational Research, 58*(6), 695–712.

Swennen, A., Lunenberg, M., & Korthagen, F. (2008). Preach what you teach! Teacher educators and congruent teaching. *Teachers and Teaching: Theory and Practice, 14*(5–6), 531–542.

Teacher Education Ministerial Advisory Group (TEMAG). (2014). *Action now: Classroom ready teachers.* Retrieved from http://www.studentsfirst.gov.au/teacher-education-ministerial-advisory-group

Vygotsky, L. (1978). *Mind in society: The development of higher psychological processes.* Cambridge, MA: Harvard University Press.

Zaranis, N. (2016). The use of ICT in kindergarten for teaching addition based on realistic mathematics education. *Education and Information Technologies, 21*(3), 589–606.

Zeichner, Z., & Liston, D. (2014). *Reflective teaching: An introduction* (2nd ed.). New York: Routledge.

Chapter 13
A Guide for Visualising Personalising Learning in Teacher Education

In this chapter, we offer a guide for visualising personalising learning in teacher education. This guide draws on the theoretical and practical examination of personalising learning which we argue is rooted in established theories of teaching and learning; operationalised through the tenets of Learner as Central, Communities of Collaboration, ICT and Lifelong Learning; and enacted through a myriad of learning pathways and possibilities to suit individuals and groups of learners. We attest that personalising learning may hold the potential to reshape the nature of teaching, schooling and teacher education in ways that speak to the persistent criticisms levelled at teaching and teacher education and address the current policy imperatives calling for more "classroom ready" teachers.

13.1 Introduction

Throughout this book we have examined the tenets of personalising learning as described by Keamy et al. (2007) and their informing theories of sociocultural, situated and lifelong learning. What is revealed in this examination is an approach to teaching, learning and assessment that brings together and supports a student-centred, constructively aligned, social outlook on how effective learning occurs. We have argued that there is nothing new per se in such an approach to teaching and learning. We have also shown how these personalising approaches align with other established and emerging pedagogies of higher education and teacher education specifically. Perhaps what is relatively new though, is ensuring all of these aspects, alongside the meaningful inclusion of ICT for learning, are attended to as a collective, and it is this collective that is termed and understood as personalising learning.

Whilst there has been something of a global movement towards some form of personalising learning in education (Keamy 2009), it has not infiltrated teacher education anywhere near to the extent, if at all, as it has in other sectors. In some

© Springer Nature Singapore Pte Ltd. 2018
M. Jones, K. McLean, *Personalising Learning in Teacher Education*,
https://doi.org/10.1007/978-981-10-7930-6_13

countries (e.g. England) personalising learning has become a politicised agenda for schooling (Keamy 2009), although thankfully, to date, this has not occurred in Australia. How much these approaches have actually been adopted in the educational practices of these countries, and not just paid lip service, is less well evidenced. Also unclear is whether approaches to personalising learning have infiltrated higher education sectors of these countries and teacher education in particular.

The ongoing inquiries into teacher education in Australia (and indeed, worldwide) consistently call for teacher education to enhance its effectiveness in preparing "classroom ready" teachers (e.g. TEMAG 2014). Personalising learning holds potential in providing the types of changes that may indeed reshape the nature of teaching, schooling and teacher education in ways that help to meet these demands. In this concluding chapter, we summarise the informing theories, the supporting characteristics and the potential outcomes of personalising learning. We present these notions, with supporting literature and evidence from practice, in a guide for visualising personalising learning in teacher education. We believe this guide supports established ideas about effective learning and teacher education and extends on them to offer a way of speaking to the persistent criticisms levelled at teaching and teacher education that may help to address current policy and stakeholder imperatives regarding the quality and effectiveness of teacher education.

13.2   Theoretical Foundations for Personalising Learning

Personalising learning is rooted in sociocultural theory and its antecedent situated learning theory through Communities of Practice. These theories are manifested through Keamy et al.'s (2007) key tenets for personalising learning: Learner as Central and Communities of Collaboration. Together, these tenets, alongside the Lifelong Learning tenet of personalising learning, provide a holistic view of the teaching and learning process.

Cases of this personalisation and holistic learning were shown in our examples (Chaps. 8, 9, 10 and 11) where pre-service teachers' learning needs were addressed by:

- Allowing choice of content focus (e.g. designing their own teaching plans, selecting which text-types to adopt and which ICTs to engage with)
- Providing authenticity (learning that is relevant to pre-service teachers' lives by situating it in schools or linking it to their life experiences)
- Enabling self-paced progression through learning tasks (moving the learning outside of the scheduled timetable to allow flexibility and alternate settings)

Moreover, these examples also drew from key approaches associated with effective pedagogy specific to teacher education. This was evident in the work integrated learning (Patrick et al. 2008) of the school-based learning depicted in Chaps. 8, 9 and 10. Elements of explicit modelling (Loughran 2006) and congruent teaching (Swennen et al. 2008) were also described in these chapters. Core practices (Grossman et al. 2009), which allow for rehearsal of high-frequency teaching skills, were embedded in the examples illustrated in Chaps. 9, 10 and 11. All of the examples provided showed strong constructive alignment between learning, teaching and assessment. As such it is clear that the focus on personalisation in each of these examples is supportive of these other established teacher education pedagogies, particularly in regard to the design and enactment of the teaching that took place.

Assessment was also closely aligned to the teaching and learning strategy in our examples of personalising learning. This constructive alignment (Biggs and Tang 2011) was evident through the marriage of outcomes around learning to plan, teach and assess literacy and science learning with tasks that directly assessed pre-service teachers' planning, and assessment of children's and their own learning after a teaching period in schools. This example of assessment *for* learning aligns with the overarching approach to personalising learning where it is expected that the links between learning and assessment tasks allow for learning to occur through the completion of assessment tasks. As such, assessment "serves the purpose of promoting students' learning" (Black et al. 2003, p. 17). Value-added assessment, targeted in the Foundation Education unit (Chap. 11), further promoted personalisation of learning through increasing pre-service teachers' motivation by guaranteeing a measure of success based on the impact of the learning experience on their actual, individual knowledge and skill development. Such an approach is in contrast to the traditional forms of assessment that generally operate in universities, where students are assessed according to how they rank against their peers (Anderman et al. 2010).

The elements of personalising learning described above are practices that support the tenet of placing the Learner as Central. It is characterised by a focus on students' needs and interests, through providing them with choice and giving them a voice in the selection of content and resources and, ultimately, ensuring that assessment is meaningfully aligned with the learning experience. These elements of placing the Learner as Central makes teaching, learning and assessment *student-centred*, a concept broadly represented in the research literature as founded in social constructivism and informed by sociocultural theory (Smit et al. 2014).

Student-centred approaches to teaching and learning respond to the large body of evidence that has seen understanding of learning move from individualistic, behavioural approaches to those that are more cognitively and socially informed, that is, social constructivism. Social constructivism builds on the work of cognitive psychologists such as Piaget (1936) who purported that learning is an outcome of meaningful construction of ideas based on existing understandings in the learner's mind. Expanding on this notion, Vygotsky (1978) emphasised the importance of the social element in this construction of new ideas, indicating that learning is not an outcome of what happens in the learner's mind alone but is also influenced by the broader social and cultural interactions in which the learner is involved. In education, this

Fig. 13.1 Theoretical foundations for personalising learning

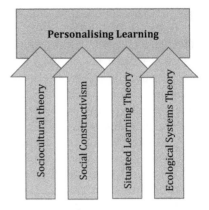

translates into the interactions the learner engages in with peers and teachers. A student-centred focus of such an approach requires the learning design to leverage these social interactions such that individuals learn with and from one another as much, or perhaps even more, as they do by themselves.

Situated learning theory (Lave and Wenger 1991) expands on this again. Rather than viewing learning as defined by the cognitive development that occurs, as constructivism (in its various forms) does, situated learning theory claims that learning is a function of participation. In situated learning theory, learners gradually assimilate and adopt the ideas and practices of the broader community in which they participate. The differences between this and social constructivism are subtle as they are both strongly defined by social interaction.

We see the two working together. At times the learner is developing personal meanings and understandings through the thought processes initiated by their experiences, including their social interactions, as well as experiencing a gradual assimilation brought about by their active participation and collaboration in the practices of the community in which they are situated. Together, these theories of learning marry with the ideas of a systems-based approach to thinking about learning and development, a system that also incorporates the broader contexts of the learner and how these contexts interact with one another. This system, in which the *ecology* of the learner is recognised, is represented in ecological systems theory (Bronfenbrenner 1977).

The collective contribution that sociocultural theory, personal and social constructivism, situated learning theory and ecological systems theory make is foundational to personalising learning. These established and widely accepted theories of learning and development provide a grounding stability to the ways in which personalising learning is understood and enacted. Ultimately, as long as the educator is true to the underpinning theories, other variations in the approaches to personalising learning can be generally managed. They form the basis, or the roots for personalising learning, which is represented diagrammatically in Fig. 13.1.

13.3   Structure and Support for Personalising Learning

Keamy et al.'s (2007) tenets of Learner as Central, Communities of Collaboration, ICT and Lifelong Learning help to provide a support structure for achievement of personalising learning. The tenets provide a scaffold to help ensure that key aspects of the learning design are incorporated. Each tenet is underpinned by the established theories of learning noted above: that is, sociocultural theory, social constructivism, situated learning and ecological systems theory. The elements of these theories manifest in the student-centred learning, the collaborative group work and the focus on learning processes rather than products that help to instil a Lifelong Learning mindset (Aspin and Chapman 2012).

13.3.1   Learner as Central

We see Learners as Central through approaches that are problem- and inquiry-based that provide authentic, differentiated learning that is situated in meaningful contexts. Placing the Learner as Central also means there is some level of open-ended, negotiated learning; hence the design of teaching, learning and assessment must have flexibility in order to remain responsive to individual learning needs. These traits of student-centred learning are represented through the five characteristics of student-centred learning environments identified by Smit et al. (2014), which are operationalised through tasks, teacher activities, student activities, sources of information and assessment. Smit et al. discuss tasks as being negotiated, problem-based and situated in rich, authentic contexts; teacher activities as serving to facilitate the setting, achievement and evaluation of students' learning goals; student activities as self-regulated and requiring active participation; sources of information as broad-ranging and accessible within and beyond the classroom; and assessment as reflective and ongoing. A more detailed and robust discussion of these characteristics and how they pertain to the Learner as Central tenet is presented in Chap. 5.

13.3.2   Communities of Collaboration

Communities of Collaboration are also engendered through the Learner as Central tenet, as the active participation they each call for ultimately leads to a strong emphasis on collaborative group work. This group work encourages peer-to-peer interaction, as well as interaction with teachers and other education support people in the learning space. Being informed by situated learning theory, the Communities of Collaboration tenet also calls for learning experiences to be situated in the particular environment in which the knowledge and skills are to be used/applied (Lave and Wenger 1991). For teacher education, this means a need for far greater work *in* and *with* schools than is often the case in current teacher education in Australia.

To maintain the rigour and theoretical support of effective learning about teaching, the university-facilitated focus on theoretically informed critical reflection must also be a strong feature in teacher education programmes. As we have noted in Chap. 3, it is through guided reflective practice that pre-service teachers are able to form another, more theory-focused Community of Practice. In this second Community of Practice, pre-service teachers collaborate and learn from one another's experiences and from their reflection on important elements of these experiences. This element of reflection on experience has long been acknowledged as being fundamental to deep learning about teaching (e.g. Loughran 2006; Korthagen 2001). Thus, it is the interconnectedness of communities within Communities of Practice, or, as Wenger (1998) describes, constellations of practice, that allows for the more complex network of different Communities of Collaboration that best supports teacher education.

13.3.3   ICT as a Key Enabler

As was illustrated in detail in Chap. 4, the place of technology, and ICT in particular, is now prolific in society and education systems worldwide. There is an imperative to access and use ICT with creativity and collaboration (Koehler et al. 2014) as well as critical thought and understanding (Selwyn 2013). These learner attributes are paramount for informed and active citizenship in present and future society, particularly given the various forms of ICT and access to the suite of both reliable and not so reliable information these bring with them. To develop such creativity, collaboration, critical thinking and understanding about ICTs means they must be incorporated into teaching, learning and assessment in pedagogically sound ways.

Following the principles of the foundational theories outlined above, ICT pedagogy needs to be active, collaborative, differentiated and flexible (Newhouse and Clarkson 2008). Applying such approaches to ICT use in learning allows the educator to encourage ICT knowledge and skill development from the student's point of need. One of the most widely acknowledged works around ICT and pedagogy to assist in achieving these approaches is Koehler and Mishra's (2009) Technological Pedagogical Content Knowledge (TPACK) framework, which aims to support the effective integration of ICT in educational settings. Frameworks such as TPACK, which began in situated cognition theory, and later developed within a learning-technology-by-design approach (Koehler and Mishra 2009), help to ensure that the focus on ICT learning moves away from the historical "tool" for learning it has had, to one that provides a more seamless integration into teaching and learning. In this way, TPACK allows for ICT to be utilised as a vehicle for learning (Jones and McLean 2012) where the use of ICT is authentic, contextualised, collaborative and facilitated by educators rather than "taught" (Koehler and Mishra 2009).

13.3.4 Lifelong Learning

Lifelong Learning is a far more abstract concept than the other tenets informing personalising learning. It is probably best understood as an attitude, or mindset (Fischer 2000), to describe a desire to engage in ongoing learning throughout the lifetime. Attitudes cannot be observed directly, but rather, are manifested through what a person says and how he/she behaves (Aiken 2002). Attitudes are thought to be influenced by what is described as tripartite origins: the cognitive, affective and behavioural dispositions of a person, developed explicitly with conscious thought and effort or implicitly through sub-conscious acquisition (Olson and Kendrick 2012).

Whether or not attitudes can be explicitly taught is something open to debate. In the early twentieth century, Lichtenstein conducted an inconclusive literature search and an empirical research study of which results demonstrated that attitude could be taught in as many cases as it could not (Lichtenstein 1934). More recent research has shown that attitudes vary in strength and persistence, conditions that appear to be connected to which part of the tripartite the attitude originated (Olson and Kendrick 2012). They vary considerably from one person to the next (Aiken 2002).

With the relationship between attitude formation and individual, social, cultural and historical constructs, it is clear why Bronfenbrenner's (1977) ecological systems theory is so important as an underpinning theory of the Lifelong Learning tenet of personalising learning. There are a myriad of factors, both internal and external to the person, that shape the formation of his/her attitudes, and the relative "invisibility" they have means we need to work with these constructs to try to influence attitudes in the way we might like. For Lifelong Learning, this means trying to instil a positive attitude towards learning and a desire to pursue knowledge and skills beyond the walls of the classroom.

Authors in the field of Lifelong Learning suggest that education needs to embrace the sorts of approaches that are already embedded in the other tenets of personalising learning to achieve the attitude and desire for ongoing learning. That is, for example, that learners are active in planning and assessing their own learning (Keamy et al. 2007; Owen 2016; Saribas 2015); given choice and voice in the content and the processes they engage in for their learning (Florian 2009); supported through holistic approaches that acknowledge the importance of broader contexts in their lives (Bronfenbrenner 1977); situated in authentic and meaningful contexts for learning, in which *they* see relevance (Keamy et al. 2007; Smit et al. 2014); and a part of a broader learning community made up of peers, mentors and teachers

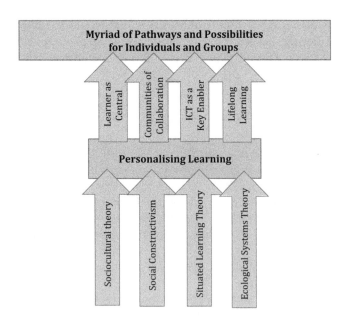

Fig. 13.2 The personalising learning collective

(Saribas 2015). Each of these considerations has been highlighted through the Learner as Central, Communities of Collaboration and ICT tenets of personalising learning. As such, Lifelong Learning is likely to be a natural consequence of applying other forms of best practice approaches embedded in the personalising learning framework.

13.3.5   The Personalising Learning Collective

The summary of the four key tenets above, that we have borrowed from Keamy et al. (2007) and elected to use as the focus for personalising learning in teacher education, demonstrates the mutually supportive ideas and concepts that each gives to the other. This alignment between the tenets arises from their strong theoretical foundations in sociocultural, social constructivism, situated learning and ecological systems theories. Having such strong foundational underpinnings means that each aspect of personalising learning will naturally encourage and support attainment of the others. The tenets help these theories of learning to be operationalised and serve collectively as both a strong support structure for effective teaching, learning and assessment, and as a bedrock for the myriad of pathways that enable individuals and groups of individuals to pursue their learning. They are represented in relationship to these underpinning factors and potential pathways in Fig. 13.2.

13.4   A Guide for Visualising Personalising Learning in Teacher Education

The personalising learning collective depicted diagrammatically in Fig. 13.2 provides the basis for visualising the personalising of learning as teacher education pedagogy. This collective can be likened to the interdependencies of different parts of a tree.

In the same way the roots of a tree anchor it to the ground, the informing theories are fortifying for the implementation of personalising learning. The tree's roots provide it a stability that assists in supporting the tree as it faces the myriad of variables in its environment. Roots are also instrumental in supplying the tree with important nutrition and hydration to support its growth and development. In personalising learning, the underpinning theories provide a similar bedrock that allows for variability in the ways in which personalising learning can be enacted and provides teacher educators with a source of core principles on which they can rely to manage and adapt the appropriate learning pathways to support individuals' growth and development in relevant skills, knowledge and understandings.

Above the ground, the trunk of the tree acts as the central support system for the tree's entire growth and development. Nutrients and water are transported from the roots through the tree's trunk for distribution to the many branches and leaves it contains. Sugars produced in the leaves through photosynthesis are also transported to different parts of the tree through the trunk, which further supports the distribution of nutrition needed for the tree's optimal growth. Moreover, the trunk of a tree provides a strong structural support that allows the tree to gain sufficient height to rise above other elements in the environment so it might flourish. The four tenets of Learner as Central, Communities of Collaboration, ICT and Lifelong Learning provide this same structural support in personalising learning. The four tenets provide a way in which underpinning theories can be considered and operationalised. They provide something tangible that teacher educators can return to as they plan for and interpret the needs of their students. The tenets are more visible than the learning theories in the same way that the tree trunk is more visible than its roots. This "visibility" assists the teacher in identifying the range of strategies that might suit the learning process for different learners and, thus, helps to operationalise learning theory and enable optimal learning. Students' response to these strategies also assists the teacher educator to interpret the level of relevance and meaning they have for individual students and thus reflect on and refine approaches to teaching accordingly. In this way, the tenets provide a similar two-way flow of information that informs and supports the overall growth and development of learners to that of the tree trunk's two-way flow of nutrients to support its growth. As a support structure, the tenets of personalising learning also provide a guide that, hopefully, allows all individuals to reach their full potential within the system in the same way the strength of the trunk supports growth of the tree to its lofty heights.

The network of branches and leaves, known as the crown of the tree, gives the tree some of its most unique attributes. Leaves can be short, flat and broad or long, pointy and needle-like. They differ in colour, texture, size, shape, scent and strength. This variability in features and characteristics is comparable to the wide variation in learners. Learners, both within and beyond a particular cohort of students, can differ physically, emotionally, mentally, culturally, linguistically and in almost every way imaginable. Some are highly capable in some contexts, and others are more capable in different contexts. Students, like leaves, make every learning setting one that is unique, special and in need of individual consideration.

The branches, small and large, twig-like or limb-like, represent the offshoots of the four tenets of personalising learning. Thick-limbed, strong, more mature, "lateral" branches represent the main teaching approaches and strategies, informed by the tenets of personalising learning and, in turn, its underpinning theories. It is these primary limbs that are attached directly to the tree's trunk that best support the collection of individual branches, twigs and leaves that grow on a particular section of the tree. Smaller limbs and less stable "twigs", and stalks of the individual leaves themselves, represent the broad network of strategies and activities as they apply in nuanced ways for different groups and individual learners.

The interdependencies of the different parts of the tree (roots, trunk, branches, limbs, twigs, stalks and leaves) must work as a collective for the optimum growth of the tree. Akin to this, the learning theories and tenets of personalising learning, and the strategies and activities utilised in teaching, learning and assessment that operationalise this approach to learning, must also work in a constructively aligned way to achieve optimum learning for individual students. We have represented this tree analogy as a guide for visualising personalising learning (Fig. 13.3). This guide draws on the informing theories and examples of practice that are represented in the chapters forming this volume and encompasses other established pedagogies of teacher education.

Certainly if there was ever a cultural-change challenge in establishing an approach to personalising learning as Keamy (2009) describes is the case for schools, then it is an even more pertinent challenge for teacher education and universities. In an age where, arguably, much school-based teaching and learning has shifted towards a more meaningful and student-centred delivery, teacher education falls significantly behind. The guiding visualisation presented in this concluding chapter is based on informing, established and generally accepted theories of effective teaching and learning, teacher education pedagogy, as well as modest levels of research into its application through our practice. We hope it offers an entry point for application and further research into the place of personalising learning for effective teacher education.

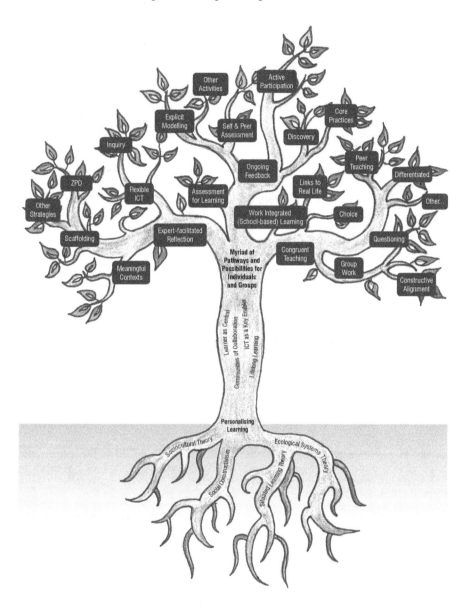

Fig. 13.3 A guide for visualising personalising learning in teacher education

References

Aiken, L. (2002). *Attitudes and related psychosocial constructs: Theories, assessment, and research*. Thousand Oaks: Sage.

Anderman, E., Anderman, L., Yough, M., & Gimbert, B. (2010). Value-added models of assessment: Implications for motivation and accountability. *Educational Psychologist, 45*(2), 123–137.

Aspin, D., & Chapman, J. (2012). Towards a philosophy of lifelong learning. In D. Aspin, J. Chapman, K. Evans, & R. Bagnall (Eds.), *Second international handbook of lifelong learning* (Vol. 26, pp. 3–35). Dordrecht: Springer.

Biggs, J., & Tang, C. (2011). *Teaching for quality learning at university: What the student does* (4th ed.). Berkshire: McGraw-Hill Education.

Black, P., Harrison, C., Lee, C., Marshall, B., & William, D. (2003). *Assessment for learning: Putting it into practice*. Berkshire: Open University Press.

Bronfenbrenner, U. (1977). Toward an experimental ecology of human development. *American Psychologist, 32*(7), 513–531.

Fischer, G. (2000). Lifelong learning – more than training. *Journal of Interactive Learning Research, 11*(3/4), 265–294.

Florian, L. (2009). Towards an inclusive pedagogy. In P. Hick, R. Kershner, & P. Farrell (Eds.), *Psychology for inclusive education* (pp. 38–51). Oxon: Routledge.

Grossman, P., Hammerness, K., & McDonald, M. (2009). Redefining teaching, re-imagining teacher education. *Teachers and Teaching, 15*(2), 273–289.

Jones, M., & McLean, K. (2012). Personalising learning in teacher education through the use of technology. *Australian Journal of Teacher Education, 37*(1), 75–92.

Keamy, K. (2009). Lining up the ducks: Personalising education and the challenges it poses for a school's leadership. *The International Journal of Learning, 16*(2), 245–255.

Keamy, R. K., Nicholas, H., Mahar, S., & Herrick, C. (2007). *Personalising education: From research to policy and practice*. (Paper No. 11. Office of Education Policy and Innovation). Melbourne: Department of Education and Early Childhood Development.

Koehler, M. J., & Mishra, P. (2009). What is technological content knowledge? *Contemporary Issues in Teacher Education, 9*(1), 60–70.

Koehler, M. J., Mishra, P., Kereluik, K., Shin, T. S., & Graham, C. R. (2014). The technological pedagogical content knowledge framework. In J. M. Spector (Ed.), *Handbook of research on educational communications and technology* (pp. 101–111). New York: Springer.

Korthagen, F. A. J. (2001). Building a realistic teacher education program. In F. A. J. Korthagen (with J. Kessels, B. Koster, B. Langerwarf, & T. Wubbels) (Eds.), *Linking practice and theory: The pedagogy of realistic teacher education* (pp. 69–87). Mahwah: Erlbaum.

Lave, J., & Wenger, E. (1991). *Situated learning: Legitimate peripheral participation (learning in doing: Social, cognitive and computational perspectives)*. Cambridge: Cambridge University Press.

Lichtenstein, A. (1934). *Can attitudes be taught?* (No. 21). Baltimore: The John Hopkins Press.

Loughran, J. (2006). *Developing a pedagogy of teacher education: Understanding teaching and learning about teaching*. New York: Routledge.

Newhouse, C. P., & Clarkson, B. (2008). Using learning environment attributes to evaluate the impact of ICT on learning in schools. *Research and Practice in Technology Enhanced Learning, 3*(2), 139–158.

Olson, M., & Kendrick, R. (2012). Attitude formation. In V. Ramachandra (Ed.), *Encyclopedia of human behaviour* (2nd ed., pp. 230–235). Oxford: Elsevier.

Owen, J. (2016). Foreword. In Foundation for Young Australians (FYA) (Ed.), *The New Basics: Big data reveals the skills young people need for the new work order* (p. 3). Melbourne: Foundation for Young Australians.

Patrick, C.-J., Peach, D., Pocknee, C., Webb, F., Fletcher, M., & Pretto, G. (2008). *The WIL [Work Integrated Learning] report: A national scoping study [Australian learning and teaching council (ALTC) final report]*. Brisbane: Queensland University of Technology. Retrieved from www.altc.edu.au and www.acen.edu.au

Piaget, J. (1936). *Origins of intelligence in the child*. London: Routledge & Kegan Paul.

Saribas, D. (2015). Investigating the relationship between pre-service teachers' scientific literacy, environmental literacy and life-long learning tendency. *Science Education International, 26*(1), 80–100.

Selwyn, N. (2013). *Education in a digital world*. London: Routledge.

Smit, K., de Brabander, C., & Martens, R. (2014). Student-centred and teacher-centred learning environment in pre-vocational secondary education: Psychological needs, and motivation. *Scandinavian Journal of Educational Research, 58*(6), 695–712.

Swennen, A., Lunenberg, M., & Korthagen, F. (2008). Preach what you teach! Teacher educators and congruent teaching. *Teachers and Teaching: Theory and Practice, 14*(5–6), 531–542.

Teacher Education Ministerial Advisory Group (TEMAG). (2014). *Action now: Classroom ready teachers*. Retrieved from http://www.studentsfirst.gov.au/teacher-education-ministerial-advisory-group

Vygotsky, L. (1978). *Mind in society. The development of higher psychological perspectives*. Cambridge, MA: Harvard University Press.

Wenger, E. (1998). *Communities of practice: Learning, meaning and identity*. New York: Cambridge University Press.

Author Index

© Springer Nature Singapore Pte Ltd. 2018
M. Jones, K. McLean, *Personalising Learning in Teacher Education*,
https://doi.org/10.1007/978-981-10-7930-6

Subject Index

© Springer Nature Singapore Pte Ltd. 2018
M. Jones, K. McLean, *Personalising Learning in Teacher Education*,
https://doi.org/10.1007/978-981-10-7930-6

CPSIA information can be obtained
at www.ICGtesting.com
Printed in the USA
LVHW05*0207140418
573478LV00009B/244/P